W9-AAC-510

THE NEW FOLGER LIBRARY SHAKESPEARE

Designed to make Shakespeare's great plays available to all readers, the New Folger Library edition of Shakespeare's plays provides accurate texts in modern spelling and punctuation, as well as scene-by-scene action summaries, full explanatory notes, many pictures clarifying Shakespeare's language, and notes recording all significant departures from the early printed versions. Each play is prefaced by a brief introduction, by a guide to reading Shakespeare's language, and by accounts of his life and theater. Each play is followed by an annotated list of further readings and by a "Modern Perspective" written by an expert on that particular play.

Barbara A. Mowat was Director of Research *emerita* at the Folger Shakespeare Library, Consulting Editor of *Shakespeare Quarterly*, and author of *The Dramaturgy of Shakespeare's Romances* and of essays on Shakespeare's plays and their editing.

Paul Werstine is Professor of English at the Graduate School and at King's University College at Western University. He is a general editor of the New Variorum Shakespeare and author of *Early Modern Playhouse Manuscripts and the Editing of Shakespeare* and of many papers and articles on the printing and editing of Shakespeare's plays.

The Folger Shakespeare Library

The Folger Shakespeare Library in Washington, D.C., a privately funded research library dedicated to Shakespeare and the civilization of early modern Europe, was founded in 1932 by Henry Clay and Emily Jordan Folger, and incorporated as part of Amherst College in Amherst, Massachusetts, one of the nation's oldest liberal arts colleges, from which Henry Folger had graduated in 1879. In addition to its role as the world's preeminent Shakespeare collection and its emergence as a leading center for Renaissance studies, the Folger Shakespeare Library offers a wide array of cultural and educational programs and services for the general public.

EDITORS

BARBARA A. MOWAT
Former Director of Research emerita
Folger Shakespeare Library

PAUL WERSTINE
Professor of English
King's University College
at Western University, Canada

Folger SHAKESPEARE LIBRARY

Henry VI

Part 1

By
WILLIAM SHAKESPEARE

EDITED BY BARBARA A. MOWAT
AND PAUL WERSTINE

Simon & Schuster Paperbacks
NEW YORK LONDON TORONTO SYDNEY NEW DELHI

The sale of this book without its cover is unauthorized. If you purchased this book without a cover, you should be aware that it was reported to the publisher as "unsold and destroyed." Neither the author nor the publisher has received payment for the sale of this "stripped book."

Simon & Schuster
1230 Avenue of the Americas
New York, NY 10020

Copyright © 2008 by The Folger Shakespeare Library

All rights reserved, including the right to reproduce this book or portions thereof in any form whatsoever. For information, address Simon & Schuster Subsidiary Rights Department, 1230 Avenue of the Americas, New York, NY 10020.

This Simon & Schuster trade paperback edition December 2020

SIMON & SCHUSTER and colophon are registered trademarks of Simon & Schuster, Inc.

For information about special discounts for bulk purchases, please contact Simon & Schuster Special Sales at 1-866-506-1949 or business@simonandschuster.com.

The Simon & Schuster Speakers Bureau can bring authors to your live event. For more information or to book an event, contact the Simon & Schuster Speakers Bureau at 1-866-248-3049 or visit our website at www.simonspeakers.com.

Manufactured in the United States of America

10 9 8 7 6 5 4 3 2 1

ISBN 978-1-9821-6497-3
ISBN 978-1-4767-8863-0 (ebook)

From the Director of the Folger Shakespeare Library

It is hard to imagine a world without Shakespeare. Since their composition more than four hundred years ago, Shakespeare's plays and poems have traveled the globe, inviting those who see and read his works to make them their own.

Readers of the New Folger Editions are part of this ongoing process of "taking up Shakespeare," finding our own thoughts and feelings in language that strikes us as old or unusual and, for that very reason, new. We still struggle to keep up with a writer who could think a mile a minute, whose words paint pictures that shift like clouds. These expertly edited texts, presented here with accompanying explanatory notes and up-to-date critical essays, are distinctive because of what they do: they allow readers not simply to keep up, but to engage deeply with a writer whose works invite us to think, and think again.

These New Folger Editions of Shakespeare's plays and poems are also special because of where they come from. The Folger Shakespeare Library in Washington, D.C., where the Editions are produced, is the single greatest documentary source of Shakespeare's works. An unparalleled collection of early modern books, manuscripts, and artwork connected to Shakespeare, the Folger's holdings have been consulted extensively in the preparation of these texts. The Editions also reflect the expertise gained through the regular performance of Shakespeare's works in the Folger's Elizabethan Theatre.

I want to express my deep thanks to editors Barbara Mowat and Paul Werstine for creating these indispensable editions of Shakespeare's works, which incorporate the best of textual scholarship with a richness of commentary that is both inspired and engaging. Readers who want to know more about Shakespeare and his plays can follow the paths these distinguished scholars have trod by visiting the Folger itself, where a range of physical and digital resources (available online) exists to supplement the material in these texts. I commend to you these words, and hope that they inspire.

Michael Witmore
Director, Folger Shakespeare Library

Contents

Editors' Preface

In recent years, ways of dealing with Shakespeare's texts and with the interpretation of his plays have been undergoing significant change. This edition, while retaining many of the features that have always made the Folger Shakespeare so attractive to the general reader, at the same time reflects these current ways of thinking about Shakespeare. For example, modern readers, actors, and teachers have become interested in the differences between, on the one hand, the early forms in which Shakespeare's plays were first published and, on the other hand, the forms in which editors through the centuries have presented them. In response to this interest, we have based our edition on what we consider the best early printed version of a particular play (explaining our rationale in "An Introduction to This Text") and have marked our changes in the text—unobtrusively, we hope, but in such a way that the curious reader can be aware that a change has been made and can consult the "Textual Notes" to discover what appeared in the early printed version.

Current ways of looking at the plays are reflected in our brief prefaces, in many of the commentary notes, in the annotated lists of "Further Reading," and especially in each play's "Modern Perspective," an essay written by an outstanding scholar who brings to the reader his or her fresh assessment of the play in the light of today's interests and concerns.

As in the Folger Library General Reader's Shakespeare, which this edition replaces, we include explanatory notes designed to help make Shakespeare's language clearer to a modern reader, and we place the notes on the page facing the text they explain. We also follow the earlier edition in including illustrations—of objects, of clothing, of mythological figures—from books and manuscripts in the Folger Shakespeare Library collection. We provide fresh accounts of the life of Shakespeare, of the publishing of his plays, and of the theaters in which his plays were performed, as well as an introduction to the text itself. We also include "Reading Shakespeare's Language," in which we try to help readers learn to "break the code" of Elizabethan poetic language.

For each section of each volume, we are indebted to a host of generous experts and fellow scholars. The "Reading Shakespeare's Language" sections, for example, could not have been written had not Arthur King, of Brigham Young University, and Randall Robinson, author of *Unlocking Shakespeare's Language*, led the way in untangling Shakespearean language puzzles and shared their insights and methodologies generously with us. "Shakespeare's Life" profited by the careful reading given it by the late S. Schoenbaum; "Shakespeare's Theater" was strengthened by Andrew Gurr, John Astington, and William Ingram; and "The Publication of Shakespeare's Plays" is indebted to the comments of Peter W. M. Blayney. We, as editors, take sole responsibility for any errors in our editions.

We are grateful to the authors of the "Modern Perspectives"; to the Huntington and Newberry Libraries for fellowship support; to King's University College for the grants it has provided to Paul Werstine; to the Social Sciences and Humanities Research Council of Canada, which provided him with a Research Time Stipend for 1990–91; to R. J. Shroyer of the University of Western Ontario for essential computer support; to the Folger Institute's Center for Shakespeare Studies for its sponsorship of a workshop on "Shakespeare's

Texts for Students and Teachers" (funded by the National Endowment for the Humanities and led by Richard Knowles of the University of Wisconsin), a workshop from which we learned an enormous amount about what is wanted by college and high-school teachers of Shakespeare today; to Alice Falk for her expert copyediting; and especially to Stephen Llano, our production editor at Washington Square Press.

Our biggest debt is to the Folger Shakespeare Library—to Gail Kern Paster, Director of the Library, whose interest and support are unfailing (and whose scholarly expertise is an invaluable resource), and to Werner Gundersheimer, the Library's Director from 1984 to 2002, who made possible our edition; to Deborah Curren-Aquino, who provides extensive editorial and production support; to Jean Miller, the Library's former Art Curator, who combs the Library holdings for illustrations, and to Julie Ainsworth, Head of the Photography Department, who carefully photographs them; to Peggy O'Brien, former Director of Education at the Folger and now Senior Vice President, Educational Programming and Services at the Corporation for Public Broadcasting, who gave us expert advice about the needs being expressed by Shakespeare teachers and students (and to Martha Christian and other "master teachers" who used our texts in manuscript in their classrooms); to Mary Bloodworth for her expert computer support; to the staff of the Research Division, especially Karen Rogers (whose help is crucial), Liz Pohland, Mimi Godfrey, Kathleen Lynch, Carol Brobeck, Sarah Werner, Owen Williams, and Caryn Lazzuri; and, finally, to the generously supportive staff of the Library's Reading Room.

Barbara A. Mowat and Paul Werstine

Henry VI, Part 1

Henry VI, Part 1 is an uncompromising celebration of early English nationalism and imperialism. It defines the English against the French, whom it degrades as scheming, effeminate, and willing to consort with the devil. The play idealizes the English king Henry V for his successful conquest of much of France during the Hundred Years War. But Henry V has died just as the play begins, and leadership of the English cause in France has passed to Talbot, an indomitable, fierce, almost perpetually enraged, and therefore altogether masculine warrior hero. Yet Talbot is not as fortunate as Henry V. While all of France, we are told, shakes in terror at the name of Talbot, the French still refuse to yield.

Opposed to the idealized Talbot are a number of other characters who fail to match him. One is the official leader of the French, Charles the Dauphin, whose status as a military hero suffers a blow very early in the play when he must yield in single combat to Joan la Pucelle, or Joan of Arc. She then becomes the captain of the French, showing admirable cunning and resourcefulness in devising strategy and remarkable boldness in carrying it out. She fulfills for the French her claims to have been chosen by the Virgin Mary as the chaste instrument of France's liberation from the hated English invaders. However, for the English, her shrewdness and power issue from the practice of filthy witchcraft, and her pretensions to chastity mask a characteristically French sensuality.

Also opposed to Talbot are many of the English, especially those who remain for the most part in England. They include Gloucester and Winchester, two

xiii

England's Claim to France

[Characters in this play appear in bold]

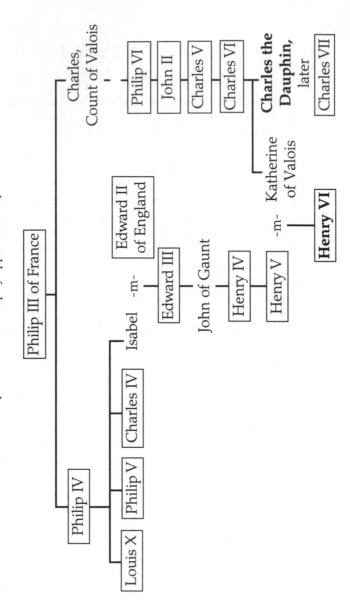

bitter rivals more intent on defeating each other than the French. Gloucester, the Protector of the boy king Henry VI and therefore ruler of England, and Winchester, a bishop and cardinal, urge their servants on to brawl openly in the streets of London. Before their quarrel can be silenced, another breaks out between the Duke of Somerset and Richard Plantagenet, soon to be powerful as Duke of York. Once in France, they and their followers seek royal permission to fight each other, rather than the French. The play demonstrates, especially from this point on, that the French owe their victory to the English defeat of themselves. Talbot and his son, despite their glorious self-sacrifice in the English military cause (presented to inspire imitation among all Englishmen), cannot prevail against the French, because the rest of the English nobility are intent on preying on each other in the service of their own ambitions.

After you have read the play, we invite you to turn to the essay printed after it, *"Henry VI, Part 1*: A Modern Perspective," by Phyllis Rackin of the University of Pennsylvania.

Ancestry of Richard Plantagenet, Duke of York

[Characters in this play appear in bold]

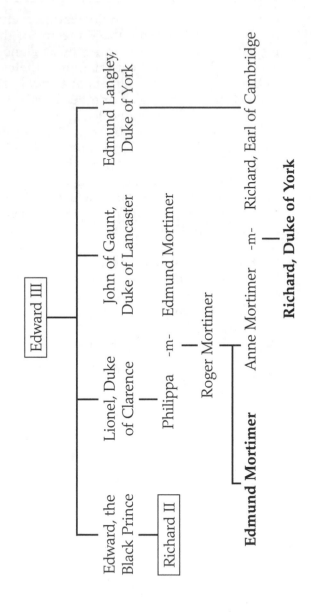

Reading Shakespeare's Language: *Henry VI, Part 1*

For many people today, reading Shakespeare's language can be a problem—but it is a problem that can be solved.* Those who have studied Latin (or even French or German or Spanish), and those who are used to reading poetry, will have little difficulty understanding the language of poetic drama. Others, though, need to develop the skills of untangling unusual sentence structures and of recognizing and understanding poetic compressions, omissions, and wordplay. And even those skilled in reading unusual sentence structures may have occasional trouble with Shakespeare's words. Four hundred years of "static" intervene between his speaking and our hearing. Most of his vocabulary is still in use, but a few of his words are no longer used and many of his words now have meanings quite different from those they had in the sixteenth century. In the theater, most of these difficulties are solved for us by actors who study the language and articulate it for us so that the essential meaning is heard—or, when combined with stage action, is at least *felt*. When we are reading on our own, we must do what each actor does: go over the lines (often with a dictionary close at hand) until the puzzles are solved and the lines yield up their poetry and the characters speak in words and phrases that are, suddenly, rewarding and wonderfully memorable.

---

*For our use of the name *Shakespeare* in this essay, see our appendix "Authorship of *Henry VI, Part 1*," p. 245.

Shakespeare's Words

As you begin to read the opening scenes of a play from Shakespeare's time, you may notice occasional unfamiliar words. Some are unfamiliar simply because we no longer use them. In the early scenes of *Henry VI, Part 1,* for example, one finds the words *vaward* (i.e., vanguard), *otherwhiles* (i.e., occasionally, sometimes), *intermissive* (i.e., intermittent), and *agazed* (i.e., terrified). Words of this kind are explained in notes to the text and will become familiar the more early plays you read.

In *Henry VI, Part 1,* as in all of Shakespeare's writing, more problematic are the words that are still in use but that now have different meanings. In the opening scenes of *Henry VI, Part 1,* for example, the word *brandish* is used where we would say "scatter," *car* where we would say "chariot," *jars* where we would say "quarrels," and *porridge* where we would say "soup." Such words will be explained in the notes to the text, but they too will become familiar as you continue to read Shakespeare's language.

Some words and phrases are strange not because of the "static" introduced by changes in language over the past centuries but because these are expressions that Shakespeare is using to build a dramatic world that has its own space, time, and history. In the opening scenes of *Henry VI, Part 1,* for example, the dramatist quickly establishes a sense of an English government suffering such a loss in the death of its king that the cosmos seems to have turned against it: Henry V's "thread of life" has been cut because of "revolting stars" and "planets of mishap," and England is under the threat of becoming "a nourish of salt tears." Such language quickly constructs the overwhelming sense of disaster surrounding the death of Henry V and the succession of his young son, Henry VI; the words and the world they create will become increasingly familiar as you get further into the play.

Shakespeare's Sentences

In an English sentence, meaning is quite dependent on the place given each word. "The dog bit the boy" and "The boy bit the dog" mean very different things, even though the individual words are the same. Because English places such importance on the positions of words in sentences, on the way words are arranged, unusual arrangements can puzzle a reader. Shakespeare frequently shifts his sentences away from "normal" English arrangements—often to create the rhythm he seeks, sometimes to use a line's poetic rhythm to emphasize a particular word, sometimes to give a character his or her own speech patterns or to allow the character to speak in a special way. When we attend a good performance of the play, the actors will have worked out the sentence structures and will articulate the sentences so that the meaning is clear. When reading the play, we need to do as the actor does: that is, when puzzled by a character's speech, check to see if words are being presented in an unusual sequence.

Often Shakespeare rearranges subjects and verbs (i.e., instead of "He goes" we find "Goes he"). In *Henry VI, Part 1*, when the Messenger announces "Cropped *are the flower-de-luces*," he is using such a construction (1.1.82). So is the Third Messenger when he says "Enclosèd *were they* with their enemies" (1.1.138). The "normal" order would be "the flower-de-luces are cropped" and "they were enclosed." Shakespeare also frequently places the object before the subject and verb (i.e., instead of "I hit him," we might find "Him I hit"). Winchester provides an example of this inversion when he says *"The battles* of the Lord of Hosts *he fought"* (1.1.31) and Gloucester another example when he says *"Virtue he had"* (1.1.9). The "normal" order would be "he fought battles" and "he had virtue." With remarkable frequency, this play rearranges normal word order so that object precedes verb, which precedes subject: *"Sad tidings bring I* to you" (1.1.59); *"No leisure had he* to enrank his men" (1.1.117); *"Nor men nor money hath he* to make war" (1.2.17). Such word order is far more common in *Henry VI, Part 1* than in plays whose Shakespearean authorship is not disputed.

Inversions are not the only unusual sentence structures in Shakespeare's language. Often in his sentences words that would normally appear together are separated from each other, usually to create a particular rhythm or to stress a particular word, or else to draw attention to a needed piece of information. Take, for example, the Third Messenger's *"His soldiers,* spying his undaunted spirit, / 'À Talbot! À Talbot!' *cried* out amain" (1.1.129–30). Here the subject ("His soldiers") is separated from its verb ("cried") by a participial phrase modifying the subject ("spying his undaunted spirit") and by the object of the verb yet to come ("'À Talbot! À Talbot!'"). As the Messenger's purpose is to describe the devotion inspired by Talbot in the soldiers, the words that separate subject from verb have an importance that allows them to take precedence over the verb. Or take the Third Messenger's introduction of Talbot's plight on the battlefield:

> *this dreadful lord,*
> Retiring from the siege of Orleance,

Having full scarce six thousand in his troop,
By three and twenty thousand of the French
Was round encompassèd and set upon.

(1.1.112–16)

Here the subject and verb ("this dreadful lord . . . Was round encompassèd and set upon") are separated by the two participial phrases "Retiring from the siege of Orleance" and "Having full scarce six thousand in his troop," as well as by the adverbial phrase "By three and twenty thousand of the French." By juxtaposing the slender troop strength of the English against the large body of the French, these interruptions emphasize that Talbot's plight arises entirely from his being greatly outnumbered. In order to create sentences that seem more like the English of everyday speech, one can rearrange the words, putting together the word clusters ("Retiring from the siege of Orleance, having full scarce six thousand in his troop, this dreadful lord was round encompassed and set upon by three and twenty thousand of the French"). The result will usually be an increase in clarity but a loss of rhythm or a shift in emphasis.

Often in *Henry VI, Part 1,* rather than separating basic sentence elements, Shakespeare simply holds them back, delaying them until other material to which he wants to give greater emphasis has been presented. He puts this kind of construction in the mouth of the Third Messenger, who again is describing Talbot: "Here, there, and everywhere, enraged, *he slew*" (1.1.126). The basic sentence elements ("he slew") are delayed until the Messenger presents the nearly superhuman ubiquity of Talbot and the quality of his disposition ("enraged") that energizes his destructiveness. When Talbot himself speaks in 2.1, he is made to utter a sentence that also illustrates an even more extensive delay:

> Lord Regent, and redoubted Burgundy,
> By whose approach the regions of Artois,
> Walloon, and Picardy are friends to us,
> This happy night *the Frenchmen are secure*[.]
>
> (9–12)

Talbot's is a speech of welcome. Therefore it is appropriate for him to accentuate the importance of the newly arrived Burgundy by loading him with his titles ("Lord Regent, and redoubted Burgundy") and celebrating his influence over "the regions of Artois, Walloon, and Picardy" before identifying by subject, verb, and predicate adjective the strategic advantage yielded the English and their allies by the dangerously overconfident French: "the Frenchmen are secure [i.e., overconfident, careless]."

Finally, in Shakespeare's plays, sentences are sometimes complicated not because of unusual structures or interruptions but because the dramatist omits words that English sentences normally require. (In conversation, we, too, often omit words. We say, "Heard from him yet?" and our hearer supplies the missing "Have you.") Shakespeare captures the same conversational tone in the play's early exchange between Exeter and the Messenger. When Exeter asks how eight French towns and cities were lost, "How were they lost? What treachery was used?" the Messenger answers "No treachery, but want of men and money" (1.1.70–71). Had the Messenger answered in a full sentence, he might have said "No treachery [was used], but [they were lost through] want [i.e., lack] of men and money." Ellipsis, or the omission of words not strictly necessary to the sense, appears again in the speech of Alanson after the French have been defeated by a much smaller English army: "One to ten!" Expanded to a full sentence, Alanson's exclamation might read "[It is incredible that] one [Englishman could best] ten [Frenchmen]." So expanded, however, the speech would lose much of its dramatic force.

Shakespeare's Wordplay

Shakespeare plays with language so often and so variously that entire books are written on the topic. Here we will mention only three kinds of wordplay: similes, allusions, and puns. These figures of speech outnumber metaphors in the opening scenes of *Henry VI, Part 1* to the same extent that metaphors often outnumber similes, allusions, and puns in plays of Shakespeare's uncontested authorship. A simile is a play on words in which one object or idea is expressed as if it were something else, something with which it is said to share common features. This is also a definition of metaphor, but in a simile the comparison is made explicit through the use of "like" or "as." For instance, when Charles the Dauphin says "the famished English, *like* pale ghosts, / Faintly besiege us one hour in a month" (1.2.7–8), he uses a simile that compares the starving English soldiers to "pale ghosts" in order to call attention to their pallid complexions and to the flimsiness of their bodies. Exeter uses a more complicated simile to comment on the funeral procession for Henry V:

Upon a wooden coffin we attend,
And Death's dishonorable victory
We with our stately presence glorify,
Like captives bound to a triumphant car.

(1.1.19–22)

According to Exeter, the nobles accompanying their king's coffin are "like captives" who, in a Roman triumphal procession, would be tied to the chariot ("car") of the victorious warrior. For Exeter, the victor in this case is Death, and his chariot is the coffin.

An allusion presents itself when a text or a character in it refers to another text, thereby prompting readers or listeners to reflect on the multiple ways in which the two texts may parallel each other. Alanson, describing the English soldiers as "none but Samsons and Goliases" (1.2.33), refers to the text of the Bible, specifically the books known as Judges and 1 Samuel. In those texts Samson and Goliath are mighty warriors, and thus Alanson pays his adversaries a great compliment. Yet as we read and reflect on the texts of Judges and 1 Samuel, we may also realize that Shakespeare has also cleverly smuggled into this play a suggestion of the ultimate destruction of the English army in France, because Samson was brought down by Delilah and Goliath suffered death at the hands of the boy David.

Sometimes allusions come thick and fast in this play. Charles the Dauphin is given four different allusions in just four lines, all of them characterizing Joan la Pucelle, the newly arrived woman warrior whom he has come immediately to admire:

> Was Mahomet inspirèd with a dove?
> Thou with an eagle art inspirèd then.
> Helen, the mother of great Constantine,
> Nor yet Saint Philip's daughters were like thee.
>
> (1.2.143–46)

First Charles alludes to a then-popular slanderous story of the Prophet Muhammad in which he was accused of training a dove to eat grain from his ear and of then claiming that the dove was the Holy Spirit come to inspire him. Next, Charles contrasts this dove to the eagle, a bird that is featured in the texts of Roman history because it was the standard held in highest honor by the Roman legions. This martial bird functions in Charles's speech as a figure of Pucelle, who, Charles hopes, will conquer as the Romans did. Then Charles goes further in idealizing Pucelle by alluding to St. Helena and thereby to the legend in which she finds in Jerusalem the cross on which Jesus was crucified. According to Charles, Pucelle is greater than St. Helena and also greater than St. Philip's daughters, who are characters, like Samson and Goliath, from the text of the Bible—this time from the Acts of the Apostles, where they are said to be virgins and prophets. Pucelle has also claimed to be a virgin and has prophesied French victory. As we reflect on these multiple allusions, we may wonder if the play will ultimately vilify Pucelle the way that Christian Europe did Muhammad or celebrate her the way Europe did its saints.

A pun is a play on words that sound at least somewhat the same but that have different meanings (or on a single word that has more than one meaning). The first kind of pun is prominent in *Henry VI, Part 1*. It occurs when Winchester insults his rival Gloucester: "thou most usurping proditor— / And not Protector" (1.3.31–32). "Proditor" and "Protector" sound very much alike, but the first means "traitor" and the second "regent," the official who governs a kingdom while the monarch is a minor. Though the terms have almost opposite meanings, they sound enough alike that Winchester can use wordplay to accuse the Protector Gloucester of treason. Another pun—on the name of Joan la Pucelle—occupies a large place in *Henry VI, Part 1*. In French *pucelle* means "virgin," but *pucelle* also sounds like the English word *puzel,* which means "whore." The opposition between the meanings of these two similar-sounding words captures the antithetical ways in which the French and English respond to Pucelle.

Implied Stage Action

Finally, in reading Shakespeare's plays we should always remember that what we are reading is a performance script. The dialogue is written to be spoken by actors who, at the same time, are moving, gesturing, picking up objects, weeping, shaking their fists. Some stage action is described in what are called "stage directions"; some is signaled within the dialogue itself. We must learn to be alert to such signals as we stage the play in our imaginations.

Often the dialogue offers an immediately clear indication of the action that is to accompany it. For example, at 3.1.133, when Gloucester says "Here, Winchester, I offer thee my hand," the next character to speak is not Winchester but King Henry, who says to Winchester, "Fie, Uncle Beaufort!" (134). The king's rebuke of Winchester signals that Gloucester's offer to shake hands has been rebuffed. Thus we feel confident adding the stage direction *"Winchester refuses Gloucester's hand,"* putting it in half–square brackets to signal that it is our interpolation, rather than words appearing in the earliest printed text. Again when Warwick addresses King Henry with the words "Accept this scroll," the dialogue, we judge, allows us to add to the early printed text *"presenting a scroll"* (3.1.158). Occasionally, in *Henry VI, Part 1,* signals to the reader are not in the least clear. There is a disturbing lack of clarity very early in the play. The opening stage direction calls for the coffin of Henry V to be brought on accompanied by a large retinue. When the second scene opens, the coffin and its retinue are no longer onstage. Yet as the first scene proceeds, it is very difficult to determine when the coffin leaves the stage. At 1.1.45, Bedford, the late king's brother, orders "Let's to the altar.—Heralds, wait on us." This line appears to call for the procession, in which the nobles will be accompanied by heralds, to proceed toward an altar that may be onstage or off. Perhaps the procession begins to move again and, as some editors think, the coffin now leaves the stage. But, as the ensuing dialogue indicates, Bedford and the nobles who would form the funeral procession must remain onstage, for Bedford's speech ordering the procession to move onward is interrupted by the entrance of the first of a series of three messengers. And Bedford's later question, "What say'st thou, man, before dead Henry's corse?" (1.1.63), suggests that the coffin, too, may remain onstage. Between Bedford's line "Let's to the altar" (line 45) and the end of the scene, there is no place in the dialogue for the coffin to be removed. Our choice, then, is to have the coffin borne off only when the scene ends, although we have much less confidence in adding a stage direction to that effect than we do in many other cases where we have put in directions. Because our added direction is in half–square brackets, readers know this is our suggestion and can do with it as they will.

Practice in reading the language of stage action repays one many times over when one reaches scenes heavily dependent on stage business—for example, 3.2. This scene opens with Pucelle disguised as a peasant carrying grain; the scene moves on to her appearance on an upper level, thrusting out a lantern. On the main stage there are skirmishes and attacks, followed by the entrance of the English army with the dying Bedford carried on in a sick-chair. Pucelle throws grain down on the English nobles; they "whisper together in council," in what Pucelle calls a "Parliament" (SD 59, 60); the English and the French exit to fight, leaving Bedford and his attendants to observe Fastolf's exhibition of cowardice. When the English then chase the French across the stage, Bedford dies and is carried offstage by his attendants. The scene ends with the entrance and exultation of the English. In a scene like this, the reader's understanding of what is happening in the story is as dependent on an imaginative re-creation of stage action as it is on the scene's dialogue.

It is immensely rewarding to work carefully with Shakespeare's language—with the words, the sentences, the wordplay, and the implied stage action—as readers for the past four centuries have discovered. It may be more pleasurable to attend a good performance of a play—though not everyone has thought so. But the joy of being able to stage a Shakespeare play in one's imagination, to return to passages that continue to yield further meanings (or further questions) the more one reads them—these are pleasures that, for many, rival (or at least augment) those of the performed text, and certainly make it worth considerable effort to "break the code" of Elizabethan poetic drama and let free the remarkable language that makes up a Shakespeare text.

Shakespeare's Life

Surviving documents that give us glimpses into the life of William Shakespeare show us a playwright, poet, and actor who grew up in the market town of Stratford-upon-Avon, spent his professional life in London, and returned to Stratford a wealthy landowner. He was born in April 1564, died in April 1616, and is buried inside the chancel of Holy Trinity Church in Stratford.

We wish we could know more about the life of the world's greatest dramatist. His plays and poems are testaments to his wide reading—especially to his knowledge of Virgil, Ovid, Plutarch, Holinshed's *Chronicles*, and the Bible—and to his mastery of the English language, but we can only speculate about his education. We know that the King's New School in Stratford-upon-Avon was considered excellent. The school was one of the English "grammar schools" established to educate young men, primarily in Latin grammar and literature. As in other schools of the time, students began their studies at the age of four or five in the attached "petty school," and there learned to read and write in English, studying primarily the catechism from the Book of Common Prayer. After two years in the petty school, students entered the lower form (grade) of the grammar school, where they began the serious study of Latin grammar and Latin texts that would occupy most of the remainder of their school days. (Several Latin texts that Shakespeare used repeatedly in writing his plays and poems were texts that schoolboys memorized and recited.) Latin comedies were introduced early in the lower form; in the upper form, which the boys entered at age ten or eleven, students wrote their own Latin orations and declamations, studied Latin historians and rhetoricians, and began the study of Greek using the Greek New Testament.

Since the records of the Stratford "grammar school" do not survive, we cannot prove that William Shakespeare attended the school; however, every indication (his father's position as an alderman and bailiff of Stratford, the playwright's own knowledge of the Latin classics, scenes in the plays that recall grammar-school experiences—for example, *The Merry Wives of Windsor*, 4.1) suggests that he did. We also lack generally accepted documentation about Shakespeare's life after his schooling ended and his professional life in London began. His marriage in 1582 (at age eighteen) to Anne Hathaway and the subsequent births of his daughter Susanna (1583) and the twins Judith and Hamnet (1585) are recorded, but how he supported himself and where he lived are not known. Nor do we know when and why he left Stratford for the London theatrical world, nor how he rose to be the important figure in that world that he had become by the early 1590s.

We do know that by 1592 he had achieved some prominence in London as both an actor and a playwright. In that year was published a book by the playwright Robert Greene attacking an actor who had the audacity to write blank-verse drama and who was "in his own conceit [i.e., opinion] the only Shake-scene in a country." Since Greene's attack includes a parody of a line from one of Shakespeare's early plays, there is little doubt that it is Shakespeare to whom he refers, a "Shake-scene" who had aroused Greene's fury by successfully competing with university-educated dramatists like Greene himself. It was in 1593 that

Shakespeare became a published poet. In that year he published his long narrative poem *Venus and Adonis;* in 1594, he followed it with *The Rape of Lucrece.* Both poems were dedicated to the young earl of Southampton (Henry Wriothesley), who may have become Shakespeare's patron.

It seems no coincidence that Shakespeare wrote these narrative poems at a time when the theaters were closed because of the plague, a contagious epidemic disease that devastated the population of London. When the theaters reopened in 1594, Shakespeare apparently resumed his double career of actor and playwright and began his long (and seemingly profitable) service as an acting-company shareholder. Records for December of 1594 show him to be a leading member of the Lord Chamberlain's Men. It was this company of actors, later named the King's Men, for whom he would be a principal actor, dramatist, and shareholder for the rest of his career.

So far as we can tell, that career spanned about twenty years. In the 1590s, he wrote his plays on English history as well as several comedies and at least two tragedies (*Titus Andronicus* and *Romeo and Juliet*). These histories, comedies, and tragedies are the plays credited to him in 1598 in a work, *Palladis Tamia,* that in one chapter compares English writers with "Greek, Latin, and Italian Poets." There the author, Francis Meres, claims that Shakespeare is comparable to the Latin dramatists Seneca for tragedy and Plautus for comedy, and calls him "the most excellent in both kinds for the stage." He also names him "Mellifluous and honey-tongued Shakespeare": "I say," writes Meres, "that the Muses would speak with Shakespeare's fine filed phrase, if they would speak English." Since Meres also mentions Shakespeare's "sugared sonnets among his private friends," it is assumed that many of Shakespeare's sonnets (not published until 1609) were also written in the 1590s.

In 1599, Shakespeare's company built a theater for themselves across the river from London, naming it the Globe. The plays that are considered by many to be Shakespeare's major tragedies (*Hamlet, Othello, King Lear,* and *Macbeth*) were written while the company was resident in this theater, as were such comedies as *Twelfth Night* and *Measure for Measure*. Many of Shakespeare's plays were performed at court (both for Queen Elizabeth I and, after her death in 1603, for King James I), some were presented at the Inns of Court (the residences of London's legal societies), and some were doubtless performed in other towns, at the universities, and at great houses when the King's Men went on tour; otherwise, his plays from 1599 to 1608 were, so far as we know, performed only at the Globe. Between 1608 and 1612, Shakespeare wrote several plays—among them *The Winter's Tale* and *The Tempest*—presumably for the company's new indoor Blackfriars theater, though the plays seem to have been performed also at the Globe and at court. Surviving documents describe a performance of *The Winter's Tale* in 1611 at the Globe, for example, and performances of *The Tempest* in 1611 and 1613 at the royal palace of Whitehall.

Shakespeare wrote very little after 1612, the year in which he probably wrote *King Henry VIII*. (It was at a performance of *Henry VIII* in 1613 that the Globe caught fire and burned to the ground.) Sometime between 1610 and 1613 he seems to have returned to live in Stratford-upon-Avon, where he owned a large house and considerable property, and where his wife and his two daughters and their husbands lived. (His son Hamnet had died in 1596.) During his professional years in London, Shakespeare had presumably derived income from the acting company's profits as well as from his own career as an actor, from the sale of his play manuscripts to the acting company, and, after 1599, from his shares as an owner of the Globe. It was presumably that income, carefully invested in land and other property, which made him the wealthy man that surviving documents show him to have become. It is also assumed that William Shakespeare's growing wealth and reputation played some part in inclining the crown, in 1596, to grant John Shakespeare, William's father, the coat of arms that he had so long sought. William Shakespeare died in Stratford on April 23, 1616 (according to the epitaph carved under his bust in Holy Trinity Church) and was buried on April 25. Seven years after his death, his collected plays were published as *Mr. William Shakespeares Comedies, Histories, & Tragedies* (the work now known as the First Folio).

The years in which Shakespeare wrote were among the most exciting in English history. Intellectually, the discovery, translation, and printing of Greek and Roman classics were making available a set of works and worldviews that interacted complexly with Christian texts and beliefs. The result was a questioning, a vital intellectual ferment, that provided energy for the period's amazing dramatic and literary output and that fed directly into Shakespeare's plays. The Ghost in *Hamlet,* for example, is wonderfully complicated in part because he is a figure from Roman tragedy—the spirit of the dead returning to seek revenge—who at the same time inhabits a Christian hell (or purgatory); Hamlet's description of humankind reflects at one moment the Neoplatonic wonderment at mankind ("What a piece of work is a man!") and, at the next, the Christian disparagement of human sinners ("And yet, to me, what is this quintessence of dust?").

As intellectual horizons expanded, so also did geo-graphical and cosmological horizons. New worlds—both North and South America—were explored, and in them were found human beings who lived and wor-shiped in ways radically different from those of Renaissance Europeans and Englishmen. The universe during these years also seemed to shift and expand. Copernicus had earlier theorized that the earth was not the center of the cosmos but revolved as a planet around the sun. Galileo's telescope, created in 1609, allowed scientists to see that Copernicus had been cor-rect: the universe was not organized with the earth at the center, nor was it so nicely circumscribed as people had, until that time, thought. In terms of expanding horizons, the impact of these discoveries on people's beliefs—religious, scientific, and philosophical—can-not be overstated.

London, too, rapidly expanded and changed during the years (from the early 1590s to around 1610) that Shakespeare lived there. London—the center of England's government, its economy, its royal court, its overseas trade—was, during these years, becoming an exciting metropolis, drawing to it thousands of new citi-zens every year. Troubled by overcrowding, by poverty, by recurring epidemics of the plague, London was also a mecca for the wealthy and the aristocratic, and for those who sought advancement at court, or power in govern-ment or finance or trade. One hears in Shakespeare's plays the voices of London—the struggles for power, the fear of venereal disease, the language of buying and sell-ing. One hears as well the voices of Stratford-upon-Avon—references to the nearby Forest of Arden, to sheepherding, to small-town gossip, to village fairs and markets. Part of the richness of Shakespeare's work is the influence felt there of the various worlds in which he lived: the world of metropolitan London, the world of small-town and rural England, the world of the theater, and the worlds of craftsmen and shepherds.

That Shakespeare inhabited such worlds we know from surviving London and Stratford documents, as well as from the evidence of the plays and poems themselves. From such records we can sketch the dramatist's life. We know from his works that he was a voracious reader. We know from legal and business documents that he was a multifaceted theater man who became a wealthy landowner. We know a bit about his family life and a fair amount about his legal and financial dealings. Most scholars today depend upon such evidence as they draw their picture of the world's greatest playwright. Such, however, has not always been the case. Until the late eighteenth century, the William Shakespeare who lived in most biographies was the creation of legend and tradition. This was the Shakespeare who was supposedly caught poaching deer at Charlecote, the estate of Sir Thomas Lucy close by Stratford; this was the Shakespeare who fled from Sir Thomas's vengeance and made his way in London by taking care of horses outside a playhouse; this was the Shakespeare who reportedly could barely read but whose natural gifts were extraordinary, whose father was a butcher who allowed his gifted son sometimes to help in the butcher shop, where William supposedly killed calves "in a high style," making a speech for the occasion. It was this legendary William Shakespeare whose Falstaff (in *1* and *2 Henry IV*) so pleased Queen Elizabeth that she demanded a play about Falstaff in love, and demanded that it be written in fourteen days (hence the existence of *The Merry Wives of Windsor*). It was this legendary Shakespeare who reached the top of his acting career in the roles of the Ghost in *Hamlet* and old Adam in *As You Like It*— and who died of a fever contracted by drinking too hard at "a merry meeting" with the poets Michael Drayton and Ben Jonson. This legendary Shakespeare is a rambunctious, undisciplined man, as attractively "wild" as his plays were seen by earlier generations to be. Unfortunately, there is no trace of evidence to support these wonderful stories.

Perhaps in response to the disreputable Shakespeare of legend—or perhaps in response to the fragmentary and, for some, all-too-ordinary Shakespeare documented by surviving records—some people since the mid–nineteenth century have argued that William Shakespeare could not have written the plays that bear his name. These persons have put forward some dozen names as more likely authors, among them Queen Elizabeth, Sir Francis Bacon, Edward de Vere (earl of Oxford), and Christopher Marlowe. Such attempts to find what for these people is a more believable author of the plays is a tribute to the regard in which the plays are held. Unfortunately for their claims, the documents that exist that provide evidence for the facts of Shakespeare's life tie him inextricably to the body of plays and poems that bear his name. Unlikely as it seems to those who want the works to have been written by an aristocrat, a university graduate, or an "important" person, the plays and poems seem clearly to have been produced by a man from Stratford-upon-Avon with a very good "grammar school" education and a life of experience in London and in the world of the London theater. How this particular man produced the works that dominate the cultures of much of the world almost four hundred years after his death is one of life's mysteries—and one that will continue to tease our imaginations as we continue to delight in his plays and poems.

Shakespeare's Theater

The actors of Shakespeare's time performed plays in a great variety of locations. They played at court (that is, in the great halls of such royal residences as Whitehall, Hampton Court, and Greenwich); they played in halls at the universities of Oxford and Cambridge, and at the Inns of Court (the residences in London of the legal societies); and they also played in the private houses of great lords and civic officials. Sometimes acting companies went on tour from London into the provinces, often (but not only) when outbreaks of bubonic plague in the capital forced the closing of theaters to reduce the possibility of contagion in crowded audiences. In the provinces the actors usually staged their plays in churches (until around 1600) or in guildhalls. Though surviving records show only a handful of occasions when actors played at inns while on tour, London inns were important playing places up until the 1590s.

The building of theaters in London had begun only shortly before Shakespeare wrote his first plays in the 1590s. These theaters were of two kinds: outdoor or public playhouses that could accommodate large numbers of playgoers, and indoor or private theaters for much smaller audiences. What is usually regarded as the first London outdoor public playhouse was called simply the Theatre. James Burbage—the father of Richard Burbage, who was perhaps the most famous actor in Shakespeare's company—built it in 1576 in an area north of the city of London called Shoreditch. Among the more famous of the other public playhouses that capitalized on the new fashion were the Curtain and the Fortune (both also built north of the city), and the Rose, the Swan, the Globe, and the Hope (all located on the Bankside, a region just across the Thames south of the city of London). All these playhouses had to be built outside the jurisdiction of the city of London because many civic officials were hostile to the performance of drama and repeatedly petitioned the royal council to abolish it.

The theaters erected on the Bankside (a region under the authority of the Church of England, whose head was the monarch) shared the neighborhood with houses of prostitution and with the Paris Garden, where the blood sports of bearbaiting and bullbaiting were carried on. There may have been no clear distinction between playhouses and buildings for such sports, for the Hope was used for both plays and baiting, and Philip Henslowe, owner of the Rose and, later, partner in the ownership of the Fortune, was also a partner in a monopoly on baiting. All these forms of entertainment were easily accessible to Londoners by boat across the Thames or over London Bridge.

Evidently Shakespeare's company prospered on the Bankside. They moved there in 1599. Threatened by difficulties in renewing the lease on the land where their first playhouse (the Theatre) had been built, Shakespeare's company took advantage of the Christmas holiday in 1598 to dismantle the Theatre and transport its timbers across the Thames to the Bankside, where, in 1599, these timbers were used in the building of the Globe. The weather in late December 1598 is recorded as having been especially harsh. It was so cold that the Thames was "nigh [nearly] frozen," and there was heavy snow. Perhaps the weather aided Shakespeare's company in eluding their landlord, the snow hiding their activity and the freezing of the Thames allowing them to slide the timbers across to the Bankside without paying tolls for repeated trips over London

Bridge. Attractive as this narrative is, it remains just as likely that the heavy snow hampered transport of the timbers in wagons through the London streets to the river. It also must be remembered that the Thames was, according to report, only "nigh frozen" and therefore as impassable as it ever was. Whatever the precise circumstances of this fascinating event in English theater history, Shakespeare's company was able to begin playing at their new Globe theater on the Bankside in 1599. After the first Globe burned down in 1613 during the staging of Shakespeare's *Henry VIII* (its thatch roof was set alight by cannon fire called for by the performance), Shakespeare's company immediately rebuilt on the same location. The second Globe seems to have been a grander structure than its predecessor. It remained in use until the beginning of the English Civil War in 1642, when Parliament officially closed the theaters. Soon thereafter it was pulled down.

The public theaters of Shakespeare's time were very different buildings from our theaters today. First of all, they were open-air playhouses. As recent excavations of the Rose and the Globe confirm, some were polygonal or roughly circular in shape; the Fortune, however, was square. The most recent estimates of their size put the diameter of these buildings at 72 feet (the Rose) to 100 feet (the Globe), but they were said to hold vast audiences of two or three thousand, who must have been squeezed together quite tightly. Some of these spectators paid extra to sit or stand in the two or three levels of roofed galleries that extended, on the upper levels, all the way around the theater and surrounded an open space. In this space were the stage and, perhaps, the tiring house (what we would call dressing rooms), as well as the so-called yard. In the yard stood the spectators who chose to pay less, the ones whom Hamlet contemptuously called "groundlings." For a roof they had only the sky, and so they were exposed to all kinds of weather. They stood on a floor that was sometimes made of mortar and sometimes of ash mixed with the shells of hazelnuts, which, it has recently been discovered, were standard flooring material in the period.

Unlike the yard, the stage itself was covered by a roof. Its ceiling, called "the heavens," is thought to have been elaborately painted to depict the sun, moon, stars, and planets. Just how big the stage was remains hard to determine. We have a single sketch of part of the interior of the Swan. A Dutchman named Johannes de Witt visited this theater around 1596 and sent a sketch of it back to his friend, Arend van Buchel. Because van Buchel found de Witt's letter and sketch of interest, he copied both into a book. It is van Buchel's copy, adapted, it seems, to the shape and size of the page in his book, that survives. In this sketch, the stage appears to be a large rectangular platform that thrusts far out into the yard, perhaps even as far as the center of the circle formed by the surrounding galleries. This drawing, combined with the specifications for the size of the stage in the building contract for the Fortune, has led scholars to conjecture that the stage on which Shakespeare's plays were performed must have measured approximately 43 feet in width and 27 feet in depth, a vast acting area. But the digging up of a large part of the Rose by archaeologists has provided evidence of a quite different stage design. The Rose stage was a platform tapered at the corners and much shallower than what seems to be depicted in the van Buchel sketch. Indeed, its measurements seem to be about 37.5 feet across at its widest point and only 15.5 feet deep. Because the surviving indications of stage size and design differ from each other so much, it is possible that the stages in other playhouses, like the

Theatre, the Curtain, and the Globe (the outdoor play-houses where Shakespeare's plays were performed), were different from those at both the Swan and the Rose.

After about 1608 Shakespeare's plays were staged not only at the Globe but also at an indoor or private playhouse in Blackfriars. This theater had been constructed in 1596 by James Burbage in an upper hall of a former Dominican priory or monastic house. Although Henry VIII had dissolved all English monasteries in the 1530s (shortly after he had founded the Church of England), the area remained under church, rather than hostile civic, control. The hall that Burbage had purchased and renovated was a large one in which Parliament had once met. In the private theater that he constructed, the stage, lit by candles, was built across the narrow end of the hall, with boxes flanking it. The rest of the hall offered seating room only. Because there was no provision for standing room, the largest audience it could hold was less than a thousand, or about a quarter of what the Globe could accommodate. Admission to Blackfriars was correspondingly more expensive. Instead of a penny to stand in the yard at the Globe, it cost a minimum of sixpence to get into Blackfriars. The best seats at the Globe (in the Lords' Room in the gallery above and behind the stage) cost sixpence; but the boxes flanking the stage at Blackfriars were half a crown, or five times sixpence. Some spectators who were particularly interested in displaying themselves paid even more to sit on stools on the Blackfriars stage.

Whether in the outdoor or indoor playhouses, the stages of Shakespeare's time were different from ours. They were not separated from the audience by the dropping of a curtain between acts and scenes. Therefore the playwrights of the time had to find other ways of signaling to the audience that one scene (to be imagined as occurring in one location at a given time) had ended and the next (to be imagined at perhaps a different location at a later time) had begun. The customary way used by Shakespeare and many of his contemporaries was to have everyone onstage exit at the end of one scene and have one or more different characters enter to begin the next. In a few cases, where characters remain onstage from one scene to another, the dialogue or stage action makes the change of location clear, and the characters are generally to be imagined as having moved from one place to another. For example, in *Romeo and Juliet,* Romeo and his friends remain onstage in Act 1 from scene 4 to scene 5, but they are represented as having moved between scenes from the street that leads to Capulet's house into Capulet's house itself. The new location is signaled in part by the appearance onstage of Capulet's servingmen carrying napkins, something they would not take into the streets. Playwrights had to be quite resourceful in the use of hand properties, like the napkin, or in the use of dialogue to specify where the action was taking place in their plays because, in contrast to most of today's theaters, the playhouses of Shakespeare's time did not use movable scenery to dress the stage and make the setting precise. As another consequence of this difference, however, the playwrights of Shakespeare's time did not have to specify exactly where the action of their plays was set when they did not choose to do so, and much of the action of their plays is tied to no specific place.

Usually Shakespeare's stage is referred to as a "bare stage," to distinguish it from the stages of the past two or three centuries with their elaborate sets. But the stage in Shakespeare's time was not completely bare. Philip Henslowe, owner of the Rose, lists in his inventory of stage properties a rock, three tombs, and two mossy banks. Stage directions in plays of the time also call for such things as thrones (or "states"), banquets (presumably tables with plaster replicas of food on them), and beds and tombs to be pushed onto the stage. Thus the stage often held more than the actors.

The actors did not limit their performing to the stage alone. Occasionally they went beneath the stage, as the Ghost appears to do in the first act of *Hamlet*. From there they could emerge onto the stage through a trapdoor. They could retire behind the hangings across the back of the stage (or the front of the tiring house), as, for example, the actor playing Polonius does when he hides behind the arras. Sometimes the hangings could be drawn back during a performance to "discover" one or more actors behind them. When performance required that an actor appear "above," as when Juliet is imagined to stand at the window of her chamber in the famous and misnamed "balcony scene," then the actor probably climbed the stairs to the gallery over the back of the stage and temporarily shared it with some of the spectators. The stage was also provided with ropes and winches so that actors could descend from, and re-ascend to, the "heavens."

Perhaps the greatest difference between dramatic performances in Shakespeare's time and ours was that in Shakespeare's England the roles of women were played by boys. (Some of these boys grew up to take male roles in their maturity.) There were no women in the acting companies, only in the audience. It had not always been so in the history of the English stage. There are records of women on English stages in the thirteenth and fourteenth centuries, two hundred years before Shakespeare's plays were performed. After the accession of James I in 1603, the queen of England and her ladies took part in entertainments at court called masques, and with the reopening of the theaters in 1660 at the restoration of Charles II, women again took their place on the public stage.

The chief competitors for the companies of adult actors such as the one to which Shakespeare belonged and for which he wrote were companies of exclusively boy actors. The competition was most intense in the early 1600s. There were then two principal children's companies: the Children of Paul's (the choirboys from St. Paul's Cathedral, whose private playhouse was near the cathedral); and the Children of the Chapel Royal (the choirboys from the monarch's private chapel, who performed at the Blackfriars theater built by Burbage in 1596, which Shakespeare's company had been stopped from using by local residents who objected to crowds). In *Hamlet* Shakespeare writes of "an aerie [nest] of children, little eyases [hawks], that cry out on the top of question and are most tyrannically clapped for 't. These are now the fashion and . . . berattle the common stages [attack the public theaters]." In the long run, the adult actors prevailed. The Children of Paul's dissolved around 1606. By about 1608 the Children of the Chapel Royal had been forced to stop playing at the Blackfriars theater, which was then taken over by the King's company of players, Shakespeare's own troupe.

Acting companies and theaters of Shakespeare's time seem to have been organized in different ways. With the building of the Globe, Shakespeare's company apparently managed itself, with the principal actors, Shakespeare among them, having the status of "sharers" and the right to a share in the takings, as well as the responsibility for a part of the expenses.

Five of the sharers, including Shakespeare, owned the Globe. As actor, as sharer in an acting company and in ownership of theaters, and as playwright, Shakespeare was about as involved in the theatrical industry as one could imagine. Although Shakespeare and his fellows prospered, their status under the law was conditional upon the protection of powerful patrons. "Common players"—those who did not have patrons or masters—were classed in the language of the law with "vagabonds and sturdy beggars." So the actors had to secure for themselves the official rank of servants of patrons. Among the patrons under whose protection Shakespeare's company worked were the lord chamberlain and, after the accession of King James in 1603, the king himself.

In the early 1990s we seemed on the verge of learning a great deal more about the theaters in which Shakespeare and his contemporaries performed—or, at least, opening up new questions about them. At that time about 70 percent of the Rose had been excavated, as had about 10 percent of the second Globe, the one built in 1614. It was then hoped that more would become available for study. However, excavation was halted at that point, and it is not known if or when it will resume.

The Publication of Shakespeare's Plays

Eighteen of Shakespeare's plays found their way into print during the playwright's lifetime, but there is nothing to suggest that he took any interest in their publication. These eighteen appeared separately in editions called quartos. Their pages were not much larger than the one you are now reading, and these little books were sold unbound for a few pence. The earliest of the quartos that still survive were printed in 1594, the year that both *Titus Andronicus* and a version of the play now called *Henry VI, Part 2* became available. While almost every one of these early quartos displays on its title page the name of the acting company that performed the play, only about half provide the name of the playwright, Shakespeare. The first quarto edition to bear the name Shakespeare on its title page is *Love's Labor's Lost* of 1598. A few of these quartos were popular with the book-buying public of Shakespeare's lifetime; for example, quarto *Richard II* went through five editions between 1597 and 1615. But most of the quartos were far from best sellers; *Love's Labor's Lost* (1598), for instance, was not reprinted in quarto until 1631. After Shakespeare's death, two more of his plays appeared in quarto format: *Othello* in 1622 and *The Two Noble Kinsmen*, coauthored with John Fletcher, in 1634.

In 1623, seven years after Shakespeare's death, *Mr. William Shakespeares Comedies, Histories, & Tragedies* was published. This printing offered readers in a single book thirty-six of the thirty-eight plays now thought to have been written by Shakespeare, including eighteen that had never been printed before. And it offered them in a style that was then reserved for serious literature and scholarship. The plays were arranged in double columns on pages nearly a foot high. This large page size is called "folio," as opposed to the smaller "quarto," and the 1623 volume is usually called the Shakespeare First Folio. It is reputed to have sold for the lordly price of a pound. (One copy at the Folger Shakespeare Library is marked fifteen shillings—that is, three-quarters of a pound.)

In a preface to the First Folio entitled "To the great Variety of Readers," two of Shakespeare's former fellow actors in the King's Men, John Heminge and Henry Condell, wrote that they themselves had collected their dead companion's plays. They suggested that they had seen his own papers: "we have scarce received from him a blot in his papers." The title page of the Folio declared that the plays within it had been printed "according to the True Original Copies." Comparing the Folio to the quartos, Heminge and Condell disparaged the quartos, advising their readers that "before you were abused with divers stolen and surreptitious copies, maimed, and deformed by the frauds and stealths of injurious impostors." Many Shakespeareans of the eighteenth and nineteenth centuries believed Heminge and Condell and regarded the Folio plays as superior to anything in the quartos.

Once we begin to examine the Folio plays in detail, it becomes less easy to take at face value the word of Heminge and Condell about the superiority of the Folio texts. For example, of the first nine plays in the Folio (one-quarter of the entire collection), four were essentially reprinted from earlier quarto printings that Heminge and Condell had disparaged; and four have now been identified as printed from copies written in the hand of a professional scribe of the 1620s named Ralph Crane; the ninth, *The Comedy of Errors,* was apparently also printed from a manuscript, but one whose origin cannot be readily identified. Evidently, then, eight of the first nine plays in the First Folio were not printed, in spite of what the Folio title page announces, "according to the True Original Copies," or Shakespeare's own papers, and the source of the ninth is unknown. Since today's editors have been forced to treat Heminge and Condell's pronouncements with skepticism, they must choose whether to base their own editions upon quartos or the Folio on grounds other than Heminge and Condell's story of where the quarto and Folio versions originated.

Editors have often fashioned their own narratives to explain what lies behind the quartos and Folio. They have said that Heminge and Condell meant to criticize only a few of the early quartos, the ones that offer much shorter and sometimes quite different, often garbled, versions of plays. Among the examples of these are the 1600 quarto of *Henry V* (the Folio offers a much fuller version) or the 1603 *Hamlet* quarto (in 1604 a different, much longer form of the play got into print as a quarto). Early-twentieth-century editors speculated that these questionable texts were produced when someone in the audience took notes from the plays' dialogue during performances and then employed "hack poets" to fill out the notes. The poor results were then sold to a publisher and presented in print as Shakespeare's plays. More recently this story has given way to another in which the shorter versions are said to be re-creations from memory of Shakespeare's plays by actors who wanted to stage them in the provinces but lacked manuscript copies. Most of the quartos offer much better texts than these so-called bad quartos. Indeed, in most of the quartos we find texts that are at least equal to or better than what is printed in the Folio. Many Shakespeare enthusiasts persuaded themselves that most of the quartos were set into type directly from Shakespeare's own papers, although there is nothing on which to base this conclusion except the desire for it to be true. Thus speculation continues about how the Shakespeare plays got to be printed. All that we have are the printed texts.

The book collector who was most successful in bringing together copies of the quartos and the First Folio was Henry Clay Folger, founder of the Folger Shakespeare Library in Washington, D.C. While it is estimated that there survive around the world only about 230 copies of the First Folio, Mr. Folger was able to acquire more than seventy-five copies, as well as a large number of fragments, for the library that bears his name. He also amassed a substantial number of quartos. For example, only fourteen copies of the First Quarto of *Love's Labor's Lost* are known to exist, and three are at the Folger Shakespeare Library. As a consequence of Mr. Folger's labors, scholars visiting the Folger Library have been able to learn a great deal about sixteenth- and seventeenth-century printing and, particularly, about the printing of Shakespeare's plays. And Mr. Folger did not stop at the First Folio, but collected many copies of later editions of Shakespeare, beginning with the Second Folio (1632), the Third (1663–64), and the Fourth (1685). Each of these later folios was based on its immediate predecessor and was edited anonymously. The first editor of Shakespeare whose name we know was Nicholas Rowe, whose first edition came out in 1709. Mr. Folger collected this edition and many, many more by Rowe's successors.

An Introduction to This Text

Henry VI, Part 1 was first printed in the 1623 collection of Shakespeare's plays now known as the First Folio. The present edition is based directly upon that printing.* For the convenience of the reader, we have modernized the punctuation and the spelling of the Folio. Sometimes we go so far as to modernize certain old forms of words; for example, usually when *a* means *he,* we change it to *he;* we change *mo* to *more,* and *ye* to *you.* But it is not our practice in editing any of the plays to modernize words that sound distinctly different from modern forms. For example, when the early printed texts read *sith* or *apricocks* or *porpentine,* we have not modernized to *since, apricots, porcupine.* When the forms *an, and,* or *and if* appear instead of the modern form *if,* we have reduced *and* to *an* but have not changed any of these forms to their modern equivalent, *if.* We also modernize and, where necessary, correct passages in foreign languages, unless an error in the early printed text can be reasonably explained as a joke.

Whenever we change the wording of the First Folio or add anything to its stage directions, we mark the change by enclosing it in superior half-brackets (⌜ ⌝). We want our readers to be immediately aware when we have intervened. (Only when we correct an obvious typographical error in the First Folio does the change not get marked.) Whenever we change the

---

*We have also consulted the computerized text of the First Folio provided by the Text Archive of the Oxford University Computing Centre, to which we are grateful.

1

First Folio's wording or its punctuation so that meaning changes, we list the change in the textual notes at
the back of the book, even if all we have done is fix an
obvious error.

We regularize spellings of a number of the proper
names in the dialogue and stage directions, as is the
usual practice in editions of the play. For example, the
First Folio uses the forms "Reigneir," "Reignard," and
"Reignier"; the forms "Burgonie," "Burgundie," and
"Burgundy"; and the forms "Puzel" and "Pucell," but
our edition uses only the spellings "Reignier," "Burgundy," and "Pucelle." (This last form is a modern
French spelling of the word.) However, it is not our
practice always to render names of French characters
or places in modern French. Instead, to ease pronunciation in the play's verse, we retain the First Folio's
anglicized spellings of the following names: "Alanson"
for Alençon, "Callice" for Calais, "Dennis" for Denis,
"Orleance" for Orléans, and "Roan" for Rouen. (For
more detail, see longer note to 1.1.61, page 235.)

This edition differs from many earlier ones in its
efforts to aid the reader in imagining the play as a performance rather than as a novel or a series of actual
events. Thus some stage directions are edited with reference to the stage. For example, in 2.4 a group of noblemen quarrel over a case at law and divide into two
parties. They identify themselves as members of their
parties by plucking and wearing roses of different colors. One party is led by Richard Plantagenet and wears
the white rose. His chief follower is the Earl of Warwick.
The opposing party is headed by the Duke of Somerset,
whose principal supporter is the Earl of Suffolk; they
wear the red rose. Once these parties have formed in
this scene, thereafter in stage productions each time
they enter their members square off against each other
belligerently as they display the roses that signal their

allegiances. To emphasize this stage presentation of factionalism in our edition, and to help the reader identify characters with their proper factions, we reorganize the First Folio's entrance directions. The Folio opens 3.1 with the following stage direction: *"Enter . . . Warwick, Somerset, Suffolk, Richard Plantagenet."* In our edition, this direction appears as *"Enter . . . Richard Plantagenet* ⌜*and*⌝ *Warwick,* ⌜*with white roses;*⌝ *Somerset* ⌜*and*⌝ *Suffolk,* ⌜*with red roses.*⌝*"* Through this intervention we hope to help our readers stage the play in their own imaginations in a way that more closely approximates an experience in the theater.

Whenever it is reasonably certain, in our view, that a speech is accompanied by a particular action, we provide a stage direction describing the action, setting the added direction in brackets to signal that it is not found in the Folio. (Occasional exceptions to this general rule occur when the action is so obvious that to add a stage direction would insult the reader.) Stage directions for the entrance of a character in mid-scene are, with rare exceptions, placed so that they immediately precede the character's participation in the scene, even though these entrances may appear somewhat earlier in the early printed texts. Whenever we move a stage direction, we record this change in the textual notes. Latin stage directions (e.g., *Exeunt*) are translated into English (e.g., *They exit*).

We expand the often severely abbreviated forms of names used as speech headings in early printed texts into the full names of the characters. We also regularize the speakers' names in speech headings, using only a single designation for each character (with the exception of Richard Plantagenet, discussed below), even though the early printed texts sometimes use a variety of designations. Such variety is evident in connection with the character Beaufort, whose official name is Henry Beaufort, Bishop of Winchester. Beaufort is almost always called Winchester in the First Folio, but he is called Cardinal in 5.4, his final scene. (The direction for his entrance is *"Enter Cardinall,"* and he speaks as *"Car."*) We regularize his speech prefix in this scene to WINCHESTER because in all other cases in the play his prefix is *"Win.,"* *"Winch.,"* or *"Winchest."* In making this change, we record it in the textual notes, as we do all regularizations of speech prefixes. (For the argument that Beaufort's speech prefixes should be CARDINAL and not WINCHESTER in 5.4, see longer note to 1.3.36, page 239.)

Because we accept the argument that Winchester's status does not actually change in the last act, we do not change the speech prefixes of this character. However, we take a different approach when a character's status does indeed alter in the course of the play, as is the case with Richard Plantagenet. This change of status occurs at 3.1.178–82, when Richard, up to that point known as Plantagenet, is created "princely Duke of York" by Henry VI. To indicate this transformation of status, as well as to indicate the name by which he is henceforth known, we change his speech prefix from PLANTAGENET to YORK.

In the present edition, as well, we mark with a dash any change of address within a speech, unless a stage direction intervenes. When the -ed ending of a word is to be pronounced, we mark it with an accent. Like editors for the past two centuries, we print metrically linked lines in the following way:

TALBOT
  A maid, they say.

BEDFORD   A maid? And be so martial?
                                (2.1.22–23)

However, when there are a number of short verse-lines that can be linked in more than one way, we do not, with rare exceptions, indent any of them.

The Explanatory Notes

The notes that appear on the pages facing the text are designed to provide readers with the help that they may need to enjoy the play. Whenever the meaning of a word in the text is not readily accessible in a good contemporary dictionary, we offer the meaning in a note. Sometimes we provide a note even when the relevant meaning is to be found in the dictionary but when the word has acquired since Shakespeare's time other potentially confusing meanings. In our notes, we try to offer modern synonyms for Shakespeare's words. We also try to indicate to the reader the connection between the word in the play and the modern synonym. For example, Shakespeare sometimes uses the word *head* to mean *source,* but, for modern readers, there may be no connection evident between these two words. We provide the connection by explaining Shakespeare's usage as follows: "**head:** fountainhead, source." On some occasions, a whole phrase or clause needs explanation. Then we rephrase in our own words the difficult passage, and add at the end synonyms for individual words in the passage. When scholars have been unable to determine the meaning of a word or phrase, we acknowledge the uncertainty. Bible quotations are from the Geneva Bible (1560), modernized.

HENRY VI
Part 1

English Ancestry of King Henry VI
[Characters in this play appear in bold]

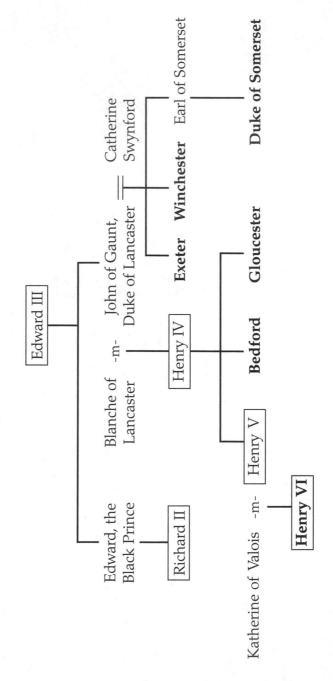

Characters in the Play

The English

KING HENRY VI
Lord TALBOT, afterwards Earl of Shrewsbury
JOHN TALBOT, his son
Duke of GLOUCESTER, the king's uncle, and Lord Protector
Duke of BEDFORD, the king's uncle, and Regent of France
Duke of EXETER, the king's great-uncle
Cardinal, Bishop of WINCHESTER, the king's great-uncle
Duke of SOMERSET
Richard PLANTAGENET, later Duke of YORK,
    and Regent of France
Earl of WARWICK
Earl of SALISBURY
Earl of SUFFOLK, William de la Pole
Edmund MORTIMER, Earl of March
Sir William GLANSDALE
Sir Thomas GARGRAVE
Sir John FASTOLF
Sir William LUCY
WOODVILLE, Lieutenant of the Tower of London
VERNON, of the White Rose or York faction
BASSET, of the Red Rose or Lancaster faction
A LAWYER
JAILORS to Mortimer
A LEGATE
MAYOR of London
Heralds, Attendants, three MESSENGERS, SERVINGMEN in
    blue coats and in tawny coats, two WARDERS, Officers,
    Soldiers, Captains, WATCH, Trumpeters, Drummer,
    Servant, two Ambassadors

3

The French

CHARLES, Dauphin of France
Joan la PUCELLE, also Joan of Arc
REIGNIER, Duke of Anjou and Maine, King of Naples
MARGARET, his daughter
Duke of ALANSON
Bastard of ORLEANCE
Duke of BURGUNDY
GENERAL of the French forces at Bordeaux
COUNTESS of Auvergne
Her PORTER
MASTER GUNNER of Orleance
BOY, his son
SERGEANT of a Band
A SHEPHERD, Pucelle's father
Drummer, Soldiers, two SENTINELS, MESSENGER,
    Soldiers, Governor of Paris, Herald, SCOUT, Fiends
    accompanying Pucelle

HENRY VI
Part 1

ACT 1

1.1   The funeral procession for Henry V is interrupted first by a quarrel between Gloucester and Winchester and then by messengers from France. The messengers report the loss of England's lands in France and the French capture of Talbot, the English military commander.

———————

0 SD. **Dead March:** somber music played for a funeral procession; **funeral:** i.e., coffin (and its bearers)

1. **the heavens:** (1) the sky; (2) the ceiling of the roof over the stage (See Shakespeare's Theater, page xl.)

2. **importing:** (1) signifying; (2) portending; (3) bringing in; **states:** (1) governments; (2) conditions

3. **Brandish:** scatter; **crystal:** i.e., bright (See picture of comet, page 220.)

4. **revolting:** rebelling (**Stars** and planets were thought to influence the fates of people, particularly the great.)

9. **Virtue:** moral excellence; physical force; courage

10. **his beams:** i.e., its (reflected) rays of light

14. **fierce bent:** fiercely turned

16. **lift:** i.e., lifted

19. **wooden:** lifeless, insensitive

ACT 1

Scene 1

*Dead March. Enter the funeral of King Henry the Fifth,
attended on by the Duke of Bedford, Regent of France;
the Duke of Gloucester, Protector; the Duke of Exeter;
⌈the Earl of⌉ Warwick; the Bishop of Winchester; and
the Duke of Somerset, ⌈with Heralds and Attendants.⌉*

BEDFORD
  Hung be the heavens with black, yield day to night!
  Comets, importing change of times and states,
  Brandish your crystal tresses in the sky,
  And with them scourge the bad revolting stars
  That have consented unto Henry's death: 5
  King Henry the Fifth, too famous to live long.
  England ne'er lost a king of so much worth.
GLOUCESTER
  England ne'er had a king until his time.
  Virtue he had, deserving to command;
  His brandished sword did blind men with his beams;   10
  His arms spread wider than a dragon's wings;
  His sparkling eyes, replete with wrathful fire,
  More dazzled and drove back his enemies
  Than midday sun fierce bent against their faces.
  What should I say? His deeds exceed all speech.   15
  He ne'er lift up his hand but conquerèd.
EXETER
  We mourn in black; why mourn we not in blood?
  Henry is dead and never shall revive.
  Upon a wooden coffin we attend,
  And Death's dishonorable victory   20

22. **car:** chariot (Lines 20–22 allude to the Roman custom of honoring a victorious warrior with a triumphal procession in which his **captives** were tied to his chariot; here it is as if the nobles are celebrating Death as the victor.) See picture of a victorious Death, page 44.

23. **planets of mishap:** i.e., **planets** exercising an evil influence

25. **subtle-witted:** crafty, treacherous

26. **Conjurers:** magicians who call up spirits; **sorcerers:** practitioners of witchcraft (See picture, page 128.)

27. **magic verses:** i.e., charms, spells

28. **of:** i.e., by; **King of kings:** "**King of kings** and Lord of lords" (Revelation 19.16)

29. **Judgment Day:** i.e., Doomsday, the **day** the dead will arise and be judged (in Christian theology) See picture, page 172.

30. **his sight:** the **sight** of Henry V

31. **Lord of Hosts:** "The **Lord of Hosts** numbreth the host of the battle" (Isaiah 13.4).

32. **Church's:** i.e., Roman Catholic **Church's**

33. **prayed:** with wordplay on *preyed*

34. **thread of life:** duration **of life** (as, in mythology, determined by the three Fates: Clotho, who spun the **thread of life**; Lachesis, who measured it out; and Atropos, who cut it) See picture, page 200.

35. **do you:** i.e., **do you churchmen** (line 33); **effeminate:** Boys were considered comparable to women in their lack of physical strength and of autonomy. (Henry VI's youth is stressed throughout the play.)

(continued)

We with our stately presence glorify,
Like captives bound to a triumphant car.
What? Shall we curse the planets of mishap
That plotted thus our glory's overthrow?
Or shall we think the subtle-witted French   25
Conjurers and sorcerers, that, afraid of him,
By magic verses have contrived his end?

WINCHESTER
He was a king blest of the King of kings;
Unto the French the dreadful Judgment Day
So dreadful will not be as was his sight.   30
The battles of the Lord of Hosts he fought;
The Church's prayers made him so prosperous.

GLOUCESTER
The Church? Where is it? Had not churchmen prayed,
His thread of life had not so soon decayed.
None do you like but an effeminate prince   35
Whom like a schoolboy you may overawe.

WINCHESTER
Gloucester, whate'er we like, thou art Protector
And lookest to command the Prince and realm.
Thy wife is proud; she holdeth thee in awe
More than God or religious churchmen may.   40

GLOUCESTER
Name not religion, for thou lov'st the flesh,
And ne'er throughout the year to church thou go'st,
Except it be to pray against thy foes.

BEDFORD
Cease, cease these jars, and rest your minds in peace!
Let's to the altar.—Heralds, wait on us.—   45
Instead of gold, we'll offer up our arms,
Since arms avail not, now that Henry's dead.
Posterity, await for wretched years
When at their mothers' moistened eyes babes shall
    suck,   50

38. **lookest to command:** i.e., expect **to command;** anticipate or look forward to commanding

39. **holdeth thee in awe:** controls you through fear

44. **jars:** quarrels

45. **wait on:** attend on, accompany

46. **arms:** armor, weapons

48. **await for:** expect

51. **Our . . . tears:** i.e., (instead of milk) England will produce nothing to sustain its children but **tears   nourish:** wet nurse

53. **invocate:** invoke, summon in prayer

54. **Prosper:** promote the success of; **broils:** turmoil

55. **adverse planets:** i.e., **planets** influencing England's fate adversely (See note to 1.1.4, above.)

57. **Julius Caesar:** Roman statesman and general (100–44 B.C.E.), whose soul is imagined as transformed into **a star** in Ovid's *Metamorphoses* 15.843–51

60. **discomfiture:** defeat in battle

61. **Guyen:** For discussion of the relation of events in the play to history as it was recorded in Shakespeare's time, see note to Saccio's essay in Further Reading, page 287. **Roan, Orleance:** i.e., Rouen, Orléans (For this edition's use of the Folio spellings, see longer note, page 235.)

65. **lead:** See longer note, page 235.

68–69. **yield the ghost:** i.e., die, give up the spirit (Henry V had reconquered much of **France** and had been made heir to the French throne, a title that passed to Henry VI on his father's death.)

(continued)

Our isle be made a nourish of salt tears,
And none but women left to wail the dead.
Henry the Fifth, thy ghost I invoke:
Prosper this realm, keep it from civil broils,
Combat with adverse planets in the heavens.   55
A far more glorious star thy soul will make
Than Julius Caesar or bright—

Enter a Messenger.

MESSENGER
My honorable lords, health to you all.
Sad tidings bring I to you out of France,
Of loss, of slaughter, and discomfiture: 60
Guyen, Champaigne, Rheims, ⌐Roan,¬ Orleance,
Paris, Gisors, Poitiers, are all quite lost.
BEDFORD
What say'st thou, man, before dead Henry's corse?
Speak softly, or the loss of those great towns
Will make him burst his lead and rise from death.   65
GLOUCESTER
Is Paris lost? Is Roan yielded up?
If Henry were recalled to life again,
These news would cause him once more yield the
    ghost.
EXETER
How were they lost? What treachery was used?   70
MESSENGER
No treachery, but want of men and money.
Amongst the soldiers, this is mutterèd:
That here you maintain several factions
And, whilst a field should be dispatched and fought,
You are disputing of your generals.   75
One would have ling'ring wars with little cost;
Another would fly swift, but wanteth wings;
A third thinks, without expense at all,

71. **want:** lack

73. **several:** separate, private

74. **field . . . fought:** i.e., armed force **should be dispatched** and battle **should be fought** (wordplay on **field,** which means both "army" and "battle")

75. **of:** i.e., about

76. **would:** wishes to, wants to

77. **wanteth:** lacks (Proverbial: "He would fain [gladly] fly but he wants [lacks] feathers.")

79. **fair:** specious, flattering

81. **begot:** begotten, acquired

82. **Cropped:** picked, plucked; **flower-de-luces:** fleurs-de-lis, heraldic lilies borne on the French royal coat of **arms** and, beginning with Edward III, also on the English coat of **arms** (along with the English lion) to indicate England's conquest over the French (See pictures of the shields carried by Henry V, page 112, and Henry VI, page 138.)

83. **coat: coat** of arms

84. **wanting to:** i.e., lacking at

85. **her:** i.e., **England's** (line 83)

86. **Me they concern:** i.e., **these tidings** (line 85) are my concern

87. **steelèd coat:** i.e., **coat** of steel, armor; **for France:** to win back **France**

88. **wailing:** i.e., funeral

89. **lend:** give, deal

90. **intermissive:** intermittent (here, resuming after an intermission)

91. **mischance:** disaster, calamity

94. **Dauphin:** accent throughout on first syllable (See longer note to 1.1.61, page 235, and picture, page 64.)

(continued)

By guileful fair words peace may be obtained.
Awake, awake, English nobility!   80
Let not sloth dim your honors new begot.
Cropped are the flower-de-luces in your arms;
Of England's coat, one half is cut away.   ⌐*He exits.*⌐

EXETER
Were our tears wanting to this funeral,
These tidings would call forth her flowing tides.   85

BEDFORD
Me they concern; regent I am of France.
Give me my steelèd coat, I'll fight for France.
Away with these disgraceful wailing robes.
Wounds will I lend the French instead of eyes
To weep their intermissive miseries.   90

Enter to them another Messenger, ⌐with papers.⌐

SECOND MESSENGER
Lords, view these letters, full of bad mischance.
France is revolted from the English quite,
Except some petty towns of no import.
The Dauphin Charles is crownèd king in Rheims;
The Bastard of Orleance with him is joined;   95
Reignier, Duke of Anjou, doth take his part;
The Duke of Alanson flieth to his side.   *He exits.*

EXETER
The Dauphin crownèd king? All fly to him?
O, whither shall we fly from this reproach?

GLOUCESTER
We will not fly but to our enemies' throats.—   100
Bedford, if thou be slack, I'll fight it out.

BEDFORD
Gloucester, why doubt'st thou of my forwardness?
An army have I mustered in my thoughts,
Wherewith already France is overrun.

Enter another Messenger.

97. **flieth:** rushes (In lines 98–100, the word **fly** means, alternately, "rush" and "flee"; in line 100, it also has the sense of "**fly** at" or attack violently.)

99. **reproach:** disgrace, shame

102. **forwardness:** promptness, zeal

106. **hearse:** (1) coffin; (2) corpse

107. **dismal:** disastrous, calamitous

111. **circumstance:** details

114. **full scarce:** i.e., barely (**Full** is an intensive.)

117. **enrank his men:** i.e., draw up **his men** in order of battle

118. **wanted:** lacked

123. **above:** beyond

125. **stand him:** face him without retreating or flinching

128. **agazed on:** terrified by; astounded or amazed at

130. **À Talbot:** to **Talbot** (a rallying cry); **amain:** with all their might

131. **bowels:** center

132. **sealed up:** secured

133. **Sir John Fastolf:** See longer note, page 236.

134. **vaward:** vanguard, the foremost division of the army; **placed behind:** perhaps, **placed behind** those in the first ranks of the vanguard

135. **them:** i.e., the soldiers in the first ranks of the vanguard

137. **wrack:** wreck, disaster

THIRD MESSENGER
   My gracious lords, to add to your laments,   105
   Wherewith you now bedew King Henry's hearse,
   I must inform you of a dismal fight
   Betwixt the stout Lord Talbot and the French.
WINCHESTER
   What? Wherein Talbot overcame, is 't so?
THIRD MESSENGER
   O no, wherein Lord Talbot was o'erthrown.   110
   The circumstance I'll tell you more at large.
   The tenth of August last, this dreadful lord,
   Retiring from the siege of Orleance,
   Having full scarce six thousand in his troop,
   By three and twenty thousand of the French   115
   Was round encompassèd and set upon.
   No leisure had he to enrank his men.
   He wanted pikes to set before his archers,
   Instead whereof, sharp stakes plucked out of hedges
   They pitchèd in the ground confusedly   120
   To keep the horsemen off from breaking in.
   More than three hours the fight continuèd,
   Where valiant Talbot, above human thought,
   Enacted wonders with his sword and lance.
   Hundreds he sent to hell, and none durst stand him; 125
   Here, there, and everywhere, enraged, he slew.
   The French exclaimed the devil was in arms;
   All the whole army stood agazed on him.
   His soldiers, spying his undaunted spirit,
   "À Talbot! À Talbot!" cried out amain   130
   And rushed into the bowels of the battle.
   Here had the conquest fully been sealed up
   If Sir John Fastolf had not played the coward.
   He, being in the vaward, placed behind
   With purpose to relieve and follow them,   135
   Cowardly fled, not having struck one stroke.
   Hence grew the general wrack and massacre.

138. **with their:** i.e., by their

139. **base Walloon:** lowborn soldier from southeast Belgium; **grace:** favor, good opinion

146. **wanting:** lacking

147. **dastard:** cowardly

148. **took:** i.e., taken

151. **there . . . I:** i.e., only I

152. **hale:** pull, haul

154. **change:** exchange

155. **will I:** i.e., **I will** go

157. **Saint George's feast:** the feast day (April 23) of the patron saint of England; **withal:** with (See picture of Saint George, below.)

160. **'fore Orleance besieged:** before **besieged** Orléans

162. **supply:** reinforcements of troops

163. **hardly:** with difficulty

165. **your . . . sworn:** i.e., the oath that each of you swore to **Henry** V (on his deathbed)

166. **quell:** crush, destroy

Saint George. (1.1.157; 4.2.55; 4.6.1)
From [Jacobus de Voragine,] *Here begynneth the legende named in latyn legenda aurea . . .* [1493].

Enclosèd were they with their enemies.
A base Walloon, to win the Dauphin's grace,
Thrust Talbot with a spear into the back,   140
Whom all France, with their chief assembled
    strength,
Durst not presume to look once in the face.

BEDFORD
Is Talbot slain then? I will slay myself
For living idly here, in pomp and ease,   145
Whilst such a worthy leader, wanting aid,
Unto his dastard foemen is betrayed.

THIRD MESSENGER
O, no, he lives, but is took prisoner,
And Lord Scales with him, and Lord Hungerford;
Most of the rest slaughtered or took likewise.   150

BEDFORD
His ransom there is none but I shall pay.
I'll hale the Dauphin headlong from his throne;
His crown shall be the ransom of my friend.
Four of their lords I'll change for one of ours.
Farewell, my masters; to my task will I.   155
Bonfires in France forthwith I am to make,
To keep our great Saint George's feast withal.
Ten thousand soldiers with me I will take,
Whose bloody deeds shall make all Europe quake.

THIRD MESSENGER
So you had need; 'fore Orleance besieged,   160
The English army is grown weak and faint;
The Earl of Salisbury craveth supply
And hardly keeps his men from mutiny,
Since they so few watch such a multitude.
                                                      ⌜*He exits.*⌝

EXETER
Remember, lords, your oaths to Henry sworn: 165
Either to quell the Dauphin utterly
Or bring him in obedience to your yoke.

170. **Tower: Tower** of London, a fortress, prison, and armory (See pictures, pages 32 and 226.)

173. **Eltham:** royal palace nine miles southeast of London (in what is now a London suburb)

174. **ordained:** appointed; **governor:** one in charge of a young man's education; tutor to a prince or young noble

176. **place:** office, duty; **attend:** look after, apply himself to

178. **Jack-out-of-office:** a proverbial term for one who has been dismissed from his **office**

180. **sit . . . weal:** i.e., occupy the chief seat in the government of the state   **stern:** rudder (of the ship of state)

1.2   Charles the Dauphin, leader of the French, is defeated by a small English force that is besieging Orleance. He is then introduced to Pucelle, who declares herself chosen by the Virgin Mary to free France from the English. Charles challenges her to single combat, loses, and grants her authority as a military leader.

———————

0 SD. **flourish:** fanfare of trumpets; **Drum:** drummer

1. **Mars his:** Mars's (**Mars,** the Roman god of war, is here imagined to control the outcome of battle.) See longer note, page 237, and picture, page 52.)

3. **Late:** recently

6. **At pleasure:** as we please; **lie:** reside

7. **Otherwhiles:** occasionally, sometimes

8. **Faintly:** timidly, weakly

BEDFORD
  I do remember it, and here take my leave
  To go about my preparation.   *Bedford exits.*
GLOUCESTER
  I'll to the Tower with all the haste I can   170
  To view th' artillery and munition,
  And then I will proclaim young Henry king.
                                    Gloucester exits.

EXETER
  To Eltham will I, where the young king is,
  Being ordained his special governor;
  And for his safety there I'll best devise.   *He exits.* 175
WINCHESTER, ⌜*aside*⌝
  Each hath his place and function to attend.
  I am left out; for me nothing remains.
  But long I will not be Jack-out-of-office.
  The King from Eltham I intend to ⌜steal,⌝
  And sit at chiefest stern of public weal.   180
              He exits ⌜at one door; at another door,
                  Warwick, Somerset, Attendants and
                      Heralds exit with the coffin.⌝

                      ⌜Scene 2⌝

          Sound a flourish. Enter Charles ⌜the Dauphin,⌝
          Alanson, and Reignier, marching with Drum
                      and Soldiers.

CHARLES
  Mars his true moving, even as in the heavens
  So in the earth, to this day is not known.
  Late did he shine upon the English side;
  Now we are victors; upon us he smiles.
  What towns of any moment but we have?   5
  At pleasure here we lie, near Orleance.
  Otherwhiles, the famished English, like pale ghosts,
  Faintly besiege us one hour in a month.

9. **want:** lack; **porridge:** thickened soup or stew

10. **dieted:** fed

12. **drownèd mice:** proverbial

13. **raise:** end (by forcing the English to withdraw)

17. **Nor men:** i.e., neither **men**

18. **alarum:** call to arms

19. **forlorn:** doomed (ironic)

21. **fly:** flee

28. **hungry prey:** i.e., **prey** of the **hungry** (transferred epithet)

29. **Froissart:** French historian of the fourteenth century

30. **Olivers and Rolands:** Oliver and Roland were legendarily great warriors who served Charlemagne (c. 800 C.E.).

33. **Samsons, Goliases:** i.e., legendary strongmen (Samson was a biblical war hero of the Israelites [Judges 14–16]; Goliath was the giant Philistine warrior slain by the young David [1 Samuel 17.4–54].)

34. **skirmish:** i.e., fight (literally, fight in small parties); **One to ten:** i.e., **one** Englishman against **ten** Frenchmen

ALANSON
  They want their porridge and their fat bull beeves.
  Either they must be dieted like mules   10
  And have their provender tied to their mouths,
  Or piteous they will look, like drownèd mice.

REIGNIER
  Let's raise the siege. Why live we idly here?
  Talbot is taken, whom we wont to fear.
  Remaineth none but mad-brained Salisbury,   15
  And he may well in fretting spend his gall;
  Nor men nor money hath he to make war.

CHARLES
  Sound, sound alarum! We will rush on them.
  Now for the honor of the forlorn French!
  Him I forgive my death that killeth me   20
  When he sees me go back one foot, or fly.
            They exit. Here alarum. They are beaten
            back by the English, with great loss.

        Enter Charles, Alanson, and Reignier.

CHARLES
  Whoever saw the like? What men have I!
  Dogs, cowards, dastards! I would ne'er have fled
  But that they left me 'midst my enemies.

REIGNIER
  Salisbury is a desperate homicide.   25
  He fighteth as one weary of his life.
  The other lords, like lions wanting food,
  Do rush upon us as their hungry prey.

ALANSON
  Froissart, a countryman of ours, records
  England all Olivers and Rolands ⌐bred⌐   30
  During the time Edward the Third did reign.
  More truly now may this be verified,
  For none but Samsons and Goliases
  It sendeth forth to skirmish. One to ten!

35. **rascals:** common soldiers

37. **hare-brained:** reckless, wild; **slaves:** term of contempt

38–40. **And hunger . . . siege:** Proverbial: "**Hunger** breaks stone **walls.**" **eager:** fierce

41. **gimmers:** gimmals, mechanical parts for transmitting motion (as in clockwork)

42. **still:** always, continually

44. **By my consent:** i.e., in my opinion; **even:** just

48. **Methinks:** it seems to me; **cheer:** facial expression; **appalled:** dismayed

49. **late:** recent

51. **maid:** maiden, virgin

53. **Ordainèd:** appointed, destined; **raise:** end

54. **forth:** out of

56. **Sibyls:** prophetesses (See picture, below.)

57. **descry:** perceive; reveal

59. **unfallible:** infallible

61. **try:** test

A Sibyl. (1.2.56)
From Philippus de Barberiis, *Quattuor hic compressa opuscula* . . . (c. 1495).

Lean rawboned rascals! Who would e'er suppose   35
They had such courage and audacity?
CHARLES
Let's leave this town, for they are hare-brained slaves,
And hunger will enforce them to be more eager.
Of old I know them; rather with their teeth
The walls they'll tear down than forsake the siege.   40
REIGNIER
I think by some odd gimmers or device
Their arms are set, like clocks, still to strike on;
Else ne'er could they hold out so as they do.
By my consent, we'll even let them alone.
ALANSON   Be it so.   45

Enter the Bastard of Orleance.

BASTARD
Where's the Prince Dauphin? I have news for him.
CHARLES
Bastard of Orleance, thrice welcome to us.
BASTARD
Methinks your looks are sad, your cheer appalled.
Hath the late overthrow wrought this offence?
Be not dismayed, for succor is at hand.   50
A holy maid hither with me I bring,
Which, by a vision sent to her from heaven,
Ordainèd is to raise this tedious siege
And drive the English forth the bounds of France.
The spirit of deep prophecy she hath,   55
Exceeding the nine Sibyls of old Rome.
What's past and what's to come she can descry.
Speak, shall I call her in? Believe my words,
For they are certain and unfallible.
CHARLES
Go call her in.   ⌜*Bastard exits.*⌝   60
            But first, to try her skill,
Reignier, stand thou as Dauphin in my place;

64. **sound:** seek to ascertain (as if by testing the depth of a body of water with a sounding device)

64. SD. **la Pucelle:** the virgin (French) See longer note, page 238, and picture, page 50.

69. **amazed:** confused, alarmed

72. **takes upon her:** behaves, proceeds; **bravely:** daringly; **at first dash:** i.e., right away (proverbial)

74. **wit:** intelligence; **art:** learning

75. **Our Lady gracious:** the Virgin Mary

76. **estate:** place in society

77. **waited on:** watched over

81. **base:** lowly

85. **black and swart:** i.e., tanned ("to sun's parching heat [I] displayed my cheeks" line 78), a sign of low social status, fair skin being a mark of the beauty unique to the upper classes who need not expose their skin to the elements   **swart:** swarthy

86. **clear:** bright; **infused:** shed

88. **what question . . . possible:** i.e., whatever **question** you possibly can

89 **unpremeditated:** without premeditation, without stopping to think

90. **try:** test

Question her proudly; let thy looks be stern.
By this means shall we sound what skill she hath.

Enter ⌐Bastard, with⌐ Joan ⌐la⌐ Pucelle.

REIGNIER, ⌐*as Charles*⌐
Fair maid, is 't thou wilt do these wondrous feats?   65
PUCELLE
Reignier, is 't thou that thinkest to beguile me?
Where is the Dauphin?—Come, come from behind.
I know thee well, though never seen before.
Be not amazed; there's nothing hid from me.
In private will I talk with thee apart.—   70
Stand back, you lords, and give us leave a while.
REIGNIER
She takes upon her bravely at first dash.
                 ⌐*Alanson, Reignier, and Bastard exit.*⌐
PUCELLE
Dauphin, I am by birth a shepherd's daughter,
My wit untrained in any kind of art.
Heaven and Our Lady gracious hath it pleased   75
To shine on my contemptible estate.
Lo, whilst I waited on my tender lambs,
And to sun's parching heat displayed my cheeks,
God's Mother deignèd to appear to me,
And in a vision full of majesty   80
Willed me to leave my base vocation
And free my country from calamity.
Her aid she promised and assured success.
In complete glory she revealed herself;
And whereas I was black and swart before,   85
With those clear rays which she infused on me
That beauty am I blest with, which you may see.
Ask me what question thou canst possible,
And I will answer unpremeditated.
My courage try by combat, if thou dar'st,   90
And thou shalt find that I exceed my sex.

92. **Resolve on:** be satisfied with, be convinced of

94. **high terms:** arrogant **words** (line 97)

95. **proof:** test

96. **buckle:** grapple

100. **Decked:** adorned

104. **a':** i.e., in

105. **fly:** flee

106. **Stay, stay thy hands:** cease your attack; **Amazon:** legendary female warrior (See picture, below.)

107. **Deborah:** a biblical judge and prophet who aided the Israelites in their victory over the Canaanites (Judges 4–5) See picture, page 118.

108. **else:** otherwise

110. **thy desire:** i.e., **desire** for you

113. **servant:** i.e., lover

114. **sueth to:** pleads **to**; courts, woos

115. **rights:** with wordplay on *rites*

116. **profession's:** vow is; **sacred:** consecrated, hallowed

Amazon Ja archibus Jacobi Philipi Libenari. 43

An Amazon. (1.2.106)
From Giovanni Battista Cavalleriis,
Antiquarum statuarum . . . (1585–94).

Resolve on this: thou shalt be fortunate
If thou receive me for thy warlike mate.

CHARLES
Thou hast astonished me with thy high terms.
Only this proof I'll of thy valor make: 95
In single combat thou shalt buckle with me,
And if thou vanquishest, thy words are true;
Otherwise I renounce all confidence.

PUCELLE
I am prepared. Here is my keen-edged sword,
Decked with fine flower-de-luces on each side—   100
⌈*Aside.*⌉ The which at Touraine, in Saint Katherine's
    churchyard,
Out of a great deal of old iron I chose forth.

CHARLES
Then come, a' God's name! I fear no woman.

PUCELLE
And while I live, I'll ne'er fly from a man.   105
                            Here they fight, and
                Joan ⌈*la*⌉ *Pucelle overcomes.*

CHARLES
Stay, stay thy hands! Thou art an Amazon,
And fightest with the sword of Deborah.

PUCELLE
Christ's mother helps me; else I were too weak.

CHARLES
Whoe'er helps thee, 'tis thou that must help me.
Impatiently I burn with thy desire.   110
My heart and hands thou hast at once subdued.
Excellent Pucelle, if thy name be so,
Let me thy servant and not sovereign be.
'Tis the French Dauphin sueth to thee thus.

PUCELLE
I must not yield to any rights of love,   115
For my profession's sacred from above.

119. gracious: with favor; **prostrate:** i.e., submissive (and, perhaps, adoring); **thrall:** captive

120. methinks: it seems to me

121. shrives . . . smock: i.e., questions **this woman** thoroughly   **smock:** undergarment

123. keeps no mean: exercises no moderation

125. shrewd: cunning, artful

127. devise you on: i.e., do you decide

132. English scourge: instrument of divine punishment of the **English**

134. Saint Martin's summer: a season of fine weather around **Saint Martin's** day, November 11; **halcyons' days:** proverbial for "peaceful times" (The halcyon is fabled to breed in a nest on the sea around December 21 and thus to calm the winter sea. See picture below.)

139. Henry's: i.e., Henry V's

A halcyon and its young. (1.2.134)
From George Wither, *A collection of emblemes* . . . (1635).

When I have chasèd all thy foes from hence,
Then will I think upon a recompense.

CHARLES
Meantime look gracious on thy prostrate thrall.

⌜*Enter Reignier and Alanson.*⌝

REIGNIER, ⌜*aside to Alanson*⌝
My lord, methinks, is very long in talk.   120

ALANSON, ⌜*aside to Reignier*⌝
Doubtless he shrives this woman to her smock,
Else ne'er could he so long protract his speech.

REIGNIER, ⌜*aside to Alanson*⌝
Shall we disturb him, since he keeps no mean?

ALANSON, ⌜*aside to Reignier*⌝
He may mean more than we poor men do know.
These women are shrewd tempters with their   125
    tongues.

REIGNIER, ⌜*to Charles*⌝
My lord, where are you? What devise you on?
Shall we give o'er Orleance, or no?

PUCELLE
Why, no, I say. Distrustful recreants,
Fight till the last gasp. I'll be your guard.   130

CHARLES
What she says I'll confirm: we'll fight it out.

PUCELLE
Assigned am I to be the English scourge.
This night the siege assuredly I'll raise.
Expect Saint Martin's summer, halcyons' days,
Since I have enterèd into these wars.   135
Glory is like a circle in the water,
Which never ceaseth to enlarge itself
Till by broad spreading it disperse to naught.
With Henry's death, the English circle ends;
Dispersèd are the glories it included.   140

141–42. **Now . . . once:** See longer note, page 238. **insulting:** boasting, bragging

143. **Was . . . dove:** It was believed by many that God spoke to the Prophet Muhammad through **a dove.** (See longer note, page 239.)   **with:** i.e., by

144. **eagle:** bird of war (because it was the standard of the Roman legions [pictured on page 40]), in contrast to the **dove,** the bird of peace

145. **Helen:** i.e., (not even) St. Helena, who was reputed to have discovered the cross on which Jesus was crucified; **Constantine:** Roman emperor, who in 313 proclaimed the toleration of Christianity throughout the empire

146. **Saint Philip's daughters:** See Acts 21.9: "[Philip the evangelist] had four daughters, virgins, which did prophesy."

147. **star of Venus:** the planet, which is both morning **star** and evening **star**

152. **Presently:** immediately

1.3   Gloucester visits the Tower of London, only to be denied entry by Winchester. The servants of the two nobles skirmish until all are ordered away by the mayor.

———————

0 SD. **blue**: In line 47, below, Gloucester refers to his men as **"blue coats."** (**Blue** was the customary color of servants' coats.)

1. **Tower: Tower** of London (See note to 1.1.170.)

2. **conveyance:** stealing

3. **wait:** keep watch

Now am I like that proud insulting ship
Which Caesar and his fortune bare at once.
CHARLES
Was Mahomet inspirèd with a dove?
Thou with an eagle art inspirèd then.
Helen, the mother of great Constantine,   145
Nor yet Saint Philip's daughters were like thee.
Bright star of Venus, fall'n down on the earth,
How may I reverently worship thee enough?
ALANSON
Leave off delays, and let us raise the siege.
REIGNIER
Woman, do what thou canst to save our honors.   150
Drive them from Orleance and be immortalized.
CHARLES
Presently we'll try. Come, let's away about it.
No prophet will I trust if she prove false.
                                        They exit.

⌜Scene 3⌝

Enter Gloucester with his Servingmen ⌜*in blue coats.*⌝

GLOUCESTER
I am come to survey the Tower this day.
Since Henry's death I fear there is conveyance.
Where be these warders that they wait not here?—
Open the gates! 'Tis Gloucester that calls.
                    ⌜*Servingmen knock at the gate.*⌝
FIRST WARDER, ⌜*within*⌝
Who's there that knocks so imperiously?   5
FIRST SERVINGMAN
It is the noble Duke of Gloucester.
SECOND WARDER, ⌜*within*⌝
Whoe'er he be, you may not be let in.

8. **Villains:** lowborn, base-minded men

10. **willed:** ordered

13. **Break up: break** open; **warrantize:** permission, authorization

14. **flouted:** insulted, mocked; **dunghill:** cowardly; **grooms:** servants

14 SD. **within:** offstage

26. **shut thee out:** perhaps, deny you entry to the Tower; or, perhaps, deprive you of your office

28 SD. **tawny:** "the shade adopted by dignitaries of the Church" for their servants' livery (*Shakespeare's England* [Oxford, 1916], 2:113)

The Tower of London. (1.1.170; 1.3.1)
From John Seller, *A book of the prospects of the remarkable places in . . . London . . .* [c. 1700?].

FIRST SERVINGMAN
  Villains, answer you so the Lord Protector?
FIRST WARDER, ⌜*within*⌝
  The Lord protect him, so we answer him.
  We do no otherwise than we are willed.   10
GLOUCESTER
  Who willed you? Or whose will stands but mine?
  There's none Protector of the realm but I.—
  Break up the gates! I'll be your warrantize.
  Shall I be flouted thus by dunghill grooms?
            Gloucester's men rush at the Tower gates, and
                Woodville, the lieutenant, speaks within.
WOODVILLE
  What noise is this? What traitors have we here?   15
GLOUCESTER
  Lieutenant, is it you whose voice I hear?
  Open the gates. Here's Gloucester that would enter.
WOODVILLE
  Have patience, noble duke, I may not open.
  The Cardinal of Winchester forbids.
  From him I have express commandment   20
  That thou nor none of thine shall be let in.
GLOUCESTER
  Fainthearted Woodville, prizest him 'fore me?
  Arrogant Winchester, that haughty prelate
  Whom Henry, our late sovereign, ne'er could brook?
  Thou art no friend to God or to the King.   25
  Open the gates, or I'll shut thee out shortly.
SERVINGMEN
  Open the gates unto the Lord Protector,
  Or we'll burst them open if that you come not quickly.

Enter, to the Protector at the Tower gates, Winchester
  ⌜*in cardinal's robes*⌝ *and his men in tawny coats.*

WINCHESTER
  How now, ambitious Humphrey, what means this?

30. **Peeled:** tonsured (See picture, page 108.)

31. **proditor:** betrayer, traitor

34. **Thou . . . lord:** The historical Gloucester did accuse Winchester of conspiring to have Henry V killed as an infant.

35. **giv'st . . . sin:** an attack on the bishop as the official responsible for the Bankside, location of brothels **indulgences:** documents for forgiveness of the punishment for **sin,** available in return for donations to the church

36. **canvass:** toss (as in a blanket or canvas sheet); **cardinal's hat:** See longer note, page 239.

39–40. **This . . . Abel:** Winchester alludes to the fratricide of **Abel** by **Cain** to call attention to his and Gloucester's kinship, which Gloucester does not like to acknowledge. (See 3.1.42–44.) **Damascus:** legendarily the location of Abel's death (For **Cain** and **Abel,** see Genesis 4.1–16, and picture, page 100.)

42. **bearing-cloth:** christening robe

44. **beard:** defy

46. **for all this:** i.e., in spite of this being a; **privilegèd place:** i.e., **place** where violence is forbidden

47. **to:** against, upon (in attack)

51. **dignities:** dignitaries

53. **answer:** be accountable or responsible for

54. **Winchester goose:** slang for (1) prostitute; (2) a pustule of syphilitic infection; **a rope, a rope:** This phrase (a rhyme for **Pope,** line 53) was taught to parrots as a comic threat of death on the gallows.

GLOUCESTER
  Peeled priest, dost thou command me to be shut out?   30
WINCHESTER
  I do, thou most usurping proditor—
  And not Protector—of the King or realm.
GLOUCESTER
  Stand back, thou manifest conspirator,
  Thou that contrived'st to murder our dead lord,
  Thou that giv'st whores indulgences to sin!   35
  I'll canvass thee in thy broad cardinal's hat
  If thou proceed in this thy insolence.
WINCHESTER
  Nay, stand thou back. I will not budge a foot.
  This be Damascus; be thou cursèd Cain
  To slay thy brother Abel, if thou wilt.   40
GLOUCESTER
  I will not slay thee, but I'll drive thee back.
  Thy scarlet robes, as a child's bearing-cloth,
  I'll use to carry thee out of this place.
WINCHESTER
  Do what thou dar'st, I beard thee to thy face.
GLOUCESTER
  What, am I dared and bearded to my face?—   45
  Draw, men, for all this privilegèd place.
  Blue coats to tawny coats!   ⌈*All draw their swords.*⌉
                    Priest, beware your beard.
  I mean to tug it and to cuff you soundly.
  Under my feet ⌈I'll⌉ stamp thy cardinal's hat;   50
  In spite of pope or dignities of Church,
  Here by the cheeks I'll drag thee up and down.
WINCHESTER
  Gloucester, thou wilt answer this before the Pope.
GLOUCESTER
  Winchester goose, I cry "a rope, a rope!"—
  Now beat them hence; why do you let them stay?—   55

56. **wolf . . . array:** Matthew 7.15: "Beware of false prophets, which come to you **in sheep's** clothing but inwardly they are ravening wolves." (See picture, below.)   **array:** attire

58. **magistrates:** members of the executive government

59. **contumeliously:** arrogantly, insolently; **break:** interrupt, disturb

60. **my wrongs:** i.e., the **wrongs** done to me

61. **Beaufort:** Winchester; **nor God:** neither **God**

62. **distrained:** seized, confiscated

64. **still:** always; **motions:** brings forward

65. **O'ercharging:** overloading, overburdening; **free:** generous; **fines:** fees (such as taxes, to fund wars)

69. **Prince:** ruler (i.e., Henry VI)

71. **rests:** remains

77. **several:** various, individual

78. **handle:** wield

A wolf in sheep's clothing. (1.3.56)
From August Casimir Redel, *Annus symbolicus* . . . (c. 1695).

Thee I'll chase hence, thou wolf in sheep's array.—
Out, tawny coats, out, scarlet hypocrite!

Here Gloucester's men beat out the Cardinal's men,
and enter in the hurly-burly the Mayor of London
and his Officers.

MAYOR
Fie, lords, that you, being supreme magistrates,
Thus contumeliously should break the peace!
GLOUCESTER
Peace, Mayor? Thou know'st little of my wrongs.   60
Here's Beaufort, that regards nor God nor king,
Hath here distrained the Tower to his use.
WINCHESTER
Here's Gloucester, a foe to citizens,
One that still motions war and never peace,
O'ercharging your free purses with large fines;   65
That seeks to overthrow religion
Because he is Protector of the realm,
And would have armor here out of the Tower
To crown himself king and suppress the Prince.
GLOUCESTER
I will not answer thee with words, but blows.   70
                    Here they skirmish again.
MAYOR
Naught rests for me in this tumultuous strife
But to make open proclamation.
Come, officer, as loud as e'er thou canst, cry.
                    ⌜*He hands an Officer a paper.*⌝
⌜OFFICER *reads*⌝ *All manner of men, assembled here in*
arms this day against God's peace and the King's, we   75
charge and command you, in his Highness' name, to
repair to your several dwelling places, and not to
wear, handle, or use any sword, weapon, or dagger
henceforward, upon pain of death.

81. **break:** reveal what is within; **at large:** freely, without restraint

84. **call for clubs:** rally apprentices bearing heavy staffs or **clubs**

89. **coast cleared:** proverbial

90. **these nobles:** i.e., that **these nobles**

91. **stomachs:** tempers, malice, spite

92. **year:** i.e., years

1.4 The master gunner of Orleance shows his boy how to fire on the English when they come to spy. The boy kills Gargrave and mortally wounds Salisbury, enraging the newly ransomed Talbot, who vows to avenge them.

———————

1. **Sirrah:** term of address to a male social inferior

2. **suburbs:** residential districts outside the town walls

5. **ruled:** guided, directed

A view of Orleance, or Orléans. (1.2.6)
From John Speed, *A prospect of the most famous parts of the world* . . . (1631).

GLOUCESTER
Cardinal, I'll be no breaker of the law,   80
But we shall meet and break our minds at large.
WINCHESTER
Gloucester, we'll meet to thy cost, be sure.
Thy heartblood I will have for this day's work.
MAYOR
I'll call for clubs if you will not away.
(⌈*Aside.*⌉) This cardinal's more haughty than the devil!   85
GLOUCESTER
Mayor, farewell. Thou dost but what thou mayst.
WINCHESTER
Abominable Gloucester, guard thy head,
For I intend to have it ere long.
              ⌈*Gloucester and Winchester*⌉ *exit*
          ⌈*at separate doors, with their Servingmen.*⌉
MAYOR, ⌈*to Officers*⌉
See the coast cleared, and then we will depart.
(⌈*Aside.*⌉) Good God, these nobles should such   90
     stomachs bear!
I myself fight not once in forty year.
                         They exit.

⌈Scene 4⌉

Enter the Master Gunner of Orleance and his Boy.

MASTER GUNNER
Sirrah, thou know'st how Orleance is besieged
And how the English have the suburbs won.
BOY
Father, I know, and oft have shot at them;
Howe'er, unfortunate, I missed my aim.
MASTER GUNNER
But now thou shalt not. Be thou ruled by me.   5
Chief master-gunner am I of this town;

7. **me:** myself; **grace:** favor

8. **Prince's espials:** i.e., Dauphin's spies or scouts

9. **close entrenched:** hidden or secure in fortified trenches

11. **overpeer:** look over

13. **vex:** harass, afflict

14. **intercept:** cut off, prevent; **inconvenience:** injury, misfortune

15. **piece of ordnance:** mounted gun or cannon; **'gainst:** i.e., opposite, directly facing

21. **take you no care:** i.e., don't concern yourself

24. **handled:** treated

30. **with:** i.e., for; **baser:** more lowly or lowborn; **man-of-arms:** warrior, soldier, knight

31. **bartered:** exchanged

33. **vile-esteemed:** little respected

34. **In fine:** in the end, at last; **redeemed:** liberated, ransomed

35. **Fastolf:** See longer note to 1.1.133, page 236.

The standard of a Roman legion. (1.2.144)
From Claude Paradin, *Deuises heroiques* . . . (1562).

Something I must do to procure me grace.
The Prince's espials have informèd me
How the English, in the suburbs close entrenched,
Went through a secret grate of iron bars   10
In yonder tower, to overpeer the city,
And thence discover how with most advantage
They may vex us with shot or with assault.
To intercept this inconvenience,
A piece of ordnance 'gainst it I have placed,   15
And even these three days have I watched
If I could see them. Now do thou watch,
For I can stay no longer.
If thou spy'st any, run and bring me word;
And thou shalt find me at the Governor's.   *He exits.*   20
BOY
Father, I warrant you, take you no care;
I'll never trouble you if I may spy them.   *He exits.*

Enter Salisbury and Talbot on the turrets,
with ⌐*Sir William Glansdale, Sir Thomas Gargrave,*
Attendants and⌐ *Others.*

SALISBURY
Talbot, my life, my joy, again returned!
How wert thou handled, being prisoner?
Or by what means gott'st thou to be released?   25
Discourse, I prithee, on this turret's top.
TALBOT
The ⌐Duke⌐ of Bedford had a prisoner
Called the brave Lord Ponton de Santrailles;
For him was I exchanged and ransomèd.
But with a baser man-of-arms by far   30
Once in contempt they would have bartered me,
Which I disdaining, scorned, and cravèd death
Rather than I would be so ⌐vile-esteemed.⌐
In fine, redeemed I was as I desired.
But O, the treacherous Fastolf wounds my heart,   35

38. **entertained:** treated

47. **grisly:** terrifying; **fly:** flee

50. **fear of my name:** French **fear of** Talbot's **name** was legendary. (See longer note, page 241.) **were:** i.e., was

52. **spurn:** kick or trample

53. **Wherefore . . . had:** i.e., for that reason I was guarded by selected sharpshooters

54. **every minute-while:** i.e., once a **minute**

56 SD. **linstock:** long staff used to hold a lighted match for firing a cannon (See picture, below.)

58. **revenged:** avenged

65. **make our batt'ry:** i.e., direct our bombardment

Firing a cannon with a linstock. (1.4.56 SD)
From Edward Webbe, . . . *The rare and most wonderful things . . .* (1590).

Whom with my bare fists I would execute
If I now had him brought into my power.

SALISBURY
Yet tell'st thou not how thou wert entertained.

TALBOT
With scoffs and scorns and contumelious taunts.
In open marketplace produced they me   40
To be a public spectacle to all.
"Here," said they, "is the terror of the French,
The scarecrow that affrights our children so."
Then broke I from the officers that led me,
And with my nails digged stones out of the ground   45
To hurl at the beholders of my shame.
My grisly countenance made others fly;
None durst come near for fear of sudden death.
In iron walls they deemed me not secure:
So great fear of my name 'mongst them were spread   50
That they supposed I could rend bars of steel
And spurn in pieces posts of adamant.
Wherefore a guard of chosen shot I had
That walked about me every minute-while;
And if I did but stir out of my bed,   55
Ready they were to shoot me to the heart.

Enter the Boy with a linstock.
⌜*He crosses the main stage and exits.*⌝

SALISBURY
I grieve to hear what torments you endured,
But we will be revenged sufficiently.
Now it is supper time in Orleance.
Here, through this grate, I count each one   60
And view the Frenchmen how they fortify.
Let us look in; the sight will much delight thee.
Sir Thomas Gargrave and Sir William Glansdale,
Let me have your express opinions
Where is best place to make our batt'ry next?   65

66. **stands:** i.e., stand

68. **must be:** will have to **be**

69 SD. **they shoot:** In the fiction of the play, it is the boy whom we are to imagine firing the cannon. The word **they** probably refers to those offstage who produce sound and light effects.

72. **chance:** mischance, misfortune; **crossed:** thwarted

74. **How far'st thou:** i.e., how are you (literally, how farest thou); **mirror:** paragon, model of excellence

80. **trump:** trumpet

86. **wants:** lacks

"Death's dishonorable victory." (1.1.20)
From *Todten-Tantz* . . . (1696).

GARGRAVE
　I think at the north gate, for there stands lords.
GLANSDALE
　And I, here, at the bulwark of the bridge.
TALBOT
　For aught I see, this city must be famished
　Or with light skirmishes enfeeblèd.
　　　　　　　　　Here they ⌜shoot,⌝ and Salisbury
　　　　　　　　　　　⌜*and Gargrave fall*⌝ *down.*
SALISBURY
　O Lord, have mercy on us, wretched sinners!　　　　70
GARGRAVE
　O Lord, have mercy on me, woeful man!
TALBOT
　What chance is this that suddenly hath crossed us?—
　Speak, Salisbury—at least if thou canst, speak!
　How far'st thou, mirror of all martial men?
　One of thy eyes and thy cheek's side struck off!—　　75
　Accursèd tower, accursèd fatal hand
　That hath contrived this woeful tragedy!
　In thirteen battles Salisbury o'ercame;
　Henry the Fifth he first trained to the wars.
　Whilst any trump did sound or drum struck up,　　80
　His sword did ne'er leave striking in the field.—
　Yet liv'st thou, Salisbury? Though thy speech doth fail,
　One eye thou hast to look to heaven for grace.
　The sun with one eye vieweth all the world.
　Heaven, be thou gracious to none alive　　　　85
　If Salisbury wants mercy at thy hands!—
　Sir Thomas Gargrave, hast thou any life?
　Speak unto Talbot. Nay, look up to him.—
　Bear hence his body; I will help to bury it.
　　　　　　⌜*Attendants exit with body of Gargrave.*⌝
　Salisbury, cheer thy spirit with this comfort,　　90
　Thou shalt not die whiles—

93. **As who should say:** i.e., **as** if to **say**

95. **Plantagenet:** This name was attached to the royal family of England, including both Yorks and Lancasters. Salisbury was a descendent of Edward I. **Nero:** Roman emperor (37–68 C.E.), notorious in legend for playing his fiddle while Rome was burning

97. **only in:** i.e., at the very sound of

97 SD. **alarum:** call to arms

100. **gathered head:** organized an army

103. **power:** army

107. **Pucelle or puzel:** See longer note to 1.2.64 SD, page 238. **dogfish:** term of abuse (with a reference to the Folio spelling of Dauphin as "Dolphin")

111. **try:** ascertain, put to the test; **dastard:** cowardly

1.5 Talbot attacks, fights Pucelle, fails to defeat her, and accuses her of witchcraft. The English, defeated, retreat.

0 SD. **driveth him:** forces him to flee

He beckons with his hand and smiles on me
As who should say "When I am dead and gone,
Remember to avenge me on the French."
Plantagenet, I will; and, like thee, ⌐Nero,⌐   95
Play on the lute, beholding the towns burn.
Wretched shall France be only in my name.
        Here an alarum, and it thunders and lightens.
What stir is this? What tumult's in the heavens?
Whence cometh this alarum and the noise?

                Enter a Messenger.

MESSENGER
My lord, my lord, the French have gathered head.   100
The Dauphin, with one Joan ⌐la⌐ Pucelle joined,
A holy prophetess new risen up,
Is come with a great power to raise the siege.
        Here Salisbury lifteth himself up and groans.
TALBOT
Hear, hear, how dying Salisbury doth groan;
It irks his heart he cannot be revenged.   105
Frenchmen, I'll be a Salisbury to you.
Pucelle or puzel, dauphin or dogfish,
Your hearts I'll stamp out with my horse's heels
And make a quagmire of your mingled brains.
Convey ⌐we⌐ Salisbury into his tent,   110
And then try what these dastard Frenchmen dare.
                        Alarum. They exit.

                    ⌐Scene 5⌐

*Here an alarum again, and Talbot pursueth the
Dauphin and driveth him; then enter Joan ⌐la⌐ Pucelle,
driving Englishmen before her. ⌐They cross the stage
and exit.⌐ Then enter Talbot.*

1. **my strength . . . force:** perhaps, my army
2. **retire:** retreat; **stay:** stop
5. **Devil . . . thee:** i.e., even if you are the **devil** himself, I'll control you as a sorcerer controls spirits **Devil or devil's dam:** Proverbial: "The **devil** and his **dam."   dam:** mother
6. **on thee:** i.e., from thee (This line acknowledges that Joan is not the **devil,** accusing her instead of serving the **devil** as **a witch.**)
7. **straightway:** immediately
9. **suffer:** allow
10. **My breast:** i.e., if necessary, **my breast**
12. **But I will chastise:** i.e., in order to **chastise; high-minded:** haughty, arrogant
13. **Thy hour:** i.e., the **hour** of your death
15. **O'ertake me:** reach me with a blow
16. **hunger-starvèd:** starving
17. **testament:** will
19. **potter's wheel:** See picture, page 150.
21. **Hannibal:** Carthaginian general who fought Rome in the Second Punic War (218–201 B.C.E.)
22. **lists:** pleases

TALBOT
  Where is my strength, my valor, and my force?
  Our English troops retire; I cannot stay them.
  A woman clad in armor chaseth them.

                Enter Pucelle, ⌜with Soldiers.⌝

  Here, here she comes!—I'll have a bout with thee.
  Devil or devil's dam, I'll conjure thee.   5
  Blood will I draw on thee—thou art a witch—
  And straightway give thy soul to him thou serv'st.
PUCELLE
  Come, come; 'tis only I that must disgrace thee.
                                        Here they fight.

TALBOT
  Heavens, can you suffer hell so to prevail?
  My breast I'll burst with straining of my courage,   10
  And from my shoulders crack my arms asunder,
  But I will chastise this high-minded strumpet.
                                        They fight again.

PUCELLE
  Talbot, farewell. Thy hour is not yet come.
  I must go victual Orleance forthwith.
                A short alarum. Then ⌜she prepares to⌝
                        enter the town with Soldiers.
  O'ertake me if thou canst. I scorn thy strength.   15
  Go, go, cheer up thy ⌜hunger-starvèd⌝ men.
  Help Salisbury to make his testament.
  This day is ours, as many more shall be.
                                She exits ⌜with Soldiers.⌝

TALBOT
  My thoughts are whirlèd like a potter's wheel.
  I know not where I am nor what I do.   20
  A witch by fear—not force, like Hannibal—
  Drives back our troops, and conquers as she lists.
  So bees with smoke and doves with noisome stench

28. **tear . . . coat:** See notes to 1.1.82, 83.

29. **give:** display in your **coat** of arms; **in lions' stead:** i.e., instead of lions

30. **treacherous:** treacherously (For Talbot, retreat is treachery.)

1.6 The French celebrate Pucelle's victory.

1. **Advance:** raise, lift up; **colors:** flags, standards

4. **Astraea's daughter:** i.e., **daughter** of the mythological goddess of justice, who fled the earth when the Iron Age succeeded the Golden Age

Joan la Pucelle, or Joan of Arc.
From Rene de Cerisiers, *Histoire . . . vray de siege* (1621).

Are from their hives and houses driven away.
They called us, for our fierceness, English dogs;   25
Now like to whelps we crying run away.

A short alarum. ⌜*Enter English soldiers,
chased by French soldiers.*⌝

Hark, countrymen, either renew the fight,
Or tear the lions out of England's coat.
Renounce your soil; give sheep in lions' stead.
Sheep run not half so treacherous from the wolf,   30
Or horse or oxen from the leopard,
As you fly from your oft-subduèd slaves.
                    Alarum. Here another skirmish.
It will not be! Retire into your trenches.
You all consented unto Salisbury's death,
For none would strike a stroke in his revenge.   35
Pucelle is entered into Orleance
In spite of us or aught that we could do.
                              ⌜*Soldiers exit.*⌝
O, would I were to die with Salisbury!
The shame hereof will make me hide my head.
                    Talbot exits. Alarum. Retreat.

⌜Scene 6⌝

Flourish. Enter on the walls Pucelle, ⌜*Charles the*⌝
Dauphin, Reignier, Alanson, and Soldiers.

PUCELLE
Advance our waving colors on the walls.
Rescued is Orleance from the English.
Thus Joan ⌜la⌝ Pucelle hath performed her word.
                              ⌜*She exits.*⌝
CHARLES
Divinest creature, Astraea's daughter,
How shall I honor thee for this success?   5

6. **Adonis' garden:** In Spenser's *The Faerie Queene,* Book 3, canto 6, the **garden** of Adonis is continuously both blooming and **fruitful.**

10. **hap:** luck

16. **played the men:** i.e., shown our supreme manly qualities

21. **pyramis:** pyramid

22. **Rhodophe's of Memphis:** i.e., the third pyramid legendarily built by the courtesan Rhodophe after she became queen **of Memphis**

25. **rich-jeweled coffer of Darius:** Darius's jewel-**coffer** was taken by Alexander the Great, who had it **transported** (line 26) **before** him (line 27) with the works of Homer inside it.

28. **Saint Dennis:** i.e., St. Denis, patron saint of France

Mars, the Roman god of war. (1.2.1)
From Vincenzo Cartari, *Le imagini de i dei de gli antichi* . . . (1587).

Thy promises are like Adonis' garden
That one day bloomed and fruitful were the next.
France, triumph in thy glorious prophetess.
Recovered is the town of Orleance.
More blessèd hap did ne'er befall our state.   10

REIGNIER
Why ring not bells aloud throughout the town?
Dauphin, command the citizens make bonfires
And feast and banquet in the open streets
To celebrate the joy that God hath given us.

ALANSON
All France will be replete with mirth and joy   15
When they shall hear how we have played the men.

CHARLES
'Tis Joan, not we, by whom the day is won;
For which I will divide my crown with her,
And all the priests and friars in my realm
Shall in procession sing her endless praise.   20
A statelier pyramis to her I'll rear
Than Rhodophe's ⌜of⌝ Memphis ever was.
In memory of her, when she is dead,
Her ashes, in an urn more precious
Than the rich-jeweled coffer of Darius,   25
Transported shall be at high festivals
Before the kings and queens of France.
No longer on Saint Dennis will we cry,
But Joan ⌜la⌝ Pucelle shall be France's saint.
Come in, and let us banquet royally   30
After this golden day of victory.
                    Flourish. They exit.

HENRY VI
Part 1

ACT 2

2.1   The English forces, led by Bedford, Burgundy, and Talbot, scale the walls of Orleance and drive out the French, who quarrel over who is responsible for this defeat.

---

0 SD. **Sergeant:** i.e., leader (a higher rank than today); **Band:** company or troop of soldiers

4. **court of guard:** corps de garde, guardroom or guardhouse

6. **servitors:** soldiers

8. **watch:** do our duty as sentinels; stay awake

8 SD. **scaling ladders: ladders** used in an assault on a fortified place (See pictures, pages 58 and 60.)

9. **Lord Regent:** Bedford's title; **redoubted:** respected, distinguished; dreaded

10–11. **By . . . us:** The implication of these lines is that the Duke of Burgundy's alliance with the English has brought with it the friendship of **regions** under Burgundy's control—**Artois, Walloon, and Picardy.** According to sixteenth-century chronicles, Bedford and Burgundy were co-regents of France. In Shakespeare's *Henry V* 5.2, Burgundy plays a central role in the earlier peace treaty between England and France.

12. **happy:** fortunate; **secure:** overconfident, careless

15. **quittance:** repay, requite

16. **art:** magic **art,** black **art** (See picture, page 128.)

17. **Coward of France:** i.e., the Dauphin

ACT 2

Scene 1

Enter ⌜on the walls⌝ a ⌜French⌝ Sergeant of a Band,
with two Sentinels.

SERGEANT
Sirs, take your places and be vigilant.
If any noise or soldier you perceive
Near to the walls, by some apparent sign
Let us have knowledge at the court of guard.

SENTINEL
Sergeant, you shall.   ⌜*Sergeant exits.*⌝   5
     Thus are poor servitors,
When others sleep upon their quiet beds,
Constrained to watch in darkness, rain, and cold.

Enter Talbot, Bedford, and Burgundy, ⌜below,⌝
with scaling ladders.

TALBOT
Lord Regent, and redoubted Burgundy,
By whose approach the regions of Artois,   10
Walloon, and Picardy are friends to us,
This happy night the Frenchmen are secure,
Having all day caroused and banqueted.
Embrace we then this opportunity,
As fitting best to quittance their deceit   15
Contrived by art and baleful sorcery.

BEDFORD
Coward of France, how much he wrongs his fame,
Despairing of his own arm's fortitude,
To join with witches and the help of hell!

57

22. **maid:** girl, virgin

24–26. **Pray . . . begun:** See longer note, page 242.

27. **practice:** conspire, plot; **converse:** associate; have sexual intercourse

29. **flinty:** rugged, hard, impenetrable

32. **several:** separate

33. **That:** i.e., so **that**

34. **other:** i.e., others; **rise:** offer armed resistance; **force:** army

41 SD. **in their shirts:** i.e., in their night attire

Ladders set up for scaling a wall. (2.1.8 SD)
From [John Lydgate,] *The hystorye sege and dystruccyon of Troye* [1513].

BURGUNDY
Traitors have never other company.   20
But what's that Pucelle whom they term so pure?

TALBOT
A maid, they say.

BEDFORD   A maid? And be so martial?

BURGUNDY
Pray God she prove not masculine ere long,
If underneath the standard of the French   25
She carry armor as she hath begun.

TALBOT
Well, let them practice and converse with spirits.
God is our fortress, in whose conquering name
Let us resolve to scale their flinty bulwarks.

BEDFORD
Ascend, brave Talbot. We will follow thee.   30

TALBOT
Not all together. Better far, I guess,
That we do make our entrance several ways,
That if it chance the one of us do fail,
The other yet may rise against their force.

BEDFORD
Agreed. I'll to yond corner.   35

BURGUNDY   And I to this.

TALBOT
And here will Talbot mount, or make his grave.
Now, Salisbury, for thee and for the right
Of English Henry, shall this night appear
How much in duty I am bound to both.   40
                    ⌜*Scaling the walls, they*⌝ *cry*
                    "Saint George! À Talbot!"

SENTINEL
Arm, arm! The enemy doth make assault.
          ⌜*The English, pursuing the Sentinels, exit aloft.*⌝
          The French leap o'er the walls in their shirts.

41 SD. **ready:** properly dressed

42. **How now:** a greeting requesting information about one's well-being

43. **scaped:** escaped

44. **trow:** believe

46. **followed arms:** i.e., have been a soldier

51. **sped:** proved successful (in escaping)

53. **cunning:** craft, witchcraft

54. **flatter:** encourage, inspire with hope; **withal:** therewith

57. **Wherefore:** why; **impatient:** irritable, provoked

58. **alike:** the same

59. **still:** always

61. **Improvident:** unforeseeing; heedless, unwary

62. **mischief:** misfortune, calamity; **fall'n:** happened, occurred

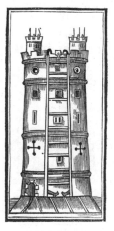

A scaling ladder. (2.1.8 SD)

From Robert Ward, *Anima'duersions of warre* . . . (1639).

*Enter several ways, Bastard, Alanson, Reignier,
half ready, and half unready.*

ALANSON
How now, my lords? What, all unready so?
BASTARD
Unready? Ay, and glad we scaped so well.
REIGNIER
'Twas time, I trow, to wake and leave our beds,
Hearing alarums at our chamber doors.   45
ALANSON
Of all exploits since first I followed arms
Ne'er heard I of a warlike enterprise
More venturous or desperate than this.
BASTARD
I think this Talbot be a fiend of hell.
REIGNIER
If not of hell, the heavens sure favor him.   50
ALANSON
Here cometh Charles. I marvel how he sped.

Enter Charles and Joan ⌐la Pucelle.¬

BASTARD
Tut, holy Joan was his defensive guard.
CHARLES
Is this thy cunning, thou deceitful dame?
Didst thou at first, to flatter us withal,
Make us partakers of a little gain   55
That now our loss might be ten times so much?
PUCELLE
Wherefore is Charles impatient with his friend?
At all times will you have my power alike?
Sleeping or waking, must I still prevail,
Or will you blame and lay the fault on me?—   60
Improvident soldiers, had your watch been good,
This sudden mischief never could have fall'n.

63. **default:** fault, failure in duty

66. **quarters:** parts (of the town); **kept:** guarded

67. **government:** command

68. **surprised:** assailed, attacked

72. **precinct:** division of the town

74. **About:** concerned with

79. **rests:** remains; **shift:** expedient; stratagem

81. **platforms:** plans, schemes; **endamage:** do harm to; **them:** i.e., the English

83–85. **The cry . . . name:** For the legendary power of Talbot's **name,** see longer note to 1.4.50, page 241.   **loaden me:** loaded myself

CHARLES
  Duke of Alanson, this was your default,
  That, being captain of the watch tonight,
  Did look no better to that weighty charge.   65
ALANSON
  Had all your quarters been as safely kept
  As that whereof I had the government,
  We had not been thus shamefully surprised.
BASTARD
  Mine was secure.
REIGNIER   And so was mine, my lord.   70
CHARLES
  And for myself, most part of all this night
  Within her quarter and mine own precinct
  I was employed in passing to and fro
  About relieving of the sentinels.
  Then how or which way should they first break in?   75
PUCELLE
  Question, my lords, no further of the case,
  How or which way; 'tis sure they found some place
  But weakly guarded, where the breach was made.
  And now there rests no other shift but this:
  To gather our soldiers, scattered and dispersed,   80
  And lay new platforms to endamage them.

    Alarum. Enter ⌐an English¬ Soldier, crying,
      "À Talbot, À Talbot!" ⌐The French¬ fly,
        leaving their clothes behind.

SOLDIER
  I'll be so bold to take what they have left.
  The cry of "Talbot" serves me for a sword,
  For I have loaden me with many spoils,
  Using no other weapon but his name.   85
                                        He exits.

2.2   The English plan a grand tomb for the dead Salisbury, in part as a monument to their recent victory. Talbot then receives an invitation to visit the Countess of Auvergne.

---

2. **pitchy:** pitch-dark
3. **retreat:** recall of a pursuing force
5. **advance it:** bring it forward; or, perhaps, lift it up (on a bier or platform)
9. **tonight:** i.e., last night
10. **hereafter:** future
16. **mournful:** deplorable
17 SD. **Funeral:** See note to 1.1.0 SD.
19. **muse:** marvel that; **the Dauphin's grace:** i.e., his **Grace** the Dauphin (See picture, below.)

"The Dauphin Charles." (1.1.94).
From Bernardo Giunti, *Cronica breve de i fatti illustri de re di Francia . . .* (1588).

⌜Scene 2⌝

Enter Talbot, Bedford, Burgundy, ⌜a Captain and Others.⌝

BEDFORD
The day begins to break and night is fled,
Whose pitchy mantle over-veiled the earth.
Here sound retreat and cease our hot pursuit.
                              Retreat ⌜sounded.⌝

TALBOT
Bring forth the body of old Salisbury,
And here advance it in the marketplace,   5
The middle center of this cursèd town.

⌜*Soldiers enter bearing the body of Salisbury,*⌝
Drums beating a dead march.

Now have I paid my vow unto his soul:
For every drop of blood was drawn from him
There hath at least five Frenchmen died tonight.
And, that hereafter ages may behold   10
What ruin happened in revenge of him,
Within their chiefest temple I'll erect
A tomb wherein his corpse shall be interred,
Upon the which, that everyone may read,
Shall be engraved the sack of Orleance,   15
The treacherous manner of his mournful death,
And what a terror he had been to France.
                              ⌜*Funeral exits.*⌝

But, lords, in all our bloody massacre,
I muse we met not with the Dauphin's grace,
His new-come champion, virtuous Joan of ⌜Arc,⌝   20
Nor any of his false confederates.

BEDFORD
'Tis thought, Lord Talbot, when the fight began,
Roused on the sudden from their drowsy beds,
They did amongst the troops of armèd men
Leap o'er the walls for refuge in the field.   25

27. **For:** despite

30. **turtledoves:** birds noted for their affection to their mates (See picture, below.)

32. **After that:** i.e., **after**

33. **all the power we have:** the whole army

35. **warlike:** valiant, skilled in war

37. **would:** wishes to

40. **vouchsafe:** condescend

41. **lies:** resides

43. **report:** (1) fame; (2) resounding noise

45. **sport:** amusement, entertainment; also, flirtation

46. **encountered with:** met (This phrase could also mean "made love to.")

47. **despise:** disregard; **suit:** petition; act of courtship

48. **Ne'er . . . then:** a proverb that here means "never **trust me** in future (if I **despise her suit**)"; **a world:** a vast quantity

50. **overruled:** prevailed

52. **attend on her:** i.e., visit her in answer to her summons

A turtledove. (2.2.30)
From Konrad Gesner, . . . *Historiae animalium* . . . (1585–1604).

BURGUNDY
   Myself, as far as I could well discern
   For smoke and dusky vapors of the night,
   Am sure I scared the Dauphin and his trull,
   When arm-in-arm they both came swiftly running,
   Like to a pair of loving turtledoves   30
   That could not live asunder day or night.
   After that things are set in order here,
   We'll follow them with all the power we have.

                 Enter a Messenger.

MESSENGER
   All hail, my lords. Which of this princely train
   Call you the warlike Talbot, for his acts   35
   So much applauded through the realm of France?
TALBOT
   Here is the Talbot. Who would speak with him?
MESSENGER
   The virtuous lady, Countess of Auvergne,
   With modesty admiring thy renown,
   By me entreats, great lord, thou wouldst vouchsafe   40
   To visit her poor castle where she lies,
   That she may boast she hath beheld the man
   Whose glory fills the world with loud report.
BURGUNDY
   Is it even so? Nay, then, I see our wars
   Will turn unto a peaceful comic sport,   45
   When ladies crave to be encountered with.
   You may not, my lord, despise her gentle suit.
TALBOT
   Ne'er trust me, then; for when a world of men
   Could not prevail with all their oratory,
   Yet hath a woman's kindness overruled.—   50
   And therefore tell her I return great thanks,
   And in submission will attend on her.—
   Will not your Honors bear me company?

54. **will:** i.e., **will** permit
57. **remedy:** alternative
58. **prove:** experience; test
61. **mean:** i.e., intend (to act)

2.3   The Countess plots to capture and kill the visiting Talbot.

---

1. **gave in charge:** ordered, commanded
4. **laid:** devised, contrived; **right:** in the required way
6. **Scythian Tamyris by Cyrus' death:** According to legend, **Tamyris,** queen of Scythia, defeated in battle Cyrus the Great, founder of the Persian Empire, and then shoved the head of his corpse into a wineskin full of human blood, all in vengeance for the death of her son after his capture by Cyrus. (See picture, page 130.)
7. **rumor:** report of the distinction; **dreadful:** formidable
8. **account:** esteem
9–10. **Fain . . . reports:** See longer note, page 242. **Fain:** gladly, with pleasure   **censure:** judgment, opinion   **rare:** (1) splendid; (2) uncommon
12. **craved:** demanded; asked for earnestly
13. **What:** interjection to introduce a question

BEDFORD
    No, truly, 'tis more than manners will;
    And I have heard it said unbidden guests   55
    Are often welcomest when they are gone.
TALBOT
    Well then, alone, since there's no remedy,
    I mean to prove this lady's courtesy.—
    Come hither, captain.   *Whispers.*
                    You perceive my mind?   60
CAPTAIN
    I do, my lord, and mean accordingly.
                                            They exit.

                    ⌐Scene 3⌐

        Enter Countess ⌐of Auvergne, with Porter.⌐

COUNTESS
    Porter, remember what I gave in charge,
    And when you have done so, bring the keys to me.
PORTER   Madam, I will.   *He exits.*
COUNTESS
    The plot is laid. If all things fall out right,
    I shall as famous be by this exploit   5
    As Scythian Tamyris by Cyrus' death.
    Great is the rumor of this dreadful knight,
    And his achievements of no less account.
    Fain would mine eyes be witness with mine ears
    To give their censure of these rare reports.   10

                Enter Messenger and Talbot.

MESSENGER
    Madam, according as your Ladyship desired,
    By message craved, so is Lord Talbot come.
COUNTESS
    And he is welcome. What, is this the man?

17. **That . . . babes:** For the power of Talbot's mere name to quiet crying babies, see longer note to 1.4.50, page 241.   **still:** silence (i.e., with terror)

18. **report:** reputation, rumor; **fabulous:** ridiculous

19. **Hercules:** in classical mythology, a hero of extraordinary strength and courage (See picture, page 80.)

20. **Hector:** eldest son of Priam, king of Troy, and leader of his forces in the Trojan War (See picture, below.) **for:** because of; **grim:** fierce; **aspect:** facial expression

21. **proportion:** size; **strong-knit:** i.e., well-**knit**

22. **silly:** defenseless, feeble

23. **be this:** i.e., **be** that **this; writhled:** withered

27. **sort:** choose

31. **Marry:** indeed (originally an oath on the name of the Virgin Mary); **for that:** because

32. **certify:** guarantee

36. **trained:** lured

37. **shadow:** image; **thrall:** slave

Hector. (2.3.20)
From [Guillaume Rouillé,] . . . *Promptuarii iconum* . . . (1553).

MESSENGER
  Madam, it is.
COUNTESS   Is this the scourge of France?   15
  Is this the Talbot, so much feared abroad
  That with his name the mothers still their babes?
  I see report is fabulous and false.
  I thought I should have seen some Hercules,
  A second Hector, for his grim aspect   20
  And large proportion of his strong-knit limbs.
  Alas, this is a child, a silly dwarf!
  It cannot be this weak and writhled shrimp
  Should strike such terror to his enemies.
TALBOT
  Madam, I have been bold to trouble you.   25
  But since your Ladyship is not at leisure,
  I'll sort some other time to visit you.
                              ⌐*He begins to exit.*⌐
COUNTESS, ⌐*to Messenger*⌐
  What means he now? Go ask him whither he goes.
MESSENGER
  Stay, my Lord Talbot, for my lady craves
  To know the cause of your abrupt departure.   30
TALBOT
  Marry, for that she's in a wrong belief,
  I go to certify her Talbot's here.

                    Enter Porter with keys.

COUNTESS, ⌐*to Talbot*⌐
  If thou be he, then art thou prisoner.
TALBOT
  Prisoner? To whom?
COUNTESS   To me, bloodthirsty lord.   35
  And for that cause I trained thee to my house.
  Long time thy shadow hath been thrall to me,
  For in my gallery thy picture hangs.

39. **substance:** solid or real thing, as proverbially opposed to appearance or **shadow** (line 37); **endure:** suffer; **the like:** the same kind of thing (i.e., being hanged)

41. **tyranny:** violence, outrage

42. **Wasted:** laid waste, destroyed

43. **captivate:** into captivity

45. **to moan:** i.e., into lamentation

46. **fond:** i.e., foolish as

48. **Whereon:** on which

55. **least proportion:** slightest portion; **humanity:** humankind

56. **frame:** human body

57. **spacious:** great, extensive; **pitch:** height

59. **merchant:** fellow; **for the nonce:** (1) on purpose, expressly; (2) for the occasion, for the time being

61. **contrarieties:** diametrical differences

62. **presently:** immediately

62 SD. **Winds:** blows

But now the substance shall endure the like,
And I will chain these legs and arms of thine,   40
That hast by tyranny these many years
Wasted our country, slain our citizens,
And sent our sons and husbands captivate.
TALBOT   Ha, ha, ha!
COUNTESS
Laughest thou, wretch? Thy mirth shall turn to moan.   45
TALBOT
I laugh to see your Ladyship so fond
To think that you have aught but Talbot's shadow
Whereon to practice your severity.
COUNTESS   Why, art not thou the man?
TALBOT   I am, indeed.   50
COUNTESS   Then have I substance too.
TALBOT
No, no, I am but shadow of myself.
You are deceived; my substance is not here,
For what you see is but the smallest part
And least proportion of humanity.   55
I tell you, madam, were the whole frame here,
It is of such a spacious lofty pitch
Your roof were not sufficient to contain 't.
COUNTESS
This is a riddling merchant for the nonce:
He will be here and yet he is not here.   60
How can these contrarieties agree?
TALBOT
That will I show you presently.
                          Winds his horn. Drums strike up;
                                   a peal of ordnance.

                     Enter Soldiers.

How say you, madam? Are you now persuaded
That Talbot is but shadow of himself?

67. **Razeth:** obliterates; **subverts:** overthrows
68. **desolate:** deserted
69. **abuse:** ill-usage; deceit
70. **I find . . . bruited:** See longer note to 2.3.9–10, page 242.   **fame:** public report   **bruited:** rumored
71. **gathered:** inferred
73. **reverence:** due respect, deference
74. **entertain:** receive
75. **misconster:** misconstrue
76–77. **did mistake . . . body:** perhaps, did not understand that it is Talbot's army that is **the outward composition of his body** (See line 65, above.) **mistake:** misunderstand
79. **satisfaction:** reparation
80. **patience:** permission, indulgence
81. **cates:** dainties, delicacies

2.4   Richard Plantagenet and Somerset, having quarreled over a case at law, withdraw into a garden, where the supporters of Plantagenet signal their commitment to him by plucking and wearing white roses, the supporters of Somerset red roses.

———————

0 SD. **Plantagenet:** See note to 1.4.95.
2. **case of truth:** a dispute between Plantagenet and Somerset, never defined by the play

These are his substance, sinews, arms, and strength,   65
With which he yoketh your rebellious necks,
Razeth your cities, and subverts your towns,
And in a moment makes them desolate.

COUNTESS
Victorious Talbot, pardon my abuse.
I find thou art no less than fame hath bruited,   70
And more than may be gathered by thy shape.
Let my presumption not provoke thy wrath,
For I am sorry that with reverence
I did not entertain thee as thou art.

TALBOT
Be not dismayed, fair lady, nor misconster   75
The mind of Talbot as you did mistake
The outward composition of his body.
What you have done hath not offended me,
Nor other satisfaction do I crave
But only, with your patience, that we may   80
Taste of your wine and see what cates you have,
For soldiers' stomachs always serve them well.

COUNTESS
With all my heart, and think me honorèd
To feast so great a warrior in my house.

They exit.

⌜Scene 4⌝

Enter Richard Plantagenet, Warwick, Somerset,
⌜*William de la*⌝ *Pole* ⌜*the Earl of Suffolk,*
Vernon, a Lawyer,⌝ *and Others.*

PLANTAGENET
Great lords and gentlemen, what means this silence?
Dare no man answer in a case of truth?

3. **Temple Hall:** the **hall** within one of the Inns of Court or the London law schools, either Inner **Temple** or Middle **Temple; were:** would have been

6. **wrangling:** (1) bickering; (2) engaging in public disputation

7. **Faith:** a mild oath (by my **faith**); **a truant in:** i.e., neglectful of my duty to study

8. **frame:** train, discipline

9. **frame:** i.e., I adapt, I fit

11. **the higher pitch:** i.e., to the greater height

12. **mouth:** bark

13. **temper:** degree of elasticity or resiliency

14. **bear him best:** i.e., behave better

17. **nice:** precise; **sharp:** acute; **quillets:** subtle distinctions

18. **daw:** (1) jackdaw, a small crow; (2) simpleton

20. **The truth . . . naked:** Proverb: "**The truth** shows best being **naked.**"

21. **purblind:** partially blind, dim-sighted

23. **clear:** bright

24. **glimmer . . . eye:** i.e., be visible to **a blind** man **glimmer:** shine brightly

26. **dumb:** silent, mute; **significants:** symbols

28. **stands upon:** is scrupulous about; claims respect for; values

29. **pleaded:** i.e., maintained by argument (literally, in a court of law)

SUFFOLK
　Within the Temple Hall we were too loud;
　The garden here is more convenient.
PLANTAGENET
　Then say at once if I maintained the truth,　　　　　5
　Or else was wrangling Somerset in th' error?
SUFFOLK
　Faith, I have been a truant in the law
　And never yet could frame my will to it,
　And therefore frame the law unto my will.
SOMERSET
　Judge you, my Lord of Warwick, then, between us.　　10
WARWICK
　Between two hawks, which flies the higher pitch,
　Between two dogs, which hath the deeper mouth,
　Between two blades, which bears the better temper,
　Between two horses, which doth bear him best,
　Between two girls, which hath the merriest eye,　　15
　I have perhaps some shallow spirit of judgment;
　But in these nice sharp quillets of the law,
　Good faith, I am no wiser than a daw.
PLANTAGENET
　Tut, tut, here is a mannerly forbearance!
　The truth appears so naked on my side　　　　　20
　That any purblind eye may find it out.
SOMERSET
　And on my side it is so well appareled,
　So clear, so shining, and so evident,
　That it will glimmer through a blind man's eye.
PLANTAGENET
　Since you are tongue-tied and so loath to speak,　　25
　In dumb significants proclaim your thoughts:
　Let him that is a trueborn gentleman
　And stands upon the honor of his birth,
　If he suppose that I have pleaded truth,
　From off this brier pluck a white rose with me.　　30

32. **party:** side

33. **thorn:** brier

34. **colors:** pretexts; false pleas in law courts; **color:** semblance, cloak (The wordplay here is based in the notion of **white** [line 36] as having **no color.**)

35. **insinuating:** ingratiating

38. **withal:** therewith; **held the right:** i.e., maintained the truth

41. **tree:** bush

42. **yield the other in:** i.e., **yield** to **the other** as having; **opinion:** legal judgment

44. **subscribe:** submit, yield

47. **maiden:** i.e., white; virginally innocent

52. **opinion:** judgment (In line 53, **opinion** means "reputation.")

54. **still:** always

55. **Well, well:** probably meant maliciously (Proverbial: "**Well, well** is a word of malice.")

56. **false:** defective

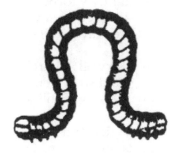

A canker. (2.4.69)
From John Johnstone, [*Opera aliquot*] (1650–62).

SOMERSET
   Let him that is no coward nor no flatterer,
   But dare maintain the party of the truth,
   Pluck a red rose from off this thorn with me.

WARWICK
   I love no colors; and, without all color
   Of base insinuating flattery,   35
   I pluck this white rose with Plantagenet.

SUFFOLK
   I pluck this red rose with young Somerset,
   And say withal I think he held the right.

VERNON
   Stay, lords and gentlemen, and pluck no more
   Till you conclude that he upon whose side   40
   The fewest roses are croppèd from the tree
   Shall yield the other in the right opinion.

SOMERSET
   Good Master Vernon, it is well objected:
   If I have fewest, I subscribe in silence.

PLANTAGENET   And I.   45

VERNON
   Then for the truth and plainness of the case,
   I pluck this pale and maiden blossom here,
   Giving my verdict on the white rose side.

SOMERSET
   Prick not your finger as you pluck it off,
   Lest, bleeding, you do paint the white rose red,   50
   And fall on my side so against your will.

VERNON
   If I, my lord, for my opinion bleed,
   Opinion shall be surgeon to my hurt
   And keep me on the side where still I am.

SOMERSET   Well, well, come on, who else?   55

LAWYER
   Unless my study and my books be false,

57. **in law:** rather than "in fact"

60. **that:** i.e., **that** which

69. **canker:** cankerworm, caterpillar (See picture, page 78.)

71, 72. **his:** i.e., its

77. **fashion:** i.e., wearing the red rose; **peevish boy:** a double insult, since **peevish** was a word expressing contempt and **boy** was an insult when addressed to a young man

79. **Pole:** Suffolk's family name is "de la **Pole.**" (See line 81.)

Hercules. (2.3.19; 4.7.61)

From Vincenzo Cartari, *Le vere e noue imagini* . . . (1615).

The argument you held was wrong in ⌜law,⌝
In sign whereof I pluck a white rose too.
PLANTAGENET
Now, Somerset, where is your argument?
SOMERSET
Here in my scabbard, meditating that   60
Shall dye your white rose in a bloody red.
PLANTAGENET
Meantime your cheeks do counterfeit our roses,
For pale they look with fear, as witnessing
The truth on our side.
SOMERSET   No, Plantagenet.   65
'Tis not for fear, but anger that thy cheeks
Blush for pure shame to counterfeit our roses,
And yet thy tongue will not confess thy error.
PLANTAGENET
Hath not thy rose a canker, Somerset?
SOMERSET
Hath not thy rose a thorn, Plantagenet?   70
PLANTAGENET
Ay, sharp and piercing, to maintain his truth,
Whiles thy consuming canker eats his falsehood.
SOMERSET
Well, I'll find friends to wear my bleeding roses
That shall maintain what I have said is true,
Where false Plantagenet dare not be seen.   75
PLANTAGENET
Now, by this maiden blossom in my hand,
I scorn thee and thy fashion, peevish boy.
SUFFOLK
Turn not thy scorns this way, Plantagenet.
PLANTAGENET
Proud Pole, I will, and scorn both him and thee.
SUFFOLK
I'll turn my part thereof into thy throat.   80

82. **yeoman:** A **yeoman** was a small farmer below the rank of a gentleman. This insult alludes to Plantagenet's family having been stripped of its lands and titles.

84. **grandfather:** i.e., ancestor (literally, great-great-grandfather) See chart, page xvi.

86. **Spring . . . root:** i.e., do **crestless yeomen** issue from such a lineage **crestless yeomen:** A crest is a figure or emblem that serves as the badge of a noble family; **yeomen** would have no such device.

87. **bears him:** presumes; **the place's privilege:** the prohibition of violence in this place (See longer note, page 242.)

93–94. **And . . . gentry:** i.e., because of his conviction of the capital crime of **treason,** according to the law, you have forfeited all real estate and personal property, your blood (i.e., family) is regarded as corrupt or tainted, and you have been excluded from all civil rights and capacities that would be yours by high birth

96. **restored:** reinstated in your former rank

97. **attachèd:** accused, charged; **attainted:** legally convicted of treason (**Cambridge** was executed on the king's direct command.)

100. **Were . . . will:** i.e., if I get the chance

101. **partaker:** supporter

103. **apprehension:** conception, view

104. **Look to it well:** i.e., beware, be very careful

105. **still:** always

106. **these colors:** i.e., the color of these red roses

107. **in spite of:** in contempt or scorn of

109. **cognizance:** token (A **cognizance** was also a device identifying a noble family.)

SOMERSET
  Away, away, good William de la Pole!
  We grace the yeoman by conversing with him.
WARWICK
  Now, by God's will, thou wrong'st him, Somerset.
  His grandfather was Lionel, Duke of Clarence,
  Third son to the third Edward, King of England.   85
  Spring crestless yeomen from so deep a root?
PLANTAGENET
  He bears him on the place's privilege,
  Or durst not for his craven heart say thus.
SOMERSET
  By Him that made me, I'll maintain my words
  On any plot of ground in Christendom.   90
  Was not thy father Richard, Earl of Cambridge,
  For treason executed in our late king's days?
  And, by his treason, stand'st not thou attainted,
  Corrupted, and exempt from ancient gentry?
  His trespass yet lives guilty in thy blood,   95
  And, till thou be restored, thou art a yeoman.
PLANTAGENET
  My father was attachèd, not attainted,
  Condemned to die for treason, but no traitor;
  And that I'll prove on better men than Somerset,
  Were growing time once ripened to my will.   100
  For your partaker Pole and you yourself,
  I'll note you in my book of memory
  To scourge you for this apprehension.
  Look to it well, and say you are well warned.
SOMERSET
  Ah, thou shalt find us ready for thee still,   105
  And know us by these colors for thy foes,
  For these my friends in spite of thee shall wear.
PLANTAGENET
  And, by my soul, this pale and angry rose,
  As cognizance of my blood-drinking hate,

112. **degree:** rank

115. **Have with thee:** i.e., I'll go with you

116. **braved:** defied

117. **object:** attribute as a crime

118. **whipped out:** i.e., driven **out** (as with a whip); or, perhaps, chastised (Many editors substitute the F2 variant "wipt **out**"—i.e., wiped **out.**)

119. **Called for the truce of:** i.e., **called for the** purpose of arranging a **truce** between

120. **York:** i.e., Duke of **York**

121. **Warwick:** i.e., Earl of **Warwick**

122. **in signal:** as a sign

124. **party:** side

126. **faction:** factious quarrel, quarrel of one party against another

129. **bound:** obliged

131. **still:** always

A rack. (2.5.3)
From Girolamo Maggi, . . . *De tintinnabulis liber postumus . . . Accedit . . . De equuleo liber . . .* (1689).

Will I forever, and my faction, wear   110
Until it wither with me to my grave
Or flourish to the height of my degree.
SUFFOLK
Go forward, and be choked with thy ambition!
And so farewell, until I meet thee next.   *He exits.*
SOMERSET
Have with thee, Pole.—Farewell, ambitious Richard.   115
                                                    He exits.
PLANTAGENET
How I am braved, and must perforce endure it!
WARWICK
This blot that they object against your house
Shall be whipped out in the next parliament,
Called for the truce of Winchester and Gloucester;
And if thou be not then created York,   120
I will not live to be accounted Warwick.
Meantime, in signal of my love to thee,
Against proud Somerset and William Pole
Will I upon thy party wear this rose.
And here I prophesy: this brawl today,   125
Grown to this faction in the Temple garden,
Shall send, between the red rose and the white,
A thousand souls to death and deadly night.
PLANTAGENET
Good Master Vernon, I am bound to you,
That you on my behalf would pluck a flower.   130
VERNON
In your behalf still will I wear the same.
LAWYER
And so will I.
PLANTAGENET   Thanks, gentle ⌜sir.⌝
Come, let us four to dinner. I dare say
This quarrel will drink blood another day.   135
                                                    They exit.

2.5 Edmund Mortimer, imprisoned by Henry IV because of his strong claim to the throne, and kept in prison by Henry V, is about to die and wishes to see Richard Plantagenet, his kinsman. The dying Mortimer encourages Richard's ambitions but counsels him to be secretive.

O SD. **Edmund: Mortimer** is named **Edmund** in line 7 below. In fact it was Sir John **Mortimer,** not **Edmund Mortimer,** who was imprisoned. But Shakespeare's historical source gives the name **Edmund.**

1. **keepers:** (1) jailers; (2) nurses

3. **new-halèd:** recently pulled or hauled; **rack:** an instrument of torture by which the joints were pulled apart (See picture, page 84.)

5. **pursuivants:** heralds who proclaim someone else's approach (Proverbial: "**Gray** hairs are death's blossoms.")

6. **Nestor-like:** In Homer, **Nestor,** king of Pylos, was of a great age, having outlived two generations. **an age:** a lifetime; **care:** sorrow, mental suffering

8. **wasting:** waning, decreasing (Proverbial: "There is no **oil** left in the lamp.")

9. **Wax:** grow; **exigent:** end, extremity

10. **overborne:** oppressed

11. **pithless:** devoid of strength, weak

12. **his:** i.e., its

13. **strengthless stay:** weak support; **numb:** i.e., paralyzed

(continued)

⌜Scene 5⌝

Enter ⌜Edmund⌝ Mortimer, brought in a chair,
and Jailers.

MORTIMER
  Kind keepers of my weak decaying age,
  Let dying Mortimer here rest himself.
  Even like a man new-halèd from the rack,
  So fare my limbs with long imprisonment;
  And these gray locks, the pursuivants of death,   5
  Nestor-like agèd in an age of care,
  Argue the end of Edmund Mortimer;
  These eyes, like lamps whose wasting oil is spent,
  Wax dim, as drawing to their exigent;
  Weak shoulders, overborne with burdening grief,   10
  And pithless arms, like to a withered vine
  That droops his sapless branches to the ground;
  Yet are these feet, whose strengthless stay is numb,
  Unable to support this lump of clay,
  Swift-wingèd with desire to get a grave,   15
  As witting I no other comfort have.
  But tell me, keeper, will my nephew come?
KEEPER
  Richard Plantagenet, my lord, will come.
  We sent unto the Temple, unto his chamber,
  And answer was returned that he will come.   20
MORTIMER
  Enough. My soul shall then be satisfied.
  Poor gentleman, his wrong doth equal mine.
  Since Henry Monmouth first began to reign,
  Before whose glory I was great in arms,
  This loathsome sequestration have I had;   25
  And even since then hath Richard been obscured,
  Deprived of honor and inheritance.
  But now the arbitrator of despairs,

14. **this lump of clay:** i.e., Mortimer's body (Genesis 2.7: "The Lord God . . . made man of the dust of the ground.")

16. **witting:** knowing

22. **his wrong:** i.e., the **wrong** he suffers

23. **Henry Monmouth:** i.e., **Henry** V, who was born in **Monmouth** in Wales

24. **Before:** prior to; **glory:** i.e., reign; **great:** extraordinary; **arms:** war

25. **sequestration:** seclusion (through imprisonment); confiscation of property

26. **Richard:** i.e., **Richard** Plantagenet

30. **enlargement:** release from confinement

31. **would his:** i.e., wish that Richard's

35. **ignobly:** dishonorably

36. **late:** recently

37. **Direct:** guide; **arms:** i.e., **arms** so that

38. **latter:** last

40. **kindly:** fittingly, affectionately; in accordance with nature (as his kinsman)

41. **stem from York's great stock:** The York lineage is here expressed in terms of a tree trunk (**stock**) and its branches (**stems**). For this lineage, see page xvi.

42. **of late:** recently; **despised:** treated with contempt

44. **ease:** state of comfort; **disease:** grievance

47. **lavish:** loose, wild; **tongue:** language, speech

49. **obloquy:** reproach; detraction

53. **alliance':** kinship's; **declare:** explain

54. **lost his head:** See picture, page 110.

Just Death, kind umpire of men's miseries,
With sweet enlargement doth dismiss me hence.   30
I would his troubles likewise were expired,
That so he might recover what was lost.

Enter Richard ⌜Plantagenet.⌝

KEEPER
My lord, your loving nephew now is come.
MORTIMER
Richard Plantagenet, my friend, is he come?
PLANTAGENET
Ay, noble uncle, thus ignobly used,   35
Your nephew, late despisèd Richard, comes.
MORTIMER, ⌜*to Jailer*⌝
Direct mine arms I may embrace his neck
And in his bosom spend my latter gasp.
O, tell me when my lips do touch his cheeks,
That I may kindly give one fainting kiss.   40
⌜*He embraces Richard.*⌝
And now declare, sweet stem from York's great stock,
Why didst thou say of late thou wert despised?
PLANTAGENET
First, lean thine agèd back against mine arm,
And in that ease I'll tell thee my disease.
This day, in argument upon a case,   45
Some words there grew 'twixt Somerset and me,
Among which terms he used his lavish tongue
And did upbraid me with my father's death;
Which obloquy set bars before my tongue,
Else with the like I had requited him.   50
Therefore, good uncle, for my father's sake,
In honor of a true Plantagenet,
And for alliance' sake, declare the cause
My father, Earl of Cambridge, lost his head.

56. **flow'ring:** vigorous, flourishing

57. **pine:** suffer, waste away

59. **Discover more at large:** reveal in greater detail

64. **nephew:** i.e., cousin; **Richard, Edward's son: Richard** II, **son** of Edward, the Black Prince (For the history of this period and its treatment here and in *Henry IV, Part 1* and *Henry V,* see "Shakespeare's Two Tetralogies," page 246.)

65–66. **first begotten . . . descent:** i.e., eldest son of Edward III (The Black Prince predeceased his father.) See charts, pages xvi and 2.

67. **whose reign:** i.e., the **reign** of **Henry the Fourth** (line 63); **Percies of the north:** "Percy" was the family name of the Earl of Northumberland. In Shakespeare's *Henry IV, Part 1,* where the events recounted in lines 63–81 are dramatized, **the Percies** include Northumberland, his brother Worcester, and his son Harry Percy or "Hotspur."

70. **reason:** i.e., **reason** that

71. **for that:** because

73. **next:** i.e., **next** in line for the throne

74. **mother:** i.e., grandmother (This apparent error may indicate that Shakespeare here follows his historical source in confusing Edmund Mortimer with his uncle of the same name.) **derivèd:** descended

76. **he: Henry the Fourth** (line 63)

78. **Being . . . line:** i.e., **John of Gaunt being** the **fourth** son of **Edward** III

79. **haughty:** lofty, high-minded; **attempt:** i.e., **attempt** in which

(continued)

MORTIMER
 That cause, fair nephew, that imprisoned me   55
 And hath detained me all my flow'ring youth
 Within a loathsome dungeon, there to pine,
 Was cursèd instrument of his decease.
PLANTAGENET
 Discover more at large what cause that was,
 For I am ignorant and cannot guess.   60
MORTIMER
 I will, if that my fading breath permit
 And death approach not ere my tale be done.
 Henry the Fourth, grandfather to this king,
 Deposed his nephew Richard, Edward's son,
 The first begotten and the lawful heir   65
 Of Edward king, the third of that descent;
 During whose reign the Percies of the north,
 Finding his usurpation most unjust,
 Endeavored my advancement to the throne.
 The reason moved these warlike lords to this   70
 Was, for that—young Richard thus removed,
 Leaving no heir begotten of his body—
 I was the next by birth and parentage;
 For by my mother I derivèd am
 From Lionel, Duke of Clarence, third son   75
 To King Edward the Third; whereas he
 From John of Gaunt doth bring his pedigree,
 Being but fourth of that heroic line.
 But mark: as in this haughty great attempt
 They laborèd to plant the rightful heir,   80
 I lost my liberty and they their lives.
 Long after this, when Henry the Fifth,
 Succeeding his father Bolingbroke, did reign,
 Thy father, Earl of Cambridge then, derived
 From famous Edmund Langley, Duke of York,   85
 Marrying my sister that thy mother was,

81. **they their lives:** In Shakespeare's *Henry IV, Part 1*, Hotspur is killed and Worcester sentenced to death. Northumberland is captured in *Henry IV, Part 2.*

82–91. **Long . . . beheaded:** Shakespeare tells this story somewhat differently in his *Henry V* 2.2. See longer note, page 243.

84. **derived:** descended

85. **Edmund . . . York:** the fifth son of Edward III (**York** is a central figure in Shakespeare's *Richard II.*)

87. **hard:** harsh, difficult to endure

88. **weening:** hoping, wishing; **redeem:** rescue

89. **the diadem:** royal power

90. **as the rest:** i.e., like **the Percies** and their followers; **fell:** was overthrown

92. **title:** i.e., **title** to the crown

93. **which:** i.e., whom (**the Mortimers**)

94. **issue:** offspring

95. **warrant:** promise, predict, presage

96. **gather:** i.e., to infer

97. **studious:** heedful, attentive

98. **admonishments:** warnings

100. **tyranny:** violence, outrage

101. **politic:** prudent, sagacious

102. **house of Lancaster:** i.e., Henry VI and his uncles, descendants of John of Gaunt, Duke of **Lancaster**

103. **like a mountain, not to be removed:** Psalms 125.1: "as mount Zion, which can not **be removed.**"

104. **removing:** departing

(continued)

Again, in pity of my hard distress,
Levied an army, weening to redeem
And have installed me in the diadem.
But, as the rest, so fell that noble earl   90
And was beheaded. Thus the Mortimers,
In whom the title rested, were suppressed.

PLANTAGENET
Of which, my lord, your Honor is the last.

MORTIMER
True, and thou seest that I no issue have
And that my fainting words do warrant death.   95
Thou art my heir; the rest I wish thee gather.
But yet be wary in thy studious care.

PLANTAGENET
Thy grave admonishments prevail with me.
But yet methinks my father's execution
Was nothing less than bloody tyranny.   100

MORTIMER
With silence, nephew, be thou politic;
Strong-fixèd is the house of Lancaster,
And, like a mountain, not to be removed.
But now thy uncle is removing hence,
As princes do their courts when they are cloyed   105
With long continuance in a settled place.

PLANTAGENET
O uncle, would some part of my young years
Might but redeem the passage of your age.

MORTIMER
Thou dost then wrong me, as that slaughterer doth
Which giveth many wounds when one will kill.   110
Mourn not, except thou sorrow for my good;
Only give order for my funeral.
And so farewell, and fair be all thy hopes,
And prosperous be thy life in peace and war.
                                            Dies.

105. **As . . . courts:** an allusion to the custom of the royal progress, according to which the monarch would pay prolonged visits to provincial nobles

106. **settled place:** i.e., **a place** in which they have **settled** or resided

107. **would:** i.e., I wish

111. **except:** unless; **my good:** i.e., the loss of the moral **good** in me

112. **give order:** i.e., make arrangements

117. **hermit:** religiously motivated recluse; **over-passed:** passed through (Proverbial: "Life is a **pilgrimage.**")

119. **imagine:** plot, plan

121. **his burial better than:** i.e., that **his burial** is superior in quality to that of

122. **Here dies . . . Mortimer:** For life as a candle, lamp, or **torch,** see *Macbeth* 5.5.26, where life is called a "brief candle." (Mortimer's **torch** dies because it is **choked** [line 123] or smothered.) **dusky:** dim

123. **with:** i.e., by; **the meaner sort:** i.e., those inferior to him

124. **for:** i.e., as **for**

125. **my house:** i.e., the Yorks

128. **restorèd to my blood:** readmitted to the privileges of rank and birth that were forfeited when my father was executed for treason

129. **make . . . good:** i.e., turn the injustice I suffer into the opportunity for my benefit

PLANTAGENET
    And peace, no war, befall thy parting soul.   115
    In prison hast thou spent a pilgrimage,
    And like a hermit overpassed thy days.—
    Well, I will lock his counsel in my breast,
    And what I do imagine, let that rest.—
    Keepers, convey him hence, and I myself   120
    Will see his burial better than his life.
           ⌜*Jailers*⌝ *exit* ⌜*carrying Mortimer's body.*⌝
    Here dies the dusky torch of Mortimer,
    Choked with ambition of the meaner sort.
    And for those wrongs, those bitter injuries,
    Which Somerset hath offered to my house,   125
    I doubt not but with honor to redress.
    And therefore haste I to the Parliament,
    Either to be restorèd to my blood,
    Or make ⌜mine ill⌝ th' advantage of my good.
                              He exits.

HENRY VI
Part 1

ACT 3

3.1 Gloucester and Winchester quarrel openly in Henry VI's royal court. Their supporters, forbidden to carry weapons, have been fighting in the streets with stones. The two nobles pretend to reconcile at Henry's behest. Then Henry, urged by Warwick, creates Richard Plantagenet Duke of York.

---

0 SD. **bill:** list (in this case, a list of accusations)

1. **deep:** earnestly; **premeditated lines:** writings composed in advance

2. **pamphlets:** treatises

4. **charge:** blame, responsibility

5. **invention:** written composition; contrivance

6. **extemporal:** offhand, unpremeditated

7. **answer:** rebut; **object:** bring as a charge

11. **preferred:** presented, submitted

13. **forged:** i.e., fabricated (a lie)

14. **rehearse:** repeat; **method:** methodical exposition

16. **lewd:** vulgar; vile; **dissentious:** quarrelsome; **pranks:** evil deeds

17. **As very:** i.e., that even

18. **pernicious:** (1) destructive, ruinous; (2) villainous; **usurer:** one who charges (sometimes excessive) interest on loans, contrary to church law

19. **Froward:** bad; difficult to deal with

20. **beseems:** befits

ACT 3

Scene 1

Flourish. Enter King ⌜Henry,⌝ Exeter, Gloucester, ⌜and⌝
Winchester; Richard Plantagenet ⌜and⌝ Warwick,
⌜with white roses;⌝ Somerset ⌜and⌝ Suffolk, ⌜with red
roses; and Others.⌝ Gloucester offers to put up a bill.
Winchester snatches it, tears it.

WINCHESTER
Com'st thou with deep premeditated lines,
With written pamphlets studiously devised?
Humphrey of Gloucester, if thou canst accuse
Or aught intend'st to lay unto my charge,
Do it without invention, suddenly,   5
As I with sudden and extemporal speech
Purpose to answer what thou canst object.

GLOUCESTER
Presumptuous priest, this place commands my
   patience,
Or thou shouldst find thou hast dishonored me.   10
Think not, although in writing I preferred
The manner of thy vile outrageous crimes,
That therefore I have forged or am not able
Verbatim to rehearse the method of my pen.
No, prelate, such is thy audacious wickedness,   15
Thy lewd, pestiferous, and dissentious pranks,
As very infants prattle of thy pride.
Thou art a most pernicious usurer,
Froward by nature, enemy to peace,
Lascivious, wanton, more than well beseems   20

99

21. **degree:** rank
25. **sifted:** narrowly scrutinized
27. **envious:** spiteful; **swelling:** proud
29. **give me hearing:** i.e., **give hearing** to
31. **how:** i.e., why
34. **preferreth:** esteems
35. **except:** unless
36. **that:** i.e., **that** which
38. **sway:** rule, govern
39. **be about:** i.e., **be** around (i.e., have access to)
44. **bastard of my grandfather:** See longer note, page 243.
47. **saucy:** insolent
49. **as an outlaw:** i.e., in the same way **as an outlaw** who; **keeps:** lives, resides
50. **patronage:** countenance, protect, defend

Cain killing Abel. (1.3.39–40)
From [Guillaume Guéroult,] *Figures de la Bible* . . . (1582).

A man of thy profession and degree.
And for thy treachery, what's more manifest,
In that thou laid'st a trap to take my life
As well at London Bridge as at the Tower?
Besides, I fear me, if thy thoughts were sifted,   25
The King, thy sovereign, is not quite exempt
From envious malice of thy swelling heart.

WINCHESTER
Gloucester, I do defy thee.—Lords, vouchsafe
To give me hearing what I shall reply.
If I were covetous, ambitious, or perverse,   30
As he will have me, how am I so poor?
Or how haps it I seek not to advance
Or raise myself, but keep my wonted calling?
And for dissension, who preferreth peace
More than I do, except I be provoked?   35
No, my good lords, it is not that offends;
It is not that that hath incensed the Duke.
It is because no one should sway but he,
No one but he should be about the King;
And that engenders thunder in his breast   40
And makes him roar these accusations forth.
But he shall know I am as good—

GLOUCESTER   As good!
Thou bastard of my grandfather!

WINCHESTER
Ay, lordly sir; for what are you, I pray,   45
But one imperious in another's throne?

GLOUCESTER
Am I not Protector, saucy priest?

WINCHESTER
And am not I a prelate of the Church?

GLOUCESTER
Yes, as an outlaw in a castle keeps,
And useth it to patronage his theft.   50

51. **Unreverent:** irreverent

53. **Touching:** in reference to; **function:** profession (as a clergyman)

54. **Rome:** i.e., the pope

56. **forbear:** refrain

57. **so:** i.e., **so** long as; **overborne:** borne down by superior force

58. **Methinks:** it seems to me; **my lord:** probably, Gloucester; **religious:** devout, conscientious

59. **know:** admit the authority of; **such:** i.e., Winchester

60. **his Lordship:** i.e., Winchester

61. **fitteth not:** i.e., is not suitable for; **plead:** contend in debate

62. **state:** office of importance; **touched so near:** affected so closely

64. **his Grace:** i.e., Gloucester

66. **sirrah:** term of address to a socially inferior male

67. **verdict:** opinion

68. **Else:** otherwise; **have a fling:** i.e., throw out a scoffing remark

70. **special:** distinguished; **weal:** state

73. **our crown:** Henry here uses the royal plural to say "my **crown.**"

74. **jar:** quarrel, dispute

75. **my tender years:** Henry's youth is stressed throughout the play (In this scene, see, e.g., line 140.) **tell:** i.e., perceive that

76. **viperous:** malignant; **worm:** serpent

77. **bowels:** center, heart

WINCHESTER
  Unreverent Gloucester!
GLOUCESTER   Thou art reverend
  Touching thy spiritual function, not thy life.
WINCHESTER
  Rome shall remedy this.
⌜GLOUCESTER⌝   Roam thither then.   55
WARWICK, ⌜*to Winchester*⌝
  My lord, it were your duty to forbear.
SOMERSET
  Ay, ⌜so⌝ the Bishop be not overborne.
  Methinks my lord should be religious,
  And know the office that belongs to such.
WARWICK
  Methinks his Lordship should be humbler.   60
  It fitteth not a prelate so to plead.
SOMERSET
  Yes, when his holy state is touched so near.
WARWICK
  State holy, or unhallowed, what of that?
  Is not his Grace Protector to the King?
PLANTAGENET, ⌜*aside*⌝
  Plantagenet, I see, must hold his tongue,   65
  Lest it be said "Speak, sirrah, when you should;
  Must your bold verdict enter talk with lords?"
  Else would I have a fling at Winchester.
KING HENRY
  Uncles of Gloucester and of Winchester,
  The special watchmen of our English weal,   70
  I would prevail, if prayers might prevail,
  To join your hearts in love and amity.
  O, what a scandal is it to our crown
  That two such noble peers as you should jar!
  Believe me, lords, my tender years can tell   75
  Civil dissension is a viperous worm
  That gnaws the bowels of the commonwealth.

79. **uproar:** insurrection

83. **Bishop:** i.e., Bishop's

84. **late:** recently

86. **banding themselves . . . parts:** banding together into mutually opposed parties

88. **giddy:** foolish; mad

89. **windows:** At the time this play is set, **windows** were latticework or shutters; at the time the play was written, **windows** might be either shutters or panes of glass. **broke down:** smashed

90 SD. **in skirmish:** fighting

91. **charge:** order; **ourself:** i.e., me

92. **hold your slaught'ring hands:** refrain from slaughter

93. **mitigate:** render less hostile

95. **fall to it with:** have recourse to

98. **peevish:** spiteful, harmful; senseless

101. **for:** because of

A noise within: "Down with the tawny coats!"

What tumult 's this?
WARWICK   An uproar, I dare warrant,
  Begun through malice of the Bishop's men.   80

A noise again: "Stones! Stones!"

Enter Mayor.

MAYOR
  O, my good lords, and virtuous Henry,
  Pity the city of London, pity us!
  The Bishop and the Duke of Gloucester's men,
  Forbidden late to carry any weapon,
  Have filled their pockets full of pebble stones   85
  And, banding themselves in contrary parts,
  Do pelt so fast at one another's pate
  That many have their giddy brains knocked out;
  Our windows are broke down in every street,
  And we, for fear, compelled to shut our shops.   90

Enter ⌜Servingmen⌝ in skirmish with bloody pates.

KING HENRY
  We charge you, on allegiance to ourself,
  To hold your slaught'ring hands and keep the peace.—
  Pray, Uncle Gloucester, mitigate this strife.
FIRST SERVINGMAN   Nay, if we be forbidden stones, we'll
  fall to it with our teeth.   95
SECOND SERVINGMAN   Do what you dare, we are as
  resolute.   *Skirmish again.*
GLOUCESTER
  You of my household, leave this peevish broil,
  And set this unaccustomed fight aside.
THIRD SERVINGMAN
  My lord, we know your Grace to be a man   100
  Just and upright, and, for your royal birth,

103. **such a prince:** i.e., Gloucester   **prince:** member of the royal family

105. **inkhorn mate:** contemptuous term for a scribbler or worthless writer, here perhaps alluding to Winchester's position as a cleric or clerk, which carried with it the meaning of someone who could read and write

109. **pitch a field:** fortify a battlefield (as if with stakes)

110. **Stay:** stop

115. **once: once** and for all

116. **pitiful:** filled with pity

117. **study:** make it your aim; **prefer:** assist in bringing about

120. **Except:** unless; **repulse:** refusal

122. **mischief:** harm, evil

123. **enacted:** performed

126. **stoop:** yield obedience

127. **his:** i.e., Winchester's; **the priest:** i.e., Winchester

128. **privilege:** preeminence; **of me:** i.e., over me

130. **moody:** angry

Inferior to none but to his Majesty;
And ere that we will suffer such a prince,
So kind a father of the commonweal,
To be disgracèd by an inkhorn mate,   105
We and our wives and children all will fight
And have our bodies slaughtered by thy foes.

FIRST SERVINGMAN
Ay, and the very parings of our nails
Shall pitch a field when we are dead.

                         Begin again.

GLOUCESTER   Stay, stay, I say!   110
And if you love me, as you say you do,
Let me persuade you to forbear awhile.

KING HENRY
O, how this discord doth afflict my soul!
Can you, my Lord of Winchester, behold
My sighs and tears, and will not once relent?   115
Who should be pitiful if you be not?
Or who should study to prefer a peace
If holy churchmen take delight in broils?

WARWICK
Yield, my Lord Protector—yield, Winchester—
Except you mean with obstinate repulse   120
To slay your sovereign and destroy the realm.
You see what mischief, and what murder too,
Hath been enacted through your enmity.
Then be at peace, except you thirst for blood.

WINCHESTER
He shall submit, or I will never yield.   125

GLOUCESTER
Compassion on the King commands me stoop,
Or I would see his heart out ere the priest
Should ever get that privilege of me.

WARWICK
Behold, my Lord of Winchester, the Duke
Hath banished moody discontented fury,   130

132. stern: uncompromising, inflexible; **tragical:** sorrowful, gloomy

134. Uncle Beaufort: i.e., Winchester (whose name was Henry **Beaufort**)

138. hath a kindly gird: has been given a reproof that is **kindly** (i.e., appropriate or kind)

143. hollow: false, insincere

145. This token: i.e., **this** handshake

147. So help me . . . as I: i.e., **God help me** to the same extent **as I**

150. contract: mutual agreement (accented throughout the play on the second syllable)

151. my masters: gentlemen, sirs

154. surgeon's: barber-surgeon's, where wounds were dressed

A "peeled" or tonsured priest. (1.3.30)
From [Abraham de Bruyn,] *Omnium pene Europae . . . gentium habitus . . .* [1581].

As by his smoothèd brows it doth appear.
Why look you still so stern and tragical?
GLOUCESTER
Here, Winchester, I offer thee my hand.
⌜*Winchester refuses Gloucester's hand.*⌝
KING HENRY
Fie, Uncle Beaufort! I have heard you preach
That malice was a great and grievous sin;   135
And will not you maintain the thing you teach,
But prove a chief offender in the same?
WARWICK
Sweet king! The Bishop hath a kindly gird.—
For shame, my Lord of Winchester, relent;
What, shall a child instruct you what to do?   140
WINCHESTER
Well, Duke of Gloucester, I will yield to thee;
Love for thy love and hand for hand I give.
⌜*They take each other's hand.*⌝
GLOUCESTER, ⌜*aside*⌝
Ay, but I fear me with a hollow heart.—
See here, my friends and loving countrymen,
This token serveth for a flag of truce   145
Betwixt ourselves and all our followers,
So help me God, as I dissemble not.
WINCHESTER, ⌜*aside*⌝
So help me God, as I intend it not.
KING HENRY
O, loving uncle—kind Duke of Gloucester—
How joyful am I made by this contract.   150
⌜*To the Servingmen.*⌝ Away, my masters, trouble us
     no more,
But join in friendship as your lords have done.
FIRST SERVINGMAN   Content. I'll to the surgeon's.
SECOND SERVINGMAN   And so will I.   155

156. **physic:** medicine
157. **affords:** provides
159. **in the right:** i.e., in support of the claim
160. **exhibit:** submit for inspection
162. **An if:** i.e., if; **mark:** consider; **circumstance:** detail
164. **for:** because of; **occasions:** facts or considerations (about which)
165. **Eltham Place:** See note to 1.1.173.
166. **of force:** persuasive, convincing
168. **restorèd to his blood:** See note to 2.5.128.
170. **his father's wrongs:** the **wrongs** suffered by **his** father
171. **will:** decree
172. **true:** loyal; **that:** i.e., restoration **to his blood**
178. **Stoop:** kneel
179. **reguerdon of:** i.e., reward for

"So fell that noble earl / And was beheaded." (2.5.90–91)
From [Richard Verstegen,] *Theatre des cruautez des hereticques de nostre temps* . . . (1607).

THIRD SERVINGMAN   And I will see what physic the tavern
  affords.

  They exit ⌐with Mayor and Others.⌐

WARWICK, *⌐presenting a scroll⌐*
  Accept this scroll, most gracious sovereign,
  Which in the right of Richard Plantagenet
  We do exhibit to your Majesty.   160

GLOUCESTER
  Well urged, my Lord of Warwick.—For, sweet prince,
  An if your Grace mark every circumstance,
  You have great reason to do Richard right,
  Especially for those occasions
  At Eltham Place I told your Majesty.   165

KING HENRY
  And those occasions, uncle, were of force.—
  Therefore, my loving lords, our pleasure is
  That Richard be restorèd to his blood.

WARWICK
  Let Richard be restorèd to his blood;
  So shall his father's wrongs be recompensed.   170

WINCHESTER
  As will the rest, so willeth Winchester.

KING HENRY
  If Richard will be true, not that alone
  But all the whole inheritance I give
  That doth belong unto the house of York,
  From whence you spring by lineal descent.   175

PLANTAGENET
  Thy humble servant vows obedience
  And humble service till the point of death.

KING HENRY
  Stoop then, and set your knee against my foot;

  ⌐Plantagenet kneels.⌐

  And in reguerdon of that duty done
  I girt thee with the valiant sword of York.   180

182. **princely:** of the royal family

184. **springs:** flourishes

185. **one:** i.e., even a single

192. **disanimates:** discourages, disheartens

194. **cuts off:** removes

195 SD. **Sennet:** trumpet fanfare marking the ceremonial exit

198. **peers:** noblemen

199. **Burns . . . love:** The image is of fire (**dissension**) that continues to burn **under** a covering of **ashes.** (Both the **ashes** and the **love** are spurious, and the **ashes** both conceal and cannot conceal the fire.)   **forged:** spurious, counterfeit

201. **members:** limbs

203. **envious:** malicious; **breed:** grow

204. **fatal:** ominous

207. **Henry born at Monmouth:** i.e., **Henry** V (See picture, below.)

King Henry V.
From John Taylor, *All the workes of* . . . (1630).

Rise, Richard, like a true Plantagenet,
And rise created princely Duke of York.
YORK, ⌜*formerly* PLANTAGENET, *standing*⌝
  And so thrive Richard as thy foes may fall!
  And as my duty springs, so perish they
  That grudge one thought against your Majesty.   185
ALL
  Welcome, high prince, the mighty Duke of York.
SOMERSET, ⌜*aside*⌝
  Perish, base prince, ignoble Duke of York.
GLOUCESTER
  Now will it best avail your Majesty
  To cross the seas and to be crowned in France.
  The presence of a king engenders love   190
  Amongst his subjects and his loyal friends,
  As it disanimates his enemies.
KING HENRY
  When Gloucester says the word, King Henry goes,
  For friendly counsel cuts off many foes.
GLOUCESTER
  Your ships already are in readiness.   195
                    Sennet. Flourish. All but Exeter exit.
EXETER
  Ay, we may march in England or in France,
  Not seeing what is likely to ensue.
  This late dissension grown betwixt the peers
  Burns under feignèd ashes of forged love
  And will at last break out into a flame.   200
  As festered members rot but by degree
  Till bones and flesh and sinews fall away,
  So will this base and envious discord breed.
  And now I fear that fatal prophecy
  Which in the time of Henry named the Fifth   205
  Was in the mouth of every sucking babe:
  That Henry born at Monmouth should win all,

208. Henry born at Windsor: i.e., **Henry** VI
210. hapless: unlucky

3.2   Pucelle and four soldiers, disguised as peasants, enter Roan. From a tower within the city, Pucelle signals to the French army where to enter. The French take the city, but the English, led by Burgundy and Talbot and observed by a dying Bedford, recapture it.

---

2. **policy:** crafty device
4. **vulgar:** ordinary, common; **market men:** people who sell their produce at a **market**
5. **gather:** acquire, gain; **corn:** grain, wheat
7. **that:** i.e., if; **watch:** watchmen, sentinels
9. **encounter:** attack
10. **mean:** i.e., means
11. **be:** i.e., shall **be**
13. **Qui là:** i.e., who goes there (literally, who there)
14. **Paysans . . . France:** peasants, the poor people of **France**

A view of Roan, or Rouen. (1.1.61; 3.2.1)
From John Speed, *A prospect of the most famous parts of the world . . .* (1631).

And Henry born at Windsor ⌐should⌐ lose all,
Which is so plain that Exeter doth wish
His days may finish ere that hapless time.   210

He exits.

Scene 2

*Enter Pucelle disguised, with four Soldiers with sacks
upon their backs.*

PUCELLE
These are the city gates, the gates of Roan,
Through which our policy must make a breach.
Take heed. Be wary how you place your words;
Talk like the vulgar sort of market men
That come to gather money for their corn.   5
If we have entrance, as I hope we shall,
And that we find the slothful watch but weak,
I'll by a sign give notice to our friends,
That Charles the Dauphin may encounter them.
SOLDIER
Our sacks shall be a mean to sack the city,   10
And we be lords and rulers over Roan;
Therefore we'll knock.

Knock.

WATCH, ⌐*within*⌐
Qui là?
PUCELLE *Paysans la pauvre gens de France:*
Poor market folks that come to sell their corn.   15
WATCH
Enter, go in. The market bell is rung.
PUCELLE, ⌐*aside*⌐
Now, Roan, I'll shake thy bulwarks to the ground.

They exit.

18. **Saint:** i.e., may **Saint; happy:** fortunate

20. **practisants:** perhaps, co-conspirators (This word is not recorded as appearing elsewhere.)

24. **discerned:** perceived; **that:** i.e., what

25. **No way . . . entered:** i.e., no entrance to the town is weaker than the one she took

26. **wedding torch:** Hymen, god of weddings, carries a **torch.** (See picture, page 204.)

28. **fatal:** deadly; **Talbonites:** followers of Talbot

31. **shine it:** i.e., may it **shine; comet:** long regarded as a herald of disastrous events (See picture, page 220.)

32. **prophet:** omen, portent

33. **Defer no time:** i.e., do not delay; **ends:** results (Proverbial: "Delay breeds danger.")

34. **presently:** immediately

35. **do execution on:** slaughter

35 SD. **in an excursion:** i.e., on a raid, sallying out

36. **treason:** Because Henry VI was, by treaty, king of France, French attacks on the English were considered **treason.**

Enter Charles, Bastard, Alanson, ⌐Reignier,
and Soldiers.⌐

CHARLES
    Saint Dennis bless this happy stratagem
    And once again we'll sleep secure in Roan.
BASTARD
    Here entered Pucelle and her practisants.   20
    Now she is there, how will she specify
    "Here is the best and safest passage in"?
REIGNIER
    By thrusting out a torch from yonder tower,
    Which, once discerned, shows that her meaning is:
    No way to that, for weakness, which she entered.   25

Enter Pucelle on the top, thrusting out a torch burning.

PUCELLE
    Behold, this is the happy wedding torch
    That joineth Roan unto her countrymen,
    But burning fatal to the Talbonites.
BASTARD
    See, noble Charles, the beacon of our friend;
    The burning torch, in yonder turret stands.   30
CHARLES
    Now shine it like a comet of revenge,
    A prophet to the fall of all our foes!
REIGNIER
    Defer no time; delays have dangerous ends.
    Enter and cry "The Dauphin!" presently,
    And then do execution on the watch.   35
                                    Alarum. ⌐They exit.⌐

An Alarum. ⌐Enter⌐ Talbot in an excursion.

TALBOT
    France, thou shalt rue this treason with thy tears,
    If Talbot but survive thy treachery.

39. **mischief:** evil, calamity; **unawares:** without warning, unexpectedly

40. **hardly:** not easily; **pride:** "haughty power" (William Warburton)

40 SD. **without:** onstage; **within:** in the gallery over the back of the stage

41. **gallants:** fine fellows (ironic); **Want you corn:** do you need grain

44. **darnel:** a weed that grows among grain

48. **starve:** die

49. **no . . . deeds:** Proverbial: "Not **words, but deeds.**"

50–51. **Break . . . a-tilt at:** i.e., joust with

51. **within:** i.e., sitting in

52. **despite:** settled malice and hatred

55. **with cowardice:** in a cowardly way

56. **Damsel:** girl (contemptuous term of address); **bout:** round of fighting

Deborah and Barak. (1.2.107)
From Gabriele Simeoni, *Figure de la Biblia* . . . (1577).

Pucelle, that witch, that damnèd sorceress,
Hath wrought this hellish mischief unawares,
That hardly we escaped the pride of France.   40
                                              He exits.

*An alarum. Excursions. Bedford brought in sick in
a chair, ⌐carried by two Attendants.¬ Enter Talbot
and Burgundy without; within, Pucelle ⌐with a sack
of grain,¬ Charles, Bastard, ⌐Alanson,¬ and Reignier
on the walls.*

PUCELLE, ⌐*to those below*¬
    Good morrow, gallants. Want you corn for bread?
                    ⌐*She scatters grain on those below.*¬
    I think the Duke of Burgundy will fast
    Before he'll buy again at such a rate.
    'Twas full of darnel. Do you like the taste?
BURGUNDY
    Scoff on, vile fiend and shameless courtesan!   45
    I trust ere long to choke thee with thine own,
    And make thee curse the harvest of that corn.
CHARLES
    Your Grace may starve, perhaps, before that time.
BEDFORD
    O, let no words, but deeds, revenge this treason.
PUCELLE
    What will you do, good graybeard? Break a lance   50
    And run a-tilt at Death within a chair?
TALBOT
    Foul fiend of France and hag of all despite,
    Encompassed with thy lustful paramours,
    Becomes it thee to taunt his valiant age
    And twit with cowardice a man half dead?   55
    Damsel, I'll have a bout with you again,
    Or else let Talbot perish with this shame.

58. **hot:** hot-tempered, angry

59. **thunder . . . follow:** Proverbial: "After **thunder** comes **rain.**"

60. **God speed:** may **God** bring success to

61. **field:** battlefield

62. **Belike:** in all likelihood

63. **try if that:** attempt to find out whether

64. **railing:** scolding, abusive; **Hecate:** in mythology, an ancient fertility goddess who later became associated with Persephone as queen of Hades and protector of witches (here pronounced with three syllables)

67. **Seigneur:** lord (French)

68. **Base:** lowborn

69. **keep:** remain on

77. **house:** family

78. **Pricked on:** provoked, impelled (Burgundy is said to have joined with the English in part because his father had been killed by the Dauphin.)

83. **Great Coeur-de-lion's heart:** the **heart** of Richard I of England, known as Richard the Lionhearted (*Coeur de lion* means "heart of lion" in French.) See picture, page 122.

PUCELLE
Are you so hot, sir? Yet, Pucelle, hold thy peace,
If Talbot do but thunder, rain will follow.
⌐*Those below*⌐ *whisper together in council.*
God speed the Parliament! Who shall be the Speaker?   60
TALBOT
Dare you come forth and meet us in the field?
PUCELLE
Belike your Lordship takes us then for fools,
To try if that our own be ours or no.
TALBOT
I speak not to that railing Hecate,
But unto thee, Alanson, and the rest.   65
Will you, like soldiers, come and fight it out?
ALANSON   Seigneur, no.
TALBOT
Seigneur, hang! Base muleteers of France,
Like peasant footboys do they keep the walls
And dare not take up arms like gentlemen.   70
PUCELLE
Away, captains. Let's get us from the walls,
For Talbot means no goodness by his looks.—
Goodbye, my lord. We came but to tell you
That we are here.   *They exit from the walls.*
TALBOT
And there will we be too, ere it be long,   75
Or else reproach be Talbot's greatest fame.—
Vow, Burgundy, by honor of thy house,
Pricked on by public wrongs sustained in France,
Either to get the town again or die.
And I, as sure as English Henry lives,   80
And as his father here was conqueror,
As sure as in this late-betrayèd town
Great Coeur-de-lion's heart was buried,
So sure I swear to get the town or die.

86. **regard:** observe
89. **crazy:** frail, infirm
92. **weal:** prosperity, success
95. **stout:** brave; **Pendragon:** in Arthurian legend, Uther **Pendragon,** father of Arthur; **litter:** stretcher
97. **Methinks:** it seems to me that
102. **out of hand:** immediately
103. **set upon:** attack
106. **like:** likely; **to have the overthrow:** i.e., to be overthrown or defeated

Richard Coeur-de-Lion. (3.2.83)
From John Rastell, *The pastyme of people* . . . [1529?].

BURGUNDY
My vows are equal partners with thy vows.   85
TALBOT
But, ere we go, regard this dying prince,
The valiant Duke of Bedford.—Come, my lord,
We will bestow you in some better place,
Fitter for sickness and for crazy age.
BEDFORD
Lord Talbot, do not so dishonor me.   90
Here will I sit, before the walls of Roan,
And will be partner of your weal or woe.
BURGUNDY
Courageous Bedford, let us now persuade you—
BEDFORD
Not to be gone from hence, for once I read
That stout Pendragon, in his litter sick,   95
Came to the field and vanquishèd his foes.
Methinks I should revive the soldiers' hearts
Because I ever found them as myself.
TALBOT
Undaunted spirit in a dying breast,
Then be it so. Heavens keep old Bedford safe!—   100
And now no more ado, brave Burgundy,
But gather we our forces out of hand
And set upon our boasting enemy.
                              He exits ⌜*with Burgundy.*⌝
                      ⌜*Bedford and Attendants remain.*⌝

An alarum. Excursions. Enter Sir John Fastolf
and a Captain.

CAPTAIN
Whither away, Sir John Fastolf, in such haste?
FASTOLF
Whither away? To save myself by flight.   105
We are like to have the overthrow again.

107. **fly:** flee

110. **ill fortune:** bad luck

113. **What . . . man:** Jeremiah 17.5: "Cursed be the **man** that trusteth in **man,** and maketh flesh his arm."

114. **of late:** recently; **daring:** bold

115. **fain:** well-pleased

122. **gentle:** noble

123. **her old familiar:** the spirit or demon associated with her or in her power (The word **old** suggests that he means the devil.)

124. **braves:** boastful, threatening behavior

124–25. **Charles his gleeks:** Charles's sharp, biting remarks

126. **all amort:** lifeless, dejected

"Triumphant Death." (4.7.3, 18)
From *Todten-Tantz . . .* (1696).

CAPTAIN
　What, will you fly and leave Lord Talbot?
FASTOLF　　　　　　　　　　　　　　　　　Ay,
　All the Talbots in the world, to save my life.
　　　　　　　　　　　　　　　　　　He exits.

CAPTAIN
　Cowardly knight, ill fortune follow thee.　　　　110
　　　　　　　　　　　　　　　　　　He exits.

Retreat. Excursions. Pucelle, Alanson, and Charles
　⌐*enter, pursued by English Soldiers, and*⌐ *fly.*

BEDFORD
　Now, quiet soul, depart when heaven please,
　For I have seen our enemies' overthrow.
　What is the trust or strength of foolish man?
　They that of late were daring with their scoffs
　Are glad and fain by flight to save themselves.　　115
　　　　　　　　　Bedford dies, and is carried
　　　　　　　　　　　in by two in his chair.

An alarum. Enter Talbot, Burgundy, and the rest.

TALBOT
　Lost and recovered in a day again!
　This is a double honor, Burgundy.
　Yet heavens have glory for this victory.
BURGUNDY
　Warlike and martial Talbot, Burgundy
　Enshrines thee in his heart, and there erects　　120
　Thy noble deeds as valor's monuments.
TALBOT
　Thanks, gentle duke. But where is Pucelle now?
　I think her old familiar is asleep.
　Now where's the Bastard's braves and Charles his
　　　gleeks?　　　　　　　　　　　　　　　125
　What, all amort? Roan hangs her head for grief

128. **take some order:** make some arrangements
129. **expert:** experienced
131. **lie:** i.e., resides
132. **wills:** determines
134. **late-deceased:** recently deceased
135. **exequies fulfilled:** funeral ceremonies performed
136. **couchèd lance:** lowered a **lance** to the position for attack
137. **gentler:** more noble; **sway:** prevail, rule
139. **that's . . . misery:** Proverbial: "Death is **the end of** every worldly sore."

3.3 As Talbot and Burgundy march separately to Paris for the coronation of Henry VI, Pucelle entices Burgundy to join the French forces led by the Dauphin.

---

1. **Dismay not:** i.e. do **not** be dismayed
3. **Care:** grief; **corrosive:** i.e., like caustic medicine (Proverbial: "**Care is no cure**"; "**Care is** a corrosive.")
5. **frantic:** wildly enraged
6. **peacock:** Proverbial: "As proud as **a peacock.**"
7. **pull:** pluck; **train:** (1) tail; (2) body of followers
8. **ruled:** subjected to guidance and discipline
10. **of thy cunning:** i.e., in your expertise, cleverness; **diffidence:** doubt
11. **foil:** defeat

That such a valiant company are fled.
Now will we take some order in the town,
Placing therein some expert officers,
And then depart to Paris to the King,   130
For there young Henry with his nobles lie.
BURGUNDY
What wills Lord Talbot pleaseth Burgundy.
TALBOT
But yet, before we go, let's not forget
The noble Duke of Bedford late-deceased,
But see his exequies fulfilled in Roan.   135
A braver soldier never couchèd lance,
A gentler heart did never sway in court.
But kings and mightiest potentates must die,
For that's the end of human misery.
                                        They exit.

Scene 3

Enter Charles, Bastard, Alanson, Pucelle, ⌜and Soldiers.⌝

PUCELLE
Dismay not, princes, at this accident,
Nor grieve that Roan is so recoverèd.
Care is no cure, but rather corrosive
For things that are not to be remedied.
Let frantic Talbot triumph for a while,   5
And like a peacock sweep along his tail;
We'll pull his plumes and take away his train,
If dauphin and the rest will be but ruled.
CHARLES
We have been guided by thee hitherto,
And of thy cunning had no diffidence.   10
One sudden foil shall never breed distrust.

12. **wit:** intelligence; **policies:** stratagems

16. **Employ thee:** busy yourself

18. **fair:** flattering

21. **Ay, marry:** i.e., yes, indeed; **sweeting:** sweetheart, darling

24. **extirpèd:** rooted out

25. **expulsed:** driven

26. **title:** legal right to possession

30. **powers:** armed forces; **unto Paris-ward:** toward **Paris**

30 SD. **sound an English march:** Presumably the marches sounded here and at line 32 SD are offstage. (See longer note, page 243.)

31. **colors:** flags, standards

34. **Fortune:** The goddess Fortuna, conventionally fickle, here grants her **favor** to the French. (See picture, page 206.)

35. **Summon:** proclaim, call

35 SD. **sound a parley:** i.e., **trumpets** signal a request for **a parley**

A conjuror. (1.1.26–27; 2.1.16)
From Christopher Marlowe, *The tragicall historie of . . .
Doctor Faustus . . .* (1631).

BASTARD, ⌜*to Pucelle*⌝
  Search out thy wit for secret policies,
  And we will make thee famous through the world.
ALANSON, ⌜*to Pucelle*⌝
  We'll set thy statue in some holy place
  And have thee reverenced like a blessèd saint.   15
  Employ thee then, sweet virgin, for our good.
PUCELLE
  Then thus it must be; this doth Joan devise:
  By fair persuasions mixed with sugared words
  We will entice the Duke of Burgundy
  To leave the Talbot and to follow us.   20
CHARLES
  Ay, marry, sweeting, if we could do that,
  France were no place for Henry's warriors,
  Nor should that nation boast it so with us,
  But be extirpèd from our provinces.
ALANSON
  Forever should they be expulsed from France,   25
  And not have title of an earldom here.
PUCELLE
  Your honors shall perceive how I will work
  To bring this matter to the wishèd end.
                          Drum sounds afar off.
  Hark! By the sound of drum you may perceive
  Their powers are marching unto Paris-ward.   30
                    Here sound an English march.
  There goes the Talbot with his colors spread,
  And all the troops of English after him.
                            French march.
  Now in the rearward comes the Duke and his.
  Fortune in favor makes him lag behind.
  Summon a parley; we will talk with him.   35
                  Trumpets sound a parley.

42. **Stay:** an injunction to pause and let the speaker make some remark

43. **over-tedious:** i.e., overly wordy

44. **Look on:** contemplate

45. **defaced:** destroyed

46. **wasting:** devastating; **ruin of:** overthrow by

47. **lowly:** humble

48. **tender-dying:** i.e., dying young

49. **pining:** consuming, wasting

59. **relent:** perhaps, yield, give way; or, perhaps, become compassionate

Tamyris with the head of Cyrus. (2.3.6)
From Sebastian Münster, *Cosmographiae uniuersalis . . .* (1554).

CHARLES
A parley with the Duke of Burgundy!

⌜*Enter Burgundy.*⌝

BURGUNDY
Who craves a parley with the Burgundy?
PUCELLE
The princely Charles of France, thy countryman.
BURGUNDY
What say'st thou, Charles?—for I am marching hence.
CHARLES, ⌜*aside to Pucelle*⌝
Speak, Pucelle, and enchant him with thy words.   40
PUCELLE
Brave Burgundy, undoubted hope of France,
Stay; let thy humble handmaid speak to thee.
BURGUNDY
Speak on, but be not over-tedious.
PUCELLE
Look on thy country, look on fertile France,
And see the cities and the towns defaced   45
By wasting ruin of the cruel foe.
As looks the mother on her lowly babe
When death doth close his tender-dying eyes,
See, see the pining malady of France:
Behold the wounds, the most unnatural wounds,   50
Which thou thyself hast given her woeful breast.
O, turn thy edgèd sword another way;
Strike those that hurt, and hurt not those that help.
One drop of blood drawn from thy country's bosom
Should grieve thee more than streams of foreign gore.   55
Return thee therefore with a flood of tears,
And wash away thy country's stainèd spots.
BURGUNDY, ⌜*aside*⌝
Either she hath bewitched me with her words,
Or nature makes me suddenly relent.

60. **exclaims on:** loudly accuses

61. **birth:** parentage, lineage; **lawful progeny:** legitimate descent

62. **lordly:** imperious, lofty

63. **but for profit's sake:** except for the **sake** of profit

64. **set footing once in:** entered **once** into (with the implication of "**once** conquered")

65. **fashioned . . . ill:** i.e., made you into an evil tool

68. **Call . . . mind:** i.e., let's remember; **mark:** consider

75. **them:** i.e., them who; **slaughtermen:** executioners

78. **haughty:** lofty, high-minded

82. **hearty:** heartfelt

83. **power:** army

85. **turn:** revolt, desert; switch position; change course

86. **fresh:** ready, eager

PUCELLE

   Besides, all French and France exclaims on thee,   60
   Doubting thy birth and lawful progeny.
   Who join'st thou with but with a lordly nation
   That will not trust thee but for profit's sake?
   When Talbot hath set footing once in France
   And fashioned thee that instrument of ill,   65
   Who then but English Henry will be lord,
   And thou be thrust out like a fugitive?
   Call we to mind, and mark but this for proof:
   Was not the Duke of Orleance thy foe?
   And was he not in England prisoner?   70
   But when they heard he was thine enemy,
   They set him free, without his ransom paid,
   In spite of Burgundy and all his friends.
   See then, thou fight'st against thy countrymen,
   And join'st with them will be thy slaughtermen.   75
   Come, come, return; return, thou wandering lord.
   Charles and the rest will take thee in their arms.

BURGUNDY, ⌈*aside*⌉

   I am vanquishèd. These haughty words of hers
   Have battered me like roaring cannon-shot,
   And made me almost yield upon my knees.—   80
   Forgive me, country, and sweet countrymen;
   And, lords, accept this hearty kind embrace.
       ⌈*He embraces Charles, Bastard, and Alanson.*⌉
   My forces and my power of men are yours.
   So, farewell, Talbot. I'll no longer trust thee.

PUCELLE, ⌈*aside*⌉

   Done like a Frenchman: turn and turn again.   85

CHARLES

   Welcome, brave duke. Thy friendship makes us fresh.

BASTARD

   And doth beget new courage in our breasts.

88. **bravely:** splendidly

90. **on:** i.e., go **on; join our powers:** combine our armies

91. **prejudice:** do injury to

3.4 In Paris, a grateful Henry VI creates Talbot Earl of Shrewsbury in recompense for his victories in France. Vernon, a supporter of York, quarrels with Basset, a supporter of Somerset.

———————

3. **truce:** temporary cessation of hostilities

4. **duty:** homage

5. **sign:** indication; **reclaimed:** subdued

7. **towns of strength:** fortified **towns**

8. **esteem:** worth, reputation

9. **Lets fall:** drops; **his:** i.e., its (referring to **this arm** [line 5])

15. **if it please:** a politeness formula

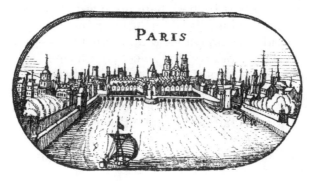

A view of Paris. (1.1.66; 3.4; 4.1)
From John Speed, *A prospect of the most famous parts of the world . . .* (1631).

ALANSON
  Pucelle hath bravely played her part in this
  And doth deserve a coronet of gold.
CHARLES
  Now let us on, my lords, and join our powers,   90
  And seek how we may prejudice the foe.
                                          They exit.

                    Scene 4

⌜*Flourish.*⌝ *Enter the King, Gloucester, Winchester,*
Exeter; York, Warwick, ⌜*and Vernon, with white roses;*⌝
  Somerset, Suffolk, ⌜*and Basset, with red roses.*⌝
      To them, with his Soldiers, Talbot.

TALBOT
  My gracious prince and honorable peers,
  Hearing of your arrival in this realm,
  I have awhile given truce unto my wars
  To do my duty to my sovereign;
  In sign whereof, this arm, that hath reclaimed   5
  To your obedience fifty fortresses,
  Twelve cities, and seven walled towns of strength,
  Besides five hundred prisoners of esteem,
  Lets fall his sword before your Highness' feet,
  And with submissive loyalty of heart   10
  Ascribes the glory of his conquest got
  First to my God, and next unto your Grace.
                                          ⌜*He kneels.*⌝
KING HENRY
  Is this the Lord Talbot, Uncle Gloucester,
  That hath so long been resident in France?
GLOUCESTER
  Yes, if it please your Majesty, my liege.   15

19. **stouter champion:** more formidable fighting man

20. **we:** i.e., I (the royal we); **resolvèd:** convinced; **truth:** allegiance, loyalty

22. **our:** i.e., my (the royal plural)

23. **reguerdoned:** rewarded

25. **deserts:** meritorious actions, excellences

27. **our coronation:** ceremony of my being crowned

27 SD. **Sennet:** trumpet fanfare marking the ceremonial exit

28. **hot:** angry

29. **Disgracing of:** reviling; **these colors:** colored device, badge (here, the white rose)

31. **the former . . . spak'st:** i.e., **the words** you spoke earlier

32. **patronage:** defend

33. **envious:** malicious; **saucy:** insolent

35. **Sirrah:** term of address to a social inferior (in this case, an insult)

37. **in witness:** as testimony

38. **law of arms:** See longer note, page 244.

39. **whoso:** whoever; **present:** immediate

40. **broach:** draw off as if through a hole in a cask

KING HENRY
   Welcome, brave captain and victorious lord.
   When I was young—as yet I am not old—
   I do remember how my father said
   A stouter champion never handled sword.
   Long since we were resolvèd of your truth, 20
   Your faithful service, and your toil in war;
   Yet never have you tasted our reward
   Or been reguerdoned with so much as thanks,
   Because till now we never saw your face.
   Therefore stand up; and for these good deserts 25
   We here create you Earl of Shrewsbury;
   And in our coronation take your place. ⌈*Talbot rises.*⌉
                 Sennet. Flourish. All except
                 Vernon and Basset exit.

VERNON
   Now, sir, to you that were so hot at sea,
   Disgracing of these colors that I wear
   In honor of my noble Lord of York, 30
   Dar'st thou maintain the former words thou spak'st?
BASSET
   Yes, sir, as well as you dare patronage
   The envious barking of your saucy tongue
   Against my lord the Duke of Somerset.
VERNON
   Sirrah, thy lord I honor as he is. 35
BASSET
   Why, what is he? As good a man as York.
VERNON
   Hark you, not so; in witness, take you that.
                      Strikes him.
BASSET
   Villain, thou knowest the law of arms is such
   That whoso draws a sword 'tis present death,
   Or else this blow should broach thy dearest blood. 40

41. **I'll unto:** i.e., **I'll** go to; **crave:** i.e., ask earnestly that
42. **venge:** avenge
43. **meet:** fight a duel with
44. **miscreant:** vile wretch
45. **after:** afterward; **would:** wish

King Henry VI.
From John Taylor, *All the workes of . . .* (1630).

But I'll unto his Majesty, and crave
I may have liberty to venge this wrong,
When thou shalt see I'll meet thee to thy cost.
⌜*He exits.*⌝

VERNON
Well, miscreant, I'll be there as soon as you,
And after meet you sooner than you would.   45
He exits.

HENRY VI
Part 1

ACT 4

4.1   Henry VI is crowned. Fastolf arrives with a letter from Burgundy and, because of his earlier cowardice in battle, is stripped of his Garter by Talbot and banished by Henry. The letter from Burgundy announces his defection, and Henry sends Talbot to attack him. Vernon and Basset seek royal permission to fight a duel, as in turn do their patrons York and Somerset. Henry denies permission to them. He then dons the red rose of Somerset's party but says he inclines no more to Somerset than to York. Henry orders York and Somerset to join forces against the French.

---

   0 SD. **Flourish:** a fanfare to announce the king's entrance
     4. **elect:** choose
     6. **pretend:** present, bring
     7. **practices:** schemes, machinations
     9. **Callice:** Calais (See picture, below.)

A view of Callice, or Calais. (4.1.9)
From John Speed, *A prospect of the most famous parts of the world* . . . (1631).

ACT 4

Scene 1

⌜*Flourish.*⌝ *Enter King, Gloucester, Winchester, Talbot, Exeter; York* ⌜*and*⌝ *Warwick,* ⌜*with white roses;*⌝ *Suffolk* ⌜*and*⌝ *Somerset,* ⌜*with red roses;*⌝ *Governor* ⌜*of Paris, and Others.*⌝

GLOUCESTER
Lord Bishop, set the crown upon his head.
WINCHESTER, ⌜*crowning King Henry*⌝
God save King Henry, of that name the Sixth!
GLOUCESTER
Now, Governor of Paris, take your oath.
⌜*Governor kneels.*⌝
That you elect no other king but him;
Esteem none friends but such as are his friends,   5
And none your foes but such as shall pretend
Malicious practices against his state:
This shall you do, so help you righteous God.
⌜*Governor rises.*⌝

Enter Fastolf.

FASTOLF
My gracious sovereign, as I rode from Callice
To haste unto your coronation,   10
A letter was delivered to my hands,
Writ to your Grace from th' Duke of Burgundy.
⌜*He hands the King a paper.*⌝
TALBOT
Shame to the Duke of Burgundy and thee!

143

15. **Garter:** badge of the highest order of English knighthood, a dark-blue velvet garter worn just below the left knee, edged and buckled with gold (See picture, page 146.)

17. **installèd:** formally instated or invested; **degree:** rank

19. **battle of Patay:** See 1.1.107–43.

20. **but in all . . . strong:** i.e., **I was in all** only **six thousand strong**

23. **Like to:** i.e., **like; trusty:** trustworthy (ironic); **squire:** term of contempt

25. **divers:** several

28. **whether that:** i.e., **whether**

30. **fact:** deed, crime

31. **ill beseeming:** not appropriate for; **common man:** i.e., commoner, one in the lower ranks of society

32. **captain:** military commander

33. **Order:** i.e., the **Order** of **the Garter; ordained:** instituted, established

35. **haughty:** exalted

36. **were grown . . . wars:** i.e., had achieved reputation in battle

37. **for distress:** because of adversity or affliction

38. **most extremes:** i.e., the greatest extremities

39. **sort:** way (i.e., with courage, resolution, etc.)

43. **degraded:** debased, lowered in rank; **hedge-born:** i.e., born in the shelter of a hedge for lack of a house (a proverbial expression); **swain:** farm laborer

44. **gentle:** noble

45. **Stain:** disgrace; **doom:** condemnation

I vowed, base knight, when I did meet thee next,
To tear the Garter from thy craven's leg,   15
                              (⌈*tearing it off*⌉)
Which I have done, because unworthily
Thou wast installèd in that high degree.—
Pardon me, princely Henry and the rest.
This dastard, at the battle of ⌈Patay,⌉
When but in all I was six thousand strong   20
And that the French were almost ten to one,
Before we met or that a stroke was given,
Like to a trusty squire did run away;
In which assault we lost twelve hundred men.
Myself and divers gentlemen besides   25
Were there surprised and taken prisoners.
Then judge, great lords, if I have done amiss,
Or whether that such cowards ought to wear
This ornament of knighthood—yea or no?
GLOUCESTER
To say the truth, this fact was infamous   30
And ill beseeming any common man,
Much more a knight, a captain, and a leader.
TALBOT
When first this Order was ordained, my lords,
Knights of the Garter were of noble birth,
Valiant and virtuous, full of haughty courage,   35
Such as were grown to credit by the wars;
Not fearing death nor shrinking for distress,
But always resolute in most extremes.
He then that is not furnished in this sort
Doth but usurp the sacred name of knight,   40
Profaning this most honorable Order,
And should, if I were worthy to be judge,
Be quite degraded, like a hedge-born swain
That doth presume to boast of gentle blood.
KING HENRY, ⌈*to Fastolf*⌉
Stain to thy countrymen, thou hear'st thy doom.   45

46. **packing:** gone
49. **uncle, Duke of Burgundy:** The families of Henry and **Burgundy** were linked through marriage.
50. **style:** tone
54. **Pretend:** portend, presage
57. **Moved:** emotionally stirred; **wrack:** ruin
63. **alliance:** family relationship
65. **revolt:** change allegiance
69. **talk with:** rebuke (understatement)

The Garter. (4.1.15, 33–34)
From Elias Ashmole, *The institution, laws & ceremonies of the . . . Order of the Garter . . .* (1672).

Be packing therefore, thou that wast a knight.
Henceforth we banish thee on pain of death.
⌐*Fastolf exits.*⌐
And now, ⌐my⌐ lord protector, view the letter
Sent from our uncle, Duke of Burgundy.
⌐*He hands the paper to Gloucester.*⌐

GLOUCESTER
What means his Grace that he hath changed his style?   50
No more but, plain and bluntly, *"To the King"*!
Hath he forgot he is his sovereign?
Or doth this churlish superscription
Pretend some alteration in good will?
What's here? (⌐*Reads.*⌐)   55
I have upon especial cause,
Moved with compassion of my country's wrack,
Together with the pitiful complaints
Of such as your oppression feeds upon,
Forsaken your pernicious faction   60
And joined with Charles, the rightful king of France.
O monstrous treachery! Can this be so?
That in alliance, amity, and oaths
There should be found such false dissembling guile?

KING HENRY
What? Doth my Uncle Burgundy revolt?   65

GLOUCESTER
He doth, my lord, and is become your foe.

KING HENRY
Is that the worst this letter doth contain?

GLOUCESTER
It is the worst, and all, my lord, he writes.

KING HENRY
Why, then, Lord Talbot there shall talk with him
And give him chastisement for this abuse.—   70
How say you, my lord, are you not content?

72. **am prevented:** i.e., have been anticipated
74. **strength:** military power; **straight:** straight-away, immediately
75. **ill we brook:** i.e., I take offense at (literally, harshly I tolerate)
77. **still:** always
78. **confusion:** destruction, ruin
79. **the combat:** i.e., the right to trial by **combat**
81. **servant:** attendant, follower
85. **wherefore:** why; **crave:** demand, beg
91. **envious:** malicious

TALBOT
  Content, my liege? Yes. But that I am prevented,
  I should have begged I might have been employed.
KING HENRY
  Then gather strength and march unto him straight;
  Let him perceive how ill we brook his treason   75
  And what offense it is to flout his friends.
TALBOT
  I go, my lord, in heart desiring still
  You may behold confusion of your foes. ⌜*He exits.*⌝

  Enter Vernon, ⌜with a white rose,⌝ and Basset,
  ⌜with a red rose.⌝

VERNON
  Grant me the combat, gracious sovereign.
BASSET
  And me, my lord, grant me the combat too.   80
YORK, ⌜*indicating Vernon*⌝
  This is my servant; hear him, noble prince.
SOMERSET, ⌜*indicating Basset*⌝
  And this is mine, sweet Henry; favor him.
KING HENRY
  Be patient, lords, and give them leave to speak.—
  Say, gentlemen, what makes you thus exclaim,
  And wherefore crave you combat, or with whom?   85
VERNON
  With him, my lord, for he hath done me wrong.
BASSET
  And I with him, for he hath done me wrong.
KING HENRY
  What is that wrong whereof you both complain?
  First let me know, and then I'll answer you.
BASSET
  Crossing the sea from England into France,   90
  This fellow here with envious carping tongue
  Upbraided me about the rose I wear,

93. **leaves:** i.e., petals

95. **repugn:** reject, contend against

96. **a certain question in the law:** See 2.4 and 2.5.45–50.

99. **rude:** ignorant, unlearned

101. **benefit of law of arms:** i.e., duel

103. **forgèd:** fabricated; **quaint:** cunning; **conceit:** device

104. **set a gloss upon:** i.e., give an attractive semblance to

108. **Bewrayed:** exposed

109. **left:** forsaken, abandoned

110. **out:** be suddenly revealed

114. **emulations:** contentions between rivals

115. **cousins:** i.e., kinsmen

117. **tried by fight:** subject to trial by combat

A potter at his wheel. (1.5.19)
From Jan Luiken, *Spiegal* . . . (1704).

Saying the sanguine color of the leaves
Did represent my master's blushing cheeks
When stubbornly he did repugn the truth   95
About a certain question in the law
Argued betwixt the Duke of York and him,
With other vile and ignominious terms.
In confutation of which rude reproach,
And in defense of my lord's worthiness,   100
I crave the benefit of law of arms.

VERNON
And that is my petition, noble lord;
For though he seem with forgèd quaint conceit
To set a gloss upon his bold intent,
Yet know, my lord, I was provoked by him,   105
And he first took exceptions at this badge,
Pronouncing that the paleness of this flower
Bewrayed the faintness of my master's heart.

YORK
Will not this malice, Somerset, be left?

SOMERSET
Your private grudge, my Lord of York, will out,   110
Though ne'er so cunningly you smother it.

KING HENRY
Good Lord, what madness rules in brainsick men
When for so slight and frivolous a cause
Such factious emulations shall arise!
Good cousins both, of York and Somerset,   115
Quiet yourselves, I pray, and be at peace.

YORK
Let this dissension first be tried by fight,
And then your Highness shall command a peace.

SOMERSET
The quarrel toucheth none but us alone;
Betwixt ourselves let us decide it then.   120

YORK, ⌜*throwing down a gage*⌝
There is my pledge; accept it, Somerset.

122. **it:** the quarrel; **rest:** remain; **where** . . . **began:** i.e., between Vernon and Basset

124. **Confounded:** i.e., cursed

125. **audacious:** shameless

127. **immodest:** impudent, arrogant; **outrage:** insolence; disorder

130. **objections:** charges

131. **take occasion . . . mouths:** i.e., **take** advantage of the opportunity provided by their words

132. **mutiny:** dispute, quarrel

136. **charge:** command, order

141. **within:** among

142. **stomachs:** dispositions

143. **rebel:** rebellion

145. **certified:** informed

146. **toy:** trifle; **regard:** importance

149. **conquest of my father:** i.e., my father's conquests

151. **That . . . that:** i.e., **for a trifle that** which

152. **umpire:** arbitrator; **doubtful:** uncertain, undecided; **strife:** dispute

VERNON, ⌜*to Somerset*⌝
  Nay, let it rest where it began at first.
BASSET, ⌜*to Somerset*⌝
  Confirm it so, mine honorable lord.
GLOUCESTER
  Confirm it so? Confounded be your strife,
  And perish you with your audacious prate!   125
  Presumptuous vassals, are you not ashamed
  With this immodest clamorous outrage
  To trouble and disturb the King and us?—
  And you, my lords, methinks you do not well
  To bear with their perverse objections,   130
  Much less to take occasion from their mouths
  To raise a mutiny betwixt yourselves.
  Let me persuade you take a better course.
EXETER
  It grieves his Highness. Good my lords, be friends.
KING HENRY
  Come hither, you that would be combatants: 135
  Henceforth I charge you, as you love our favor,
  Quite to forget this quarrel and the cause.—
  And you, my lords, remember where we are:
  In France, amongst a fickle wavering nation.
  If they perceive dissension in our looks,   140
  And that within ourselves we disagree,
  How will their grudging stomachs be provoked
  To willful disobedience and rebel!
  Besides, what infamy will there arise
  When foreign princes shall be certified   145
  That for a toy, a thing of no regard,
  King Henry's peers and chief nobility
  Destroyed themselves and lost the realm of France!
  O, think upon the conquest of my father,
  My tender years, and let us not forgo   150
  That for a trifle that was bought with blood.
  Let me be umpire in this doubtful strife.

157. **As . . . crown:** i.e., **they** could just **as well** blame **me** for wearing **my crown**

163. **institute:** appoint

166. **foot: foot** soldiers

168. **digest:** disperse

175. **promise:** assure

176. **methought:** it seemed to me; **play the orator:** proverbial

181. **iwis:** indeed, truly

King Henry VI.
From John Speed, *The theatre of the empire of Great Britaine . . .*
(1627 [i.e., 1631]).

154

I see no reason if I wear this rose
That anyone should therefore be suspicious
I more incline to Somerset than York.   155
⌜*He puts on a red rose.*⌝
Both are my kinsmen, and I love them both.
As well they may upbraid me with my crown
Because, forsooth, the King of Scots is crowned.
But your discretions better can persuade
Than I am able to instruct or teach;   160
And therefore, as we hither came in peace,
So let us still continue peace and love.
Cousin of York, we institute your Grace
To be our regent in these parts of France;—
And good my Lord of Somerset, unite   165
Your troops of horsemen with his bands of foot;
And like true subjects, sons of your progenitors,
Go cheerfully together and digest
Your angry choler on your enemies.
Ourself, my lord protector, and the rest,   170
After some respite, will return to Callice;
From thence to England, where I hope ere long
To be presented, by your victories,
With Charles, Alanson, and that traitorous rout.
    Flourish. All but York, Warwick, Exeter, Vernon exit.

WARWICK
    My Lord of York, I promise you the King   175
    Prettily, methought, did play the orator.

YORK
    And so he did, but yet I like it not
    In that he wears the badge of Somerset.

WARWICK
    Tush, that was but his fancy; blame him not.
    I dare presume, sweet prince, he thought no harm.   180

YORK
    And if ⌜iwis⌝ he did—but let it rest.
    Other affairs must now be managèd.

185. **deciphered:** revealed
188. **simple:** common (as opposed to *noble* or *gentle*)
189. **jarring:** (1) wrangling; (2) inharmonious; **discord:** (1) strife; (2) musical dissonance
190. **shouldering:** jostling
191. **bandying:** contention; **favorites:** followers
192. **ill event:** disastrous outcome
193. **'Tis much . . . children's hands:** Proverbial: "Woe to the land whose king is a child." **much:** onerous
194. **more:** worse; **envy:** malice; **unkind division:** hostile dissension
195. **confusion:** destruction, overthrow

4.2 As Talbot draws up his troops before Bordeaux, he learns that he is surrounded by much greater French forces.

———————

0 SD. **Trump and Drum:** i.e., trumpeter and drummer
3. **captains:** leaders
5. **would:** i.e., wills, decrees
8. **bloody:** cruel, bloodthirsty; **power:** army

⌜*York, Warwick and Vernon*⌝ *exit.*
Exeter remains.

EXETER
Well didst thou, Richard, to suppress thy voice,
For had the passions of thy heart burst out,
I fear we should have seen deciphered there   185
More rancorous spite, more furious raging broils,
Than yet can be imagined or supposed.
But howsoe'er, no simple man that sees
This jarring discord of nobility,
This shouldering of each other in the court,   190
This factious bandying of their favorites,
But ⌜sees⌝ it doth presage some ill event.
'Tis much when scepters are in children's hands,
But more when envy breeds unkind division:
There comes the ruin; there begins confusion.   195
He exits.

⌜Scene 2⌝

Enter Talbot with ⌜*Soldiers and*⌝ *Trump and Drum*
before Bordeaux.

TALBOT
Go to the gates of Bordeaux, trumpeter.
Summon their general unto the wall.

⌜*Trumpet*⌝ *sounds. Enter General* ⌜*and Others*⌝ *aloft.*

English John Talbot, captains, ⌜calls⌝ you forth,
Servant-in-arms to Harry, King of England,
And thus he would: open your city gates,   5
Be humble to us, call my sovereign yours,
And do him homage as obedient subjects,
And I'll withdraw me and my bloody power.
But if you frown upon this proffered peace,
You tempt the fury of my three attendants,   10

11. **quartering:** cutting (including cutting the body up into four parts)

12. **even:** level

13. **air-braving:** i.e., **air**-defying

14. **forsake:** decline, refuse

15. **fearful:** frightening; **owl of death:** Proverbial: "The screeching **owl** bodes **death**." (See picture, page 218.)

17. **period:** end; **tyranny:** violence

18. **On us:** i.e., into our city

21. **retire:** retreat; **well appointed: well** equipped (i.e., with many troops)

22. **snares:** devices for capturing birds and animals (Here begins a series of terms from hunting—**tangle, pitched, flight**—that continues into line 26 [**spoil**] and again becomes prominent in lines 45–54.)

23. **On either hand thee:** i.e., on both sides of you; **pitched:** positioned to fight

25. **turn thee:** i.e., **turn; redress:** aid

26. **front:** confront; **apparent:** clear, palpable; **spoil:** i.e., slaughter (literally, the slaughter of the quarry and its division among the hunting dogs)

27. **pale Destruction:** See Revelation 6.8: "I . . . behold a **pale** horse, and his name that sat on him was **Death**." **meets thee in the face:** i.e., directly confronts you

28. **ta'en the Sacrament:** i.e., taken Holy Communion as a confirmation of their vow

29. **rive:** burst

33. **latest:** last

34. **due thee withal:** endow you with

(continued)

Lean Famine, quartering Steel, and climbing Fire,
Who, in a moment, even with the earth
Shall lay your stately and air-braving towers,
If you forsake the offer of their love.
⌜GENERAL⌝
Thou ominous and fearful owl of death,   15
Our nation's terror and their bloody scourge,
The period of thy tyranny approacheth.
On us thou canst not enter but by death;
For I protest we are well fortified
And strong enough to issue out and fight.   20
If thou retire, the Dauphin, well appointed,
Stands with the snares of war to tangle thee.
On either hand thee, there are squadrons pitched
To wall thee from the liberty of flight;
And no way canst thou turn thee for redress   25
But Death doth front thee with apparent spoil,
And pale Destruction meets thee in the face.
Ten thousand French have ta'en the Sacrament
To rive their dangerous artillery
Upon no Christian soul but English Talbot.   30
Lo, there thou stand'st, a breathing valiant man
Of an invincible unconquered spirit.
This is the latest glory of thy praise
That I, thy enemy, due thee withal;
For ere the glass that now begins to run   35
Finish the process of his sandy hour,
These eyes, that see thee now well-colorèd,
Shall see thee withered, bloody, pale, and dead.
                                        Drum afar off.
Hark, hark, the Dauphin's drum, a warning bell,
Sings heavy music to thy timorous soul,   40
And mine shall ring thy dire departure out.
                        He exits, ⌜aloft, with Others.⌝

35–36. **For . . . hour:** i.e., before an **hour** has passed (literally, before sand finishes running through an hourglass) See picture, page 188.   **process:** progress, course   **his:** i.e., its

37. **well-colorèd:** i.e., with a healthy complexion

40. **heavy:** distressing

41. **departure:** i.e., death

42. **fables not:** i.e., does **not** lie or talk idly

43. **Out:** away; **light:** lightly armed (and therefore swift); **peruse:** survey, inspect; **wings:** divisions, one on each side of the main body of an army

44. **discipline:** military skill or training

45. **parked:** enclosed, surrounded; **bounded in a pale:** i.e., confined as if within a fenced area (The phrases anticipate reference to the English as **deer** in line 46.)

47. **Mazed:** dazed, crazed; **kennel:** pack

48. **in blood:** in full vigor

49. **rascal-like:** A **rascal** is (1) a young, lean or inferior deer; (2) a scoundrel. **pinch:** bite (i.e., of a hunting dog)

50. **moody-mad:** high-spirited, obstinate, angry

51. **bloody:** bloodthirsty

52. **at bay:** like hunted animals defending themselves, unable to flee further

53. **Sell every man:** i.e., let **every man sell; as dear as mine:** i.e., at **as** great cost **as** I do **mine**

54. **dear:** costly; glorious, honorable

55. **Saint George:** England's patron saint (See picture, page 16.)

56. **Prosper:** promote the success of; **colors:** flags, banners (and the national interest they represent)

(continued)

TALBOT
  He fables not; I hear the enemy.
  Out, some light horsemen, and peruse their wings.
                      ⌜*Some Soldiers exit.*⌝
  O, negligent and heedless discipline,
  How are we parked and bounded in a pale,   45
  A little herd of England's timorous deer
  Mazed with a yelping kennel of French curs.
  If we be English deer, be then in blood,
  Not rascal-like to fall down with a pinch,
  But rather, moody-mad and desperate stags,   50
  Turn on the bloody hounds with heads of steel
  And make the cowards stand aloof at bay.
  Sell every man his life as dear as mine
  And they shall find dear deer of us, my friends.
  God and Saint George, Talbot and England's right,   55
  Prosper our colors in this dangerous fight!
       ⌜*He exits with Soldiers, Drum and Trumpet.*⌝

⌜Scene 3⌝

Enter a Messenger that meets York. Enter York
with Trumpet and many Soldiers.

YORK
  Are not the speedy scouts returned again
  That dogged the mighty army of the Dauphin?
MESSENGER
  They are returned, my lord, and give it out
  That he is marched to Bordeaux with his power
  To fight with Talbot. As he marched along,   5
  By your espials were discoverèd
  Two mightier troops than that the Dauphin led,
  Which joined with him and made their march for
    Bordeaux.   ⌜*He exits.*⌝

4.3 Sir William Lucy urges York to help Talbot, but York refuses to march until Somerset unites his cavalry with York's army, blaming Somerset for Talbot's sure defeat.

———————

0 SD. **Trumpet:** i.e., trumpeter

3. **give it out:** report

4. **is marched:** i.e., has **marched; power:** army

6. **espials:** scouts, spies

7. **troops:** bodies of soldiers

10. **A plague upon:** i.e., may a pestilence light on

11. **my promisèd supply:** the reinforcement I have been promised (See line 4.1.166.)

13. **expect:** await

14. **louted:** treated with contempt; disgraced

15. **chevalier:** knight (French)

16. **necessity:** hardship, difficulty

17. **miscarry:** die

18. **strength:** military power

19. **needful:** necessary

21. **waist:** i.e., belt (with wordplay on *waste* or "vast expanse")

24. **Else:** otherwise

25. **that:** i.e., if only

26. **stop:** prevent the departure of; **cornets:** companies of cavalry

29. **Mad:** angry

30. **remiss:** negligent

32. **my warlike word:** i.e., **my word** as a soldier

33. **get:** gain, win

34. **long:** because

36. **who:** i.e., whom; **since:** ago

37. **warlike:** valiant

YORK
A plague upon that villain Somerset   10
That thus delays my promisèd supply
Of horsemen that were levied for this siege!
Renownèd Talbot doth expect my aid,
And I am louted by a traitor villain
And cannot help the noble chevalier.   15
God comfort him in this necessity.
If he miscarry, farewell wars in France.

Enter ⌈Sir William Lucy.⌉

⌈LUCY⌉
Thou princely leader of our English strength,
Never so needful on the earth of France,
Spur to the rescue of the noble Talbot,   20
Who now is girdled with a waist of iron
And hemmed about with grim destruction.
To Bordeaux, warlike duke! To Bordeaux, York!
Else farewell Talbot, France, and England's honor.
YORK
O God, that Somerset, who in proud heart   25
Doth stop my cornets, were in Talbot's place!
So should we save a valiant gentleman
By forfeiting a traitor and a coward.
Mad ire and wrathful fury makes me weep
That thus we die while remiss traitors sleep.   30
⌈LUCY⌉
O, send some succor to the distressed lord!
YORK
He dies, we lose; I break my warlike word;
We mourn, France smiles; we lose, they daily get,
All long of this vile traitor Somerset.
⌈LUCY⌉
Then God take mercy on brave Talbot's soul,   35
And on his son, young John, who two hours since
I met in travel toward his warlike father.

38. **This:** i.e., these; **seven years:** proverbial expression for a long time

42. **Vexation:** grief, affliction

43. **sundered:** separated; **friends:** relatives; **greet:** i.e., should **greet**

44. **No more . . . can:** i.e., **my** luck is such that I **can** do **no more**

45. **the cause:** i.e., Somerset

47. **Long all:** i.e., **all** because

48. **sedition:** violent party strife

50. **neglection:** negligence, neglect; **loss:** ruin, destruction

51. **scarce-cold:** i.e., only recently dead

52. **ever-living man of memory:** i.e., **man of ever-living memory** (transferred epithet)

53. **they:** i.e., York and Somerset; **cross:** thwart

4.4 Sir William Lucy chastises Somerset for not having helped Talbot, but Somerset blames York, who has apparently refused to communicate with him.

---

1. **them:** i.e., the cavalry

2. **This expedition:** i.e., against Bordeaux

3. **plotted:** planned, devised; **general force:** whole army

4. **a sally . . . town:** i.e., a sudden attack by the town's garrison, unaided by the approaching reinforcements

5. **buckled with:** engaged, fought with

6. **honor:** fame

7. **unheedful:** heedless

This seven years did not Talbot see his son,
And now they meet where both their lives are done.

YORK
Alas, what joy shall noble Talbot have   40
To bid his young son welcome to his grave?
Away! Vexation almost stops my breath,
That sundered friends greet in the hour of death.
Lucy, farewell. No more my fortune can
But curse the cause I cannot aid the man.   45
Maine, Blois, Poictiers, and Tours are won away,
Long all of Somerset and his delay.
⌜*York and his Soldiers*⌝ *exit.*

⌜LUCY⌝
Thus while the vulture of sedition
Feeds in the bosom of such great commanders,
Sleeping neglection doth betray to loss   50
The conquest of our scarce-cold conqueror,
That ever-living man of memory,
Henry the Fifth. Whiles they each other cross,
Lives, honors, lands, and all hurry to loss.
⌜*He exits.*⌝

⌜Scene 4⌝

Enter Somerset with his army ⌜*and a Captain
from Talbot's army.*⌝

SOMERSET
It is too late; I cannot send them now.
This expedition was by York and Talbot
Too rashly plotted. All our general force
Might with a sally of the very town
Be buckled with. The overdaring Talbot   5
Hath sullied all his gloss of former honor
By this unheedful, desperate, wild adventure.

8. **set him on:** incited him

9. **That:** i.e., so **that; bear the name:** have a reputation

13. **Whither:** Since this word means "to which place," Lucy's "**From . . . Talbot**" is a deliberate rejection of Somerset's question, or Lucy is using **whither** to mean "whence, or **from** which place." **bought and sold:** betrayed (proverbial, with a possible allusion to the betrayal of Jesus by Judas for a bribe)

16. **his weak regions:** i.e., the territory he weakly controls (**Regions** is often emended to *legions*.)

17. **captain:** leader

18. **bloody sweat:** See Luke 22.44, describing Jesus on the night before his death: "His **sweat** was like drops of blood."

19. **in advantage ling'ring:** perhaps, "suffering deadly pains (**ling'ring**) while holding a temporary **advantage**"; perhaps, "prolonging (**ling'ring**) the battle by exploiting every possible **advantage**"

20. **trust:** trustees

21. **emulation:** rivalry

23. **levied succors:** mustered reinforcements

25. **odds:** strife

28. **by:** i.e., because of

30. **upon your Grace exclaims:** accuses you

31. **host:** army (perhaps an error for **horse** [line 33], a reading supported by 4.3.11–12)

33. **sent:** i.e., **sent** a message; **horse:** cavalry

35. **take . . . him:** i.e., disdain to flatter him (The word **foul** is an intensifier.) **sending:** i.e., **sending** the forces (without his specific request); or, perhaps, **sending** a message to him

York set him on to fight and die in shame
That, Talbot dead, great York might bear the name.

⌜*Enter Sir William Lucy.*⌝

CAPTAIN
Here is Sir William Lucy, who with me   10
Set from our o'er-matched forces forth for aid.
SOMERSET
How now, Sir William, whither were you sent?
LUCY
Whither, my lord? From bought and sold Lord Talbot,
Who, ringed about with bold adversity,
Cries out for noble York and Somerset   15
To beat assailing Death from his weak regions;
And whiles the honorable captain there
Drops bloody sweat from his war-wearied limbs
And, in advantage ling'ring, looks for rescue,
You, his false hopes, the trust of England's honor,   20
Keep off aloof with worthless emulation.
Let not your private discord keep away
The levied succors that should lend him aid,
While he, renownèd noble gentleman,
Yield up his life unto a world of odds.   25
Orleance the Bastard, Charles, Burgundy,
Alanson, Reignier compass him about,
And Talbot perisheth by your default.
SOMERSET
York set him on; York should have sent him aid.
LUCY
And York as fast upon your Grace exclaims,   30
Swearing that you withhold his levied host
Collected for this expedition.
SOMERSET
York lies. He might have sent and had the horse.
I owe him little duty and less love,
And take foul scorn to fawn on him by sending.   35

36. **fraud:** faithlessness
40. **straight:** straightaway, immediately
42. **ta'en:** i.e., taken, captured
43. **fly:** flee; **would:** i.e., wished to
44. **might:** could, was able to

4.5   Talbot has been joined by his son John Talbot, whom he urges to flee certain death. John Talbot refuses to leave.

––––––––––

5.   **thy father . . . chair:** i.e., **thy father drooping to his chair** (transferred epithet) The word **chair** is here used as an attribute of old **age** (line 4).
6.   **malignant:** i.e., malign, having an evil influence
7.   **feast of Death:** "field where **death** will be feasted with slaughter" (Samuel Johnson)
8.   **unavoided:** unavoidable, inevitable

A view of Bordeaux. (4.2.1)
From John Speed, *A prospect of the most famous parts of the world . . .* (1631).

LUCY
The fraud of England, not the force of France,
Hath now entrapped the noble-minded Talbot.
Never to England shall he bear his life,
But dies betrayed to fortune by your strife.

SOMERSET
Come, go. I will dispatch the horsemen straight.   40
Within six hours they will be at his aid.

LUCY
Too late comes rescue; he is ta'en or slain,
For fly he could not if he would have fled;
And fly would Talbot never, though he might.

SOMERSET
If he be dead, brave Talbot, then adieu.   45

LUCY
His fame lives in the world, his shame in you.
                                They exit.

⌜Scene 5⌝

Enter Talbot and ⌜John Talbot,⌝ his son.

TALBOT
O young John Talbot, I did send for thee
To tutor thee in stratagems of war,
That Talbot's name might be in thee revived
When sapless age and weak unable limbs
Should bring thy father to his drooping chair.   5
But—O, malignant and ill-boding stars!—
Now thou art come unto a feast of Death,
A terrible and unavoided danger.
Therefore, dear boy, mount on my swiftest horse,
And I'll direct thee how thou shalt escape   10
By sudden flight. Come, dally not, be gone.

13. **fly:** flee

15. **make a bastard:** i.e., **make** people call me illegitimate; **slave:** figure of contempt

17. **stood:** kept his ground without budging

22. **Your loss:** i.e., the **loss** of you; **your regard:** i.e., care of you

23. **known:** revealed

25. **in you:** i.e., in your death

27. **that:** i.e., who

28. **for vantage:** i.e., in order to secure a tactical advantage

29. **bow:** retreat, go

32. **mortality:** death

"Assailing Death." (4.4.16)
From *Imagines mortis* . . . (1557).

JOHN TALBOT
Is my name Talbot? And am I your son?
And shall I fly? O, if you love my mother,
Dishonor not her honorable name
To make a bastard and a slave of me! 15
The world will say "He is not Talbot's blood,
That basely fled when noble Talbot stood."
TALBOT
Fly, to revenge my death if I be slain.
JOHN TALBOT
He that flies so will ne'er return again.
TALBOT
If we both stay, we both are sure to die. 20
JOHN TALBOT
Then let me stay and, father, do you fly.
Your loss is great; so your regard should be.
My worth unknown, no loss is known in me.
Upon my death, the French can little boast;
In yours they will; in you all hopes are lost. 25
Flight cannot stain the honor you have won,
But mine it will, that no exploit have done.
You fled for vantage, everyone will swear;
But if I bow, they'll say it was for fear.
There is no hope that ever I will stay 30
If the first hour I shrink and run away. ⌜*He kneels.*⌝
Here on my knee I beg mortality,
Rather than life preserved with infamy.
TALBOT
Shall all thy mother's hopes lie in one tomb?
JOHN TALBOT
Ay, rather than I'll shame my mother's womb. 35
TALBOT
Upon my blessing I command thee go.
JOHN TALBOT
To fight I will, but not to fly the foe.

42. **charge:** command

43. **being slain:** i.e., if you are dead

44. **death be so apparent:** i.e., **death is so** obviously the outcome

46. **age:** lifetime

50. **like:** same

52. **fair son:** a term of respectful, courteous address

53. **eclipse:** extinguish

Judgment Day. (1.1.29)
From Thomas Fisher's etching of the wall painting of Doomsday in the Guild Chapel at Stratford-upon-Avon (1807).

172

TALBOT
  Part of thy father may be saved in thee.
JOHN TALBOT
  No part of him but will be shame in me.
TALBOT
  Thou never hadst renown, nor canst not lose it.   40
JOHN TALBOT
  Yes, your renownèd name; shall flight abuse it?
TALBOT
  Thy father's charge shall clear thee from that stain.
JOHN TALBOT
  You cannot witness for me, being slain.
  If death be so apparent, then both fly.
TALBOT
  And leave my followers here to fight and die?   45
  My age was never tainted with such shame.
JOHN TALBOT
  And shall my youth be guilty of such blame?
                                   ⌜*He rises.*⌝
  No more can I be severed from your side
  Than can yourself yourself in twain divide.
  Stay, go, do what you will; the like do I,   50
  For live I will not, if my father die.
TALBOT
  Then here I take my leave of thee, fair son,
  Born to eclipse thy life this afternoon.
  Come, side by side, together live and die,
  And soul with soul from France to heaven fly.   55
                                   ⌜*They*⌝ *exit.*

4.6 Talbot again urges his son to flee and is again rebuffed.

---

0 SD. **Excursions:** skirmishes; **hemmed about:** surrounded

2. **The Regent:** i.e., York

3. **France his:** i.e., France's

8. **warlike:** valiant; **despite:** in spite

9. **To my . . . date:** i.e., you extended the term of my life **determined:** appointed, ordained **date:** limit, end of a period of time

10. **crest:** helmet

12. **leaden age:** i.e., old **age**

13. **spleen:** impetuosity, passion

15. **pride:** best; **Gallia:** France

17–18. **had the maidenhood / Of:** i.e., first drew blood from you in

20. **disgrace:** reproach, disparagement

21. **Bespoke:** addressed

23. **Mean:** ignoble; **right:** quite, very

25. **purposing:** i.e., I intending

26. **Came:** i.e., there **came; care:** object of concern

┌Scene 6┐

Alarum. Excursions, wherein Talbot's son ┌*John*┐
is hemmed about, and Talbot rescues him.

TALBOT
  Saint George, and victory! Fight, soldiers, fight!
  The Regent hath with Talbot broke his word
  And left us to the rage of France his sword.
  Where is John Talbot?—Pause, and take thy breath;
  I gave thee life and rescued thee from death.   5
JOHN TALBOT
  O, twice my father, twice am I thy son!
  The life thou gav'st me first was lost and done
  Till with thy warlike sword, despite of fate,
  To my determined time thou gav'st new date.
TALBOT
  When from the Dauphin's crest thy sword struck fire,   10
  It warmed thy father's heart with proud desire
  Of bold-faced victory. Then leaden age,
  Quickened with youthful spleen and warlike rage,
  Beat down Alanson, Orleance, Burgundy,
  And from the pride of Gallia rescued thee.   15
  The ireful Bastard Orleance, that drew blood
  From thee, my boy, and had the maidenhood
  Of thy first fight, I soon encounterèd,
  And, interchanging blows, I quickly shed
  Some of his bastard blood, and in disgrace   20
  Bespoke him thus: "Contaminated, base,
  And misbegotten blood I spill of thine,
  Mean and right poor, for that pure blood of mine
  Which thou didst force from Talbot, my brave boy."
  Here, purposing the Bastard to destroy,   25
  Came in strong rescue. Speak, thy father's care:
  Art thou not weary, John? How dost thou fare?

29. **sealed:** authenticated; **chivalry:** bravery in war, martial distinction and glory

31. **one:** i.e., John Talbot; **stands me in little stead:** provides **me** with **little** support

32–33. **O . . . boat:** Proverbial: "Venture not **all in one** bottom [**boat**]."   **wot:** know

35. **mickle:** great

39. **My death's revenge:** i.e., **revenge** for **my** death

42. **smart:** suffer

44. **On . . . shame:** i.e., to gain these benefits at the cost of **such shame** (a response to line 41: "All these are saved if thou wilt fly away.")

48. **like:** liken, compare

49. **shame's:** i.e., object of **shame's; subject:** victim

51. **An if:** i.e., **if**

52. **boot:** use

55. **Icarus:** son of inventor Daedalus, who, **desp'rate** to escape from **Crete** (line 54), devised for his son and himself wings of wax and feathers with which to escape. **Icarus,** flying too close to the sun, which melted the wax in his wings, fell to his death in the sea (Ovid, *Metamorphoses,* book 8). See picture, page 192.

57. **commendable proved:** i.e., having been **proved commendable; pride:** honor, glory

Wilt thou yet leave the battle, boy, and fly,
Now thou art sealed the son of chivalry?
Fly, to revenge my death when I am dead;   30
The help of one stands me in little stead.
O, too much folly is it, well I wot,
To hazard all our lives in one small boat.
If I today die not with Frenchmen's rage,
Tomorrow I shall die with mickle age.   35
By me they nothing gain, and, if I stay,
'Tis but the short'ning of my life one day.
In thee thy mother dies, our household's name,
My death's revenge, thy youth, and England's fame.
All these and more we hazard by thy stay;   40
All these are saved if thou wilt fly away.

JOHN TALBOT
The sword of Orleance hath not made me smart;
These words of yours draw lifeblood from my heart.
On that advantage, bought with such a shame,
To save a paltry life and slay bright fame,   45
Before young Talbot from old Talbot fly,
The coward horse that bears me fall and die!
And like me to the peasant boys of France,
To be shame's scorn and subject of mischance!
Surely, by all the glory you have won,   50
An if I fly, I am not Talbot's son.
Then talk no more of flight, it is no boot;
If son to Talbot, die at Talbot's foot.

TALBOT
Then follow thou thy desp'rate sire of Crete,
Thou Icarus; thy life to me is sweet.   55
If thou wilt fight, fight by thy father's side,
And commendable proved, let's die in pride.
                                        ⌜*They*⌝ *exit.*

4.7   Talbot, holding his dead son, dies. Sir William Lucy comes to claim their bodies from the victorious French.

---

3. **Triumphant Death:** See note to 1.1.22 and picture, page 124. **smeared with captivity:** perhaps, **smeared** with the blood of those taken captive (namely, the dead) See Ephesians 4.8: "He led **captivity** captive."

8. **stern:** fierce; **impatience:** irascibility

9. **guardant:** protector, guardian

10. **Tend'ring:** showing compassion for; taking care of; **ruin:** overthrow; **assailed of:** i.e., attacked by

11. **Dizzy-eyed:** bewildered

13. **clust'ring:** assembled; **battle:** army

14–16. **my boy . . . pride:** These lines use the story of **Icarus** to describe John Talbot's death. (See note to 4.6.55.)   **drench:** drown   **over-mounting:** i.e., flying too high

18. **antic:** jester, grotesque (The image of **Death** here is of a mocking skeleton familiar in pictures of "The dance of **Death**." See pictures, pages 44 and 124.)

19. **Anon:** immediately; soon; **insulting:** boasting, triumphing; **tyranny:** violence, cruelty

21. **lither:** yielding

22. **In thy despite:** in contemptuous defiance of you; **scape:** escape

23. **become:** are appropriate to; **hard-favored:** ugly

25. **Brave:** defy; **whither . . . no:** proverbial **whither:** whether   **will:** i.e., wishes you to speak **or no: or** not

⌜Scene 7⌝

Alarum. Excursions. Enter old Talbot
led ⌜by a Servant.⌝

TALBOT
  Where is my other life? Mine own is gone.
  O, where's young Talbot? Where is valiant John?
  Triumphant Death, smeared with captivity,
  Young Talbot's valor makes me smile at thee.
  When he perceived me shrink and on my knee,   5
  His bloody sword he brandished over me,
  And like a hungry lion did commence
  Rough deeds of rage and stern impatience;
  But when my angry guardant stood alone,
  Tend'ring my ruin and assailed of none,   10
  Dizzy-eyed fury and great rage of heart
  Suddenly made him from my side to start
  Into the clust'ring battle of the French;
  And in that sea of blood, my boy did drench
  His over-mounting spirit; and there died   15
  My Icarus, my blossom, in his pride.

Enter ⌜Soldiers⌝ with John Talbot, borne.

SERVINGMAN
  O, my dear lord, lo where your son is borne!
TALBOT
  Thou antic Death, which laugh'st us here to scorn,
  Anon from thy insulting tyranny,
  Coupled in bonds of perpetuity,   20
  Two Talbots, wingèd through the lither sky,
  In thy despite shall scape mortality.—
  O, thou whose wounds become hard-favored Death,
  Speak to thy father ere thou yield thy breath!
  Brave Death by speaking, whither he will or no.   25
  Imagine him a Frenchman and thy foe.—

27. **methinks:** it seems to me; **as who . . . say:** i.e., like one **who** would **say**

31. **bear:** (1) carry; (2) tolerate; **harms:** injuries

33 SD. **Alarums:** calls to arms

34. **rescue:** i.e., reinforcements

36. **whelp:** offspring; puppy (wordplay on *talbot*, meaning "hound"); **wood:** ferocious

37. **flesh:** initiate to bloodshed and warfare; **puny sword: sword** of a novice

39. **maiden:** untried; **maid:** virgin, girl

42. **pillage:** spoil, plunder; **giglot:** lascivious; **wench:** lewd woman

43. **rushing in:** i.e., **rushing** into; **bowels:** center, heart

44. **as unworthy fight:** i.e., **as** an **unworthy** combatant

46. **inhearsèd:** i.e., enclosed (as if in a tomb)

47. **bloody:** bloodthirsty; **nurser:** one who encourages; **his harms:** (1) the injuries he has inflicted; (2) the ones he has endured

49. **wonder:** object of astonishment

Poor boy, he smiles, methinks, as who should say
"Had Death been French, then Death had died
   today."—
Come, come, and lay him in his father's arms;   30
My spirit can no longer bear these harms.
Soldiers, adieu! I have what I would have,
Now my old arms are young John Talbot's grave.
                                Dies.
         ⌐*Alarums. Soldiers exit.*⌐

Enter Charles, Alanson, Burgundy, Bastard,
      and Pucelle, ⌐*with Forces.*⌐

CHARLES
Had York and Somerset brought rescue in,
We should have found a bloody day of this.   35
BASTARD
How the young whelp of Talbot's, raging wood,
Did flesh his puny sword in Frenchmen's blood!
PUCELLE
Once I encountered him, and thus I said:
"Thou maiden youth, be vanquished by a maid."
But with a proud majestical high scorn   40
He answered thus: "Young Talbot was not born
To be the pillage of a giglot wench."
So, rushing in the bowels of the French,
He left me proudly, as unworthy fight.
BURGUNDY
Doubtless he would have made a noble knight.   45
See where he lies inhearsèd in the arms
Of the most bloody nurser of his harms.
BASTARD
Hew them to pieces, hack their bones asunder,
Whose life was England's glory, Gallia's wonder.
CHARLES
O, no, forbear! For that which we have fled   50
During the life, let us not wrong it dead,

53. **glory of the day:** i.e., victory

54. **submissive message:** business of submission to a conquering power

55. **mere:** purely (i.e., exclusively)

56. **wot:** know

61. **Alcides:** Hercules (See picture, page 80.) **field:** battlefield

71. **Saint Michael:** a martial archangel (an allusion to the French royal order of Saint Michel); **Golden Fleece:** in mythology, the object of the quest of Jason and the Argonauts; also the name of an order of knights (See picture, below.)

72. **Great Marshal:** chief commander

74. **style:** title

75. **Turk:** sultan of Turkey

76. **Writes . . . style:** i.e., does not employ **so tedious** a title in designating himself

A portrait of the 3rd earl of Southampton wearing the collar of the Order of the Golden Fleece. (4.7.71)
By Simon van de Passe (1617).

Enter Lucy ⌈with Attendants and a French Herald.⌉

LUCY
   Herald, conduct me to the Dauphin's tent,
   To know who hath obtained the glory of the day.
CHARLES
   On what submissive message art thou sent?
LUCY
   Submission, dauphin? 'Tis a mere French word.   55
   We English warriors wot not what it means.
   I come to know what prisoners thou hast ta'en,
   And to survey the bodies of the dead.
CHARLES
   For prisoners askst thou? Hell our prison is.
   But tell me whom thou seek'st.   60
LUCY
   But where's the great Alcides of the field,
   Valiant Lord Talbot, Earl of Shrewsbury,
   Created for his rare success in arms
   Great Earl of Washford, Waterford, and Valence,
   Lord Talbot of Goodrich and Urchinfield,   65
   Lord Strange of Blackmere, Lord Verdon of Alton,
   Lord Cromwell of Wingfield, Lord Furnival of
     Sheffield,
   The thrice victorious Lord of Falconbridge,
   Knight of the noble Order of Saint George,   70
   Worthy Saint Michael, and the Golden Fleece,
   Great Marshal to Henry the Sixth
   Of all his wars within the realm of France?
PUCELLE
   Here's a silly stately style indeed.
   The Turk, that two-and-fifty kingdoms hath,   75
   Writes not so tedious a style as this.
   Him that thou magnifi'st with all these titles
   Stinking and flyblown lies here at our feet.

79. **only:** peerless

80. **black:** deadly, malignant; **Nemesis:** in mythology, the goddess of justice, who punishes pride (See picture, page 214.)

84. **fright:** frighten

86. **amaze:** terrify, alarm

88. **beseems:** is in accordance with

96. **phoenix:** a mythological creature that is unique and that consumes itself in fire, from the **ashes** of which another **phoenix** is born (See picture, below.) **afeard:** afraid

A phoenix. (4.7.96)
From Geoffrey Whitney, *A choice of emblemes* . . . (1586).

LUCY
Is Talbot slain, the Frenchmen's only scourge,
Your kingdom's terror and black Nemesis?   80
O, were mine eyeballs into bullets turned
That I in rage might shoot them at your faces!
O, that I could but call these dead to life,
It were enough to fright the realm of France.
Were but his picture left amongst you here,   85
It would amaze the proudest of you all.
Give me their bodies, that I may bear them hence
And give them burial as beseems their worth.

PUCELLE
I think this upstart is old Talbot's ghost,
He speaks with such a proud commanding spirit.   90
For God's sake, let him have him. To keep them here,
They would but stink and putrefy the air.

CHARLES
Go, take their bodies hence.

LUCY   I'll bear them hence.
But from their ashes shall be reared   95
A phoenix that shall make all France afeard.

CHARLES
So we be rid of them, do with him what thou wilt.
                    ⌜*Lucy, Servant, and Attendants exit,*
                                bearing the bodies.⌝
And now to Paris in this conquering vein.
All will be ours, now bloody Talbot's slain.
                                ⌜*They*⌝ *exit.*

HENRY VI
Part 1

ACT 5

5.1 Henry follows Gloucester's advice to make peace with France and to agree to marry the daughter of the earl of Armagnac.

---

0 SD. **Sennet:** trumpet fanfare to mark the ceremonial entrance

2. **Emperor:** Holy Roman **Emperor**
3. **intent:** desire; or, import
4. **sue:** petition
5. **concluded of:** i.e., **concluded**
7. **affect:** like; **motion:** proposal
9. **effusion:** spilling, shedding
10. **stablish:** set up securely; **quietness:** tranquility
11. **marry:** indeed
13. **immanity:** atrocious savagery
14. **professors of:** those professing belief in
16. **surer:** i.e., the more surely to
17. **near knit to Charles:** closely united to the Dauphin

An hourglass. (4.2.35–36)
From August Casimir Redel, *Apophtegmata symbolica* . . . [n.d].

⌜ACT 5⌝

⌜Scene 1⌝

Sennet. Enter King, Gloucester, and Exeter,
⌜*with Attendants.*⌝

KING HENRY, ⌜*to Gloucester*⌝
　Have you perused the letters from the Pope,
　The Emperor, and the Earl of Armagnac?
GLOUCESTER
　I have, my lord, and their intent is this:
　They humbly sue unto your Excellence
　To have a godly peace concluded of　　　　　　　　5
　Between the realms of England and of France.
KING HENRY
　How doth your Grace affect their motion?
GLOUCESTER
　Well, my good lord, and as the only means
　To stop effusion of our Christian blood
　And stablish quietness on every side.　　　　　　10
KING HENRY
　Ay, marry, uncle, for I always thought
　It was both impious and unnatural
　That such immanity and bloody strife
　Should reign among professors of one faith.
GLOUCESTER
　Besides, my lord, the sooner to effect　　　　　　15
　And surer bind this knot of amity,
　The Earl of Armagnac, near knit to Charles,
　A man of great authority in France,
　Proffers his only daughter to your Grace
　In marriage, with a large and sumptuous dowry.　20

189

22. **fitter:** i.e., more appropriate to my age
23. **dalliance:** flirtation; **paramour:** lover
26. **choice:** i.e., **choice** that
27. **weal:** welfare, prosperity
28. **What:** an interjection to introduce a question
29. **degree:** rank
30. **that will be verified: that will be** proved true
31. **Henry . . . prophesy:** i.e., which **Henry the Fifth did** once **prophesy**
32. **he:** i.e., **my Lord of Winchester** (line 28)
33. **cap:** i.e., cardinal's red hat, or biretta
34. **several:** individual; various; **suits:** petitions
37. **certainly:** fixedly
38. **draw:** write out, **draw** up
40. **presently:** immediately
42. **at large:** in full
43. **As, liking of:** i.e., that, **liking**

KING HENRY
　　Marriage, uncle? Alas, my years are young;
　　And fitter is my study and my books
　　Than wanton dalliance with a paramour.
　　Yet call th' Ambassadors and, as you please,
　　So let them have their answers every one.　　　　25
　　　　　　　　　　　　⌐*An Attendant exits.*¬
　　I shall be well content with any choice
　　Tends to God's glory and my country's weal.

　　　Enter Winchester, ⌐*dressed in cardinal's robes,*¬
　　and ⌐*the Ambassador of Armagnac, a Papal Legate,*
　　　　　　and another Ambassador.¬

EXETER, ⌐*aside*¬
　　What, is my Lord of Winchester installed
　　And called unto a cardinal's degree?
　　Then I perceive that will be verified　　　　　30
　　Henry the Fifth did sometime prophesy:
　　"If once he come to be a cardinal,
　　He'll make his cap coequal with the crown."
KING HENRY
　　My Lords Ambassadors, your several suits
　　Have been considered and debated on;　　　　35
　　Your purpose is both good and reasonable,
　　And therefore are we certainly resolved
　　To draw conditions of a friendly peace,
　　Which by my Lord of Winchester we mean
　　Shall be transported presently to France.　　　40
GLOUCESTER, ⌐*to the Ambassador of Armagnac*¬
　　And for the proffer of my lord your master,
　　I have informed his Highness so at large
　　As, liking of the lady's virtuous gifts,
　　Her beauty, and the value of her dower,
　　He doth intend she shall be England's queen.　　45

46. **In argument:** i.e., as a token

47. **jewel:** ornament made of gold, silver, or precious stones

49. **inshipped:** put into a ship

54. **these grave ornaments:** i.e., this respected attire

55. **attend upon:** await; **leisure:** i.e., convenience

56. **trow:** feel sure

62. **sack:** plunder; **mutiny:** revolt

5.2 Charles is informed that the divided English army has united and is advancing toward him.

---

1. **These news:** i.e., this **news**

2. **stout:** proud, fierce, valiant, resolute

5. **powers:** military forces; **dalliance:** delay

Icarus. (4.6.55; 4.7.16)
From Geoffrey Whitney, *A choice of emblemes* . . . (1586).

KING HENRY, ⌜*handing a jewel to the Ambassador*⌝
  In argument and proof of which contract,
  Bear her this jewel, pledge of my affection.—
  And so, my Lord Protector, see them guarded
  And safely brought to Dover, ⌜where, inshipped,⌝
  Commit them to the fortune of the sea.   50
        ⌜*All except Winchester and Legate*⌝ *exit.*

WINCHESTER
  Stay, my Lord Legate; you shall first receive
  The sum of money which I promisèd
  Should be delivered to his Holiness
  For clothing me in these grave ornaments.

LEGATE
  I will attend upon your Lordship's leisure. ⌜*He exits.*⌝   55

WINCHESTER
  Now Winchester will not submit, I trow,
  Or be inferior to the proudest peer.
  Humphrey of Gloucester, thou shalt well perceive
  That neither in birth or for authority
  The Bishop will be overborne by thee.   60
  I'll either make thee stoop and bend thy knee,
  Or sack this country with a mutiny.
                    He exits.

⌜Scene 2⌝

Enter Charles, Burgundy, Alanson, Bastard,
Reignier, and Joan ⌜*la Pucelle, with Soldiers.*⌝

CHARLES
  These news, my lords, may cheer our drooping spirits:
  'Tis said the stout Parisians do revolt
  And turn again unto the warlike French.

ALANSON
  Then march to Paris, royal Charles of France,
  And keep not back your powers in dalliance.   5

7. **Else:** otherwise; **ruin:** destruction

9. **happiness:** good fortune; **accomplices:** associates

12. **parties:** parts

13. **presently:** immediately

5.3 As the French face likely defeat, Pucelle conjures up devils, but they refuse to help, and she is captured by York. Then Suffolk captures Margaret, daughter of Reignier, who, though poor, is both King of Naples and Duke of Anjou and Maine. Suffolk falls in love with her. He offers to marry her to Henry, if her father will agree.

---

1. **Regent:** i.e., York; **fly:** flee

2–3. **Now . . . me:** For the image of Pucelle in this scene and the next, see the appendix "Joan la Pucelle, or Joan of Arc," pages 250–52. **charming:** magical **periapts:** things worn on one's person to ward off evil or misfortune **admonish me:** give me authoritative warning

PUCELLE
  Peace be amongst them if they turn to us;
  Else ruin combat with their palaces!

                Enter Scout.

SCOUT
  Success unto our valiant general,
  And happiness to his accomplices.
CHARLES
  What tidings send our scouts? I prithee speak.   10
SCOUT
  The English army that divided was
  Into two parties is now conjoined in one,
  And means to give you battle presently.
CHARLES
  Somewhat too sudden, sirs, the warning is,
  But we will presently provide for them.   15
BURGUNDY
  I trust the ghost of Talbot is not there.
  Now he is gone, my lord, you need not fear.
PUCELLE
  Of all base passions, fear is most accursed.
  Command the conquest, Charles, it shall be thine;
  Let Henry fret and all the world repine.   20
CHARLES
  Then on, my lords, and France be fortunate!
                                    They exit.

                ⌜Scene 3⌝

    Alarum. Excursions. Enter Joan ⌜la⌝ Pucelle.

PUCELLE
  The Regent conquers and the Frenchmen fly.
  Now help, you charming spells and periapts,
  And you choice spirits that admonish me,

4. **accidents:** events

5. **substitutes:** those delegated authority

6. **lordly monarch of the north:** perhaps, Lucifer (See longer note, page 244.); perhaps, the demon named Zimimar, also called the king **of the North** (Reginald Scot, *Discoverie of Witchcraft,* 1584)

8. **argues:** indicates

9. **diligence:** assiduous service; heedfulness

10. **familiar spirits:** demons who serve a human being

12. **get the field:** win the battle

13. **hold me not with:** i.e., do not keep me in

14. **Where:** whereas

15. **member:** limb

16. **In earnest:** as a foretaste or pledge

17. **condescend:** agree

18. **redress:** help, aid

19. **suit:** petition

20. **Cannot my:** i.e., can neither my

21. **Entreat:** induce, persuade; **furtherance:** assistance

23. **Before:** rather than; **foil:** defeat

25. **vail:** lower

27. **ancient:** former

28. **buckle with:** engage, fight with

And give me signs of future accidents.   *Thunder.*
You speedy helpers, that are substitutes   5
Under the lordly monarch of the north,
Appear, and aid me in this enterprise.

                    Enter Fiends.

This ⌜speed⌝ and quick appearance argues proof
Of your accustomed diligence to me.
Now, you familiar spirits that are culled   10
Out of the powerful regions under earth,
Help me this once, that France may get the field.
                              They walk, and speak not.
O, hold me not with silence overlong!
Where I was wont to feed you with my blood,
I'll lop a member off and give it you   15
In earnest of a further benefit,
So you do condescend to help me now.
                                  They hang their heads.
No hope to have redress? My body shall
Pay recompense if you will grant my suit.
                                  They shake their heads.
Cannot my body nor blood-sacrifice   20
Entreat you to your wonted furtherance?
Then take my soul—my body, soul, and all—
Before that England give the French the foil.
                                        They depart.
See, they forsake me. Now the time is come
That France must vail her lofty-plumèd crest   25
And let her head fall into England's lap.
My ancient incantations are too weak,
And hell too strong for me to buckle with.
Now, France, thy glory droopeth to the dust.
                                    ⌜*She exits.*⌝

31. **spelling charms:** magical incantations

33. **the devil's grace:** i.e., his **Grace** the devil; or, **the devil's** favor

35. **with:** in the same way as; **Circe:** in Homer, a beautiful magician who transformed Odysseus's men into swine (See picture, below.)

36. **worser:** worse

37. **proper:** handsome

39. **plaguing mischief:** pestilent calamity

40. **surprised:** captured

41. **in sleeping:** i.e., as you sleep

42. **Fell:** fierce, terrible; **banning:** cursing; **Enchantress:** witch

43. **prithee:** pray you

44 SD. **Margaret . . . hand:** i.e., holding Margaret's **hand**

45. **Be what thou wilt:** i.e., whoever you are

48. **for eternal peace:** i.e., as a pledge of **eternal peace**

Circe. (5.3.35)
From Geoffrey Whitney, *A choice of emblemes* . . . (1586).

Excursions. Burgundy and York fight hand to hand.
⌐*Burgundy and the*⌐ *French fly* ⌐*as York and English
soldiers capture Joan la Pucelle.*⌐

YORK
Damsel of France, I think I have you fast.   30
Unchain your spirits now with spelling charms,
And try if they can gain your liberty.
A goodly prize, fit for the devil's grace!
See how the ugly witch doth bend her brows
As if with Circe she would change my shape.   35
PUCELLE
Changed to a worser shape thou canst not be.
YORK
O, Charles the Dauphin is a proper man;
No shape but his can please your dainty eye.
PUCELLE
A plaguing mischief light on Charles and thee,
And may you both be suddenly surprised   40
By bloody hands in sleeping on your beds!
YORK
Fell banning hag! Enchantress, hold thy tongue.
PUCELLE
I prithee give me leave to curse awhile.
YORK
Curse, miscreant, when thou com'st to the stake.
                                    They exit.

Alarum. Enter Suffolk with Margaret in his hand.

SUFFOLK
Be what thou wilt, thou art my prisoner.   45
                                    Gazes on her.
O fairest beauty, do not fear nor fly,
For I will touch thee but with reverent hands.
I kiss these fingers for eternal peace

52. **whosoe'er:** whoever
55. **allotted:** destined; **ta'en:** taken, captured
58. **servile:** ignoble; **once:** ever
60. **pass:** go
62–63. **As . . . beam:** i.e., as when **the sun** reflects off the surface of **streams,** thus seemingly doubling each **beam**
65. **Fain:** gladly
67. **de la Pole:** Suffolk's family name; **disable . . . thyself:** i.e., do **not** deprive yourself of speech
71. **Confounds:** i.e., that it silences; **rough:** agitated; dull
75. **suit:** wooing, courtship

The Fates and the "thread of life." (1.1.34)
From Vincenzo Cartari, *Imagines deorum* . . . (1581).

And lay them gently on thy tender side.
Who art thou? Say, that I may honor thee.   50
MARGARET
    Margaret my name, and daughter to a king,
    The King of Naples, whosoe'er thou art.
SUFFOLK
    An earl I am, and Suffolk am I called.
    Be not offended, nature's miracle;
    Thou art allotted to be ta'en by me.   55
    So doth the swan her downy cygnets save,
    Keeping them prisoner underneath ⌈her⌉ wings.
    Yet if this servile usage once offend,
    Go and be free again as Suffolk's friend.
                                        She is going.
    O, stay! (⌈*Aside.*⌉) I have no power to let her pass.   60
    My hand would free her, but my heart says no.
    As plays the sun upon the glassy streams,
    Twinkling another counterfeited beam,
    So seems this gorgeous beauty to mine eyes.
    Fain would I woo her, yet I dare not speak.   65
    I'll call for pen and ink and write my mind.
    Fie, de la Pole, disable not thyself!
    Hast not a tongue? Is she not here?
    Wilt thou be daunted at a woman's sight?
    Ay. Beauty's princely majesty is such   70
    Confounds the tongue and makes the senses rough.
MARGARET
    Say, Earl of Suffolk, if thy name be so,
    What ransom must I pay before I pass?
    For I perceive I am thy prisoner.
SUFFOLK, ⌈*aside*⌉
    How canst thou tell she will deny thy suit   75
    Before thou make a trial of her love?
MARGARET
    Why speak'st thou not? What ransom must I pay?

79. **She . . . won:** Proverbial: "All women may **be won.**"

80. **accept of:** i.e., **accept**

81. **Fond:** foolish

82. **paramour:** beloved, sweetheart

84. **cooling card:** proverbial for something that cools one's passion or enthusiasm

85. **mad:** insane

86. **dispensation:** license granted by a high official of the church to exempt one from keeping a solemn oath (here, marriage vows)

87. **I would:** i.e., I wish

89. **Tush:** an exclamation of impatient contempt; **that's a wooden thing:** referring perhaps to Suffolk's plan, or perhaps to the king

91. **fancy:** love

93. **scruple:** difficulty

96. **match:** marriage

97. **captain:** military commander

SUFFOLK, ⌜*aside*⌝
  She's beautiful, and therefore to be wooed;
  She is a woman, therefore to be won.
MARGARET
  Wilt thou accept of ransom, yea or no?   80
SUFFOLK, ⌜*aside*⌝
  Fond man, remember that thou hast a wife;
  Then how can Margaret be thy paramour?
MARGARET, ⌜*aside*⌝
  I were best to leave him, for he will not hear.
SUFFOLK, ⌜*aside*⌝
  There all is marred; there lies a cooling card.
MARGARET, ⌜*aside*⌝
  He talks at random; sure the man is mad.   85
SUFFOLK, ⌜*aside*⌝
  And yet a dispensation may be had.
MARGARET
  And yet I would that you would answer me.
SUFFOLK, ⌜*aside*⌝
  I'll win this Lady Margaret. For whom?
  Why, for my king. Tush, that's a wooden thing!
MARGARET, ⌜*aside*⌝
  He talks of wood. It is some carpenter.   90
SUFFOLK, ⌜*aside*⌝
  Yet so my fancy may be satisfied,
  And peace establishèd between these realms.
  But there remains a scruple in that, too;
  For though her father be the King of Naples,
  Duke of Anjou and Maine, yet is he poor,   95
  And our nobility will scorn the match.
MARGARET
  Hear you, captain? Are you not at leisure?
SUFFOLK, ⌜*aside*⌝
  It shall be so, disdain they ne'er so much.
  Henry is youthful, and will quickly yield.—
  Madam, I have a secret to reveal.   100

101. **enthralled:** held captive

103. **vouchsafe to listen:** i.e., I beg you **to listen** to

107. **captivate:** made captive

108. **wherefore:** why

109. **cry you mercy:** beg your pardon; **quid for quo:** i.e., **quid** pro **quo,** one thing in exchange for another; tit for tat (proverbial)

110. **gentle:** noble

111. **happy:** fortunate; **to be:** i.e., if you were **to be**

113. **Than is:** i.e., **than** to be

116. **happy:** fortunate

117. **what . . . me:** i.e., how is **his freedom** my concern

Hymen, the god of marriage. (3.2.26)
From Vincenzo Cartari, *Imagines deorum* . . . (1581).

MARGARET, ⌐*aside*⌐
  What though I be enthralled, he seems a knight,
  And will not any way dishonor me.
SUFFOLK
  Lady, vouchsafe to listen what I say.
MARGARET, ⌐*aside*⌐
  Perhaps I shall be rescued by the French,
  And then I need not crave his courtesy.   105
SUFFOLK
  Sweet madam, give me hearing in a cause.
MARGARET, ⌐*aside*⌐
  Tush, women have been captivate ere now.
SUFFOLK
  Lady, wherefore talk you so?
MARGARET
  I cry you mercy, 'tis but *quid* for *quo*.
SUFFOLK
  Say, gentle princess, would you not suppose   110
  Your bondage happy, to be made a queen?
MARGARET
  To be a queen in bondage is more vile
  Than is a slave in base servility,
  For princes should be free.
SUFFOLK   And so shall you,   115
  If happy England's royal king be free.
MARGARET
  Why, what concerns his freedom unto me?
SUFFOLK
  I'll undertake to make thee Henry's queen,
  To put a golden scepter in thy hand
  And set a precious crown upon thy head,   120
  If thou wilt condescend to be my—
MARGARET   What?
SUFFOLK   His love.

125. **gentle:** noble
126. **fair:** beautiful; **dame:** woman of rank, lady
127. **portion:** share
129. **An if . . . please:** i.e., **if** it is agreeable to **my father**
130. **captains:** military leaders; **colors:** regiments
137. **unapt:** not prone
138. **exclaim on:** protest against; **Fortune's fickleness:** See note to 3.3.34, and picture, below.
140. **for . . . consent:** in return **for** your giving consent
142. **Whom:** i.e., **thy daughter** (line 141)
143. **easy-held:** i.e., lightly enforced
147. **face:** show a false face

Fickle Fortune. (3.3.34; 5.3.138)
From Giovanni Boccaccio, *A treatise . . . shewing . . . the falles of . . . princes . . .* (1554).

MARGARET
  I am unworthy to be Henry's wife.
SUFFOLK
  No, gentle madam, I unworthy am   125
  To woo so fair a dame to be his wife,
  And have no portion in the choice myself.
  How say you, madam? Are you so content?
MARGARET
  An if my father please, I am content.
SUFFOLK
  Then call our captains and our colors forth!   130
                          ⌜*A Soldier exits.*⌝
  And, madam, at your father's castle walls
  We'll crave a parley to confer with him.

    ⌜*Enter Captains and Trumpets.*⌝ *Sound* ⌜*a parley.*⌝
          Enter Reignier on the walls.

  See, Reignier, see thy daughter prisoner!
REIGNIER
  To whom?
SUFFOLK   To me.   135
REIGNIER   Suffolk, what remedy?
  I am a soldier and unapt to weep
  Or to exclaim on Fortune's fickleness.
SUFFOLK
  Yes, there is remedy enough, my lord:
  Consent, and, for thy Honor give consent,   140
  Thy daughter shall be wedded to my king,
  Whom I with pain have wooed and won thereto;
  And this her easy-held imprisonment
  Hath gained thy daughter princely liberty.
REIGNIER
  Speaks Suffolk as he thinks?   145
SUFFOLK   Fair Margaret knows
  That Suffolk doth not flatter, face, or feign.

148. **Upon . . . warrant:** i.e., relying on the royal safeguard you provide   **princely:** royal

149. **answer of:** i.e., **answer** to

150. **expect:** await

153. **happy for:** i.e., fortunate in having

155. **suit:** (1) petition; (2) courtship (on behalf of Henry)

156. **her little worth:** i.e., her (despite) her unworthiness

159. **Enjoy:** have the use or benefit of; **the country Maine and Anjou:** i.e., the land composed of **Maine and Anjou**

163. **those two counties:** i.e., **Maine and Anjou; undertake:** promise, venture to assert

166. **As deputy:** referring to Suffolk

167. **for sign:** i.e., as an indication; **plighted faith:** engagement of Henry and Margaret

169. **in traffic:** i.e., in the business or dealings

170. **methinks:** it seems to me

171. **be mine own attorney: be** my **own** agent (i.e., act for myself, not the king)

REIGNIER
Upon thy princely warrant, I descend
To give thee answer of thy just demand.
⌐*He exits from the walls.*⌐

SUFFOLK
And here I will expect thy coming.   150

Trumpets sound. Enter Reignier, ⌐*below.*⌐

REIGNIER
Welcome, brave earl, into our territories.
Command in Anjou what your Honor pleases.

SUFFOLK
Thanks, Reignier, happy for so sweet a child,
Fit to be made companion with a king.
What answer makes your Grace unto my suit?   155

REIGNIER
Since thou dost deign to woo her little worth
To be the princely bride of such a lord,
Upon condition I may quietly
Enjoy mine own, the country Maine and Anjou,
Free from oppression or the stroke of war,   160
My daughter shall be Henry's, if he please.

SUFFOLK
That is her ransom; I deliver her,
And those two counties I will undertake
Your Grace shall well and quietly enjoy.

REIGNIER
And I, again in Henry's royal name   165
As deputy unto that gracious king,
Give thee her hand for sign of plighted faith.

SUFFOLK
Reignier of France, I give thee kingly thanks
Because this is in traffic of a king.
⌐*Aside.*⌐ And yet methinks I could be well content   170
To be mine own attorney in this case.—

173. **make . . . solemnized:** i.e., have **this marriage solemnized**

179. **of Margaret:** i.e., from **Margaret**

181. **commendations:** greetings

182. **maid:** young unmarried woman

188. **taint with:** i.e., affected by

189. **withal:** in addition

191. **peevish:** silly, foolish

192. **stay:** i.e., wait a minute, pause

193–94. **Thou . . . lurk:** an allusion to the **labyrinth** (shown in picture below) built by Daedalus for King Minos of Crete to house the Minotaur, a flesh-eating monster with the body of a man and the head of a bull (Young men who "wandered" in the **labyrinth** were usually eaten.)

195. **Solicit:** allure, incite

196. **Bethink thee:** meditate; **surmount:** excel

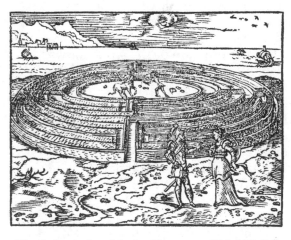

The Labyrinth with the Minotaur. (5.3.193–94)
From Gabriele Simeoni, *L'art des emblemes* . . . (1684).

I'll over then to England with this news,
And make this marriage to be solemnized.
So farewell, Reignier; set this diamond safe
In golden palaces, as it becomes.   175

REIGNIER, ⌐*embracing Suffolk*⌐

I do embrace thee, as I would embrace
The Christian prince King Henry, were he here.

MARGARET, ⌐*to Suffolk*⌐

Farewell, my lord; good wishes, praise, and prayers
Shall Suffolk ever have of Margaret.

              She is going, ⌐*as Reignier exits.*⌐

SUFFOLK

Farewell, sweet madam. But, hark you, Margaret,   180
No princely commendations to my king?

MARGARET

Such commendations as becomes a maid,
A virgin, and his servant, say to him.

SUFFOLK

Words sweetly placed and ⌐modestly⌐ directed.
But, madam, I must trouble you again: 185
No loving token to his Majesty?

MARGARET

Yes, my good lord: a pure unspotted heart,
Never yet taint with love, I send the King.

SUFFOLK   And this withal.   *Kiss her.*

MARGARET

That for thyself. I will not so presume   190
To send such peevish tokens to a king.   ⌐*She exits.*⌐

SUFFOLK

O, wert thou for myself! But, Suffolk, stay.
Thou mayst not wander in that labyrinth.
There Minotaurs and ugly treasons lurk.
Solicit Henry with her wondrous praise;   195
Bethink thee on her virtues that surmount

197. **extinguish art:** i.e., obscure **art** through superior brilliance

198. **Repeat their semblance:** reiterate the image of her **virtues** (line 196) and **graces** (line 197)

199. **That:** i.e., so **that**

200. **bereave:** rob

5.4 Pucelle, on her way to be executed by the English, is visited by her shepherd father, whom she scorns and who curses her. She pleads for a stay of execution on the grounds that she is pregnant, but her plea is denied. Cardinal Winchester enters to announce the peace between England and France, news that at first displeases both York and Charles.

---

3. **every country:** i.e., in **every** district; **far and near:** proverbial

4. **chance:** luck, fortune

5. **timeless:** untimely, premature

7. **miser:** miserable creature

8. **of a gentler blood:** from more noble parentage or lineage

9. **friend:** relative

10. **Out:** an exclamation of indignant reproach; **an please you:** i.e., if it **please you** (a conventionally polite formula)

12. **mother:** i.e., **mother** who

13. **fruit:** offspring, progeny

14. **Graceless:** i.e., wicked one

15. **argues:** indicates

16. **concludes:** sums (it) up

17. **obstacle:** i.e., obstinate (dialect form)

⌜And⌝ natural graces that extinguish art;
Repeat their semblance often on the seas,
That, when thou com'st to kneel at Henry's feet,
Thou mayst bereave him of his wits with wonder.   200

He exits.

⌜Scene 4⌝

Enter York, Warwick, Shepherd,
⌜*and*⌝ *Pucelle,* ⌜*guarded.*⌝

YORK
Bring forth that sorceress condemned to burn.
SHEPHERD
Ah, Joan, this kills thy father's heart outright.
Have I sought every country far and near,
And, now it is my chance to find thee out,
Must I behold thy timeless cruel death?   5
Ah, Joan, sweet daughter Joan, I'll die with thee.
PUCELLE
Decrepit miser, base ignoble wretch!
I am descended of a gentler blood.
Thou art no father nor no friend of mine.
SHEPHERD
Out, out!—My lords, an please you, 'tis not so!   10
I did beget her, all the parish knows;
Her mother liveth yet, can testify
She was the first fruit of my bach'lorship.
WARWICK
Graceless, wilt thou deny thy parentage?
YORK
This argues what her kind of life hath been,   15
Wicked and vile; and so her death concludes.
SHEPHERD
Fie, Joan, that thou wilt be so obstacle!

18. **collop of my flesh:** proverbial   **collop:** piece; child

22. **Of purpose:** i.e., on **purpose**

23. **noble:** English gold coin worth six shillings in 1550

27. **would:** wish

31. **keep:** guard, preserve

36. **To fill:** i.e., filling

38. **swain:** country laborer

41. **celestial:** heavenly

47. **want:** lack

48. **straight:** straightaway, immediately

Nemesis. (4.7.80)
From Geoffrey Whitney, *A choice of emblemes . . .* (1586).

God knows thou art a collop of my flesh,
And for thy sake have I shed many a tear.
Deny me not, I prithee, gentle Joan.   20
PUCELLE
Peasant, avaunt!—You have suborned this man
Of purpose to obscure my noble birth.
SHEPHERD
'Tis true, I gave a noble to the priest
The morn that I was wedded to her mother.—
Kneel down and take my blessing, good my girl.   25
Wilt thou not stoop? Now cursèd be the time
Of thy nativity! I would the milk
Thy mother gave thee when thou ⌐suck'dst⌐ her
    breast
Had been a little ratsbane for thy sake!   30
Or else, when thou didst keep my lambs afield,
I wish some ravenous wolf had eaten thee!
Dost thou deny thy father, cursèd drab?
O burn her, burn her! Hanging is too good.   *He exits.*
YORK
Take her away, for she hath lived too long   35
To fill the world with vicious qualities.
PUCELLE
First, let me tell you whom you have condemned:
Not ⌐one⌐ begotten of a shepherd swain,
But issued from the progeny of kings,
Virtuous and holy, chosen from above   40
By inspiration of celestial grace
To work exceeding miracles on earth.
I never had to do with wicked spirits.
But you, that are polluted with your lusts,
Stained with the guiltless blood of innocents,   45
Corrupt and tainted with a thousand vices,
Because you want the grace that others have,
You judge it straight a thing impossible

49. **compass:** accomplish; **but by:** except through
50. **misconceivèd:** having a misconception or wrong idea
53. **rigorously:** severely, unmercifully; **effused:** spilled, shed
56. **maid:** virgin
57. **Spare for no faggots:** i.e., use plenty of wood; **enow:** enough
58. **upon the fatal stake:** i.e., close by the **stake** to which she will be tied (The purpose of the **barrels of pitch** is to make the fire smoke so that the victim dies quickly of asphyxiation.)
59. **That so:** i.e., **so that**
60. **turn:** change
61. **discover:** reveal (See note to 5.3.2–3.)
62. **warranteth:** promises as certain; **privilege:** exemption from the death penalty
63. **bloody:** bloodthirsty
65. **hale:** drag
66. **forfend:** forbid; **maid:** virgin
68. **preciseness:** austere morality
69. **juggling:** playing tricks (with obvious sexual reference)
70. **her refuge:** the excuse in which she would take **refuge**
71. **go to:** an expression of moral condemnation
72. **must father it:** i.e., **must** be the father

To compass wonders but by help of devils.
No, misconceivèd! Joan of ⌈Arc⌉ hath been   50
A virgin from her tender infancy,
Chaste and immaculate in very thought,
Whose maiden blood, thus rigorously effused,
Will cry for vengeance at the gates of heaven.

YORK
Ay, ay.—Away with her to execution.   55

WARWICK
And hark you, sirs: because she is a maid,
Spare for no faggots; let there be enow.
Place barrels of pitch upon the fatal stake
That so her torture may be shortenèd.

PUCELLE
Will nothing turn your unrelenting hearts?   60
Then, Joan, discover thine infirmity,
That warranteth by law to be thy privilege:
I am with child, you bloody homicides.
Murder not then the fruit within my womb,
Although you hale me to a violent death.   65

YORK
Now heaven forfend, the holy maid with child?

WARWICK, ⌈*to Pucelle*⌉
The greatest miracle that e'er you wrought!
Is all your strict preciseness come to this?

YORK
She and the Dauphin have been juggling.
I did imagine what would be her refuge.   70

WARWICK
Well, go to, we'll have no bastards live,
Especially since Charles must father it.

PUCELLE
You are deceived; my child is none of his.
It was Alanson that enjoyed my love.

75. **Machiavel:** schemer, intriguer (Niccolò Machiavelli's book *The Prince* [1513] counseled ruthless deceptiveness as the way to power.)

76. **It dies an if:** i.e., the **child dies** even **if**

77. **give me leave:** i.e., let me (speak), allow me (to speak)

83. **liberal:** licentious; **free:** ready in giving, lavish

85. **brat:** term of contempt for a child

88. **reflex:** cast

89. **make abode:** live, dwell

90. **shade:** shadow

91. **mischief:** calamity

94. **minister:** agent

97. **states:** rulers

The "owl of death." (4.2.15)
From George Wither, *A collection of emblemes* . . . (1635).

YORK
Alanson, that notorious Machiavel?   75
It dies an if it had a thousand lives!

PUCELLE
O, give me leave! I have deluded you.
'Twas neither Charles nor yet the Duke I named,
But Reignier, King of Naples, that prevailed.

WARWICK
A married man? That's most intolerable.   80

YORK
Why, here's a girl! I think she knows not well—
There were so many—whom she may accuse.

WARWICK
It's sign she hath been liberal and free.

YORK
And yet, forsooth, she is a virgin pure!—
Strumpet, thy words condemn thy brat and thee.   85
Use no entreaty, for it is in vain.

PUCELLE
Then lead me hence, with whom I leave my curse:
May never glorious sun reflex his beams
Upon the country where you make abode,
But darkness and the gloomy shade of death   90
Environ you, till mischief and despair
Drive you to break your necks or hang yourselves.
She exits, ⌜led by Guards.⌝

YORK
Break thou in pieces, and consume to ashes,
Thou foul accursèd minister of hell!

Enter ⌜Winchester, as⌝ Cardinal.

WINCHESTER
Lord Regent, I do greet your Excellence   95
With letters of commission from the King.
For know, my lords, the states of Christendom,

98. **remorse of:** i.e., compassion, sorrow for; **outrageous:** violent; **broils:** tumults

101. **train:** retinue

103. **travail:** work; agony

104. **peers:** nobles

105. **captains:** military leaders

106. **quarrel:** violent contention; **overthrown:** destroyed

116. **As little:** i.e., that **little**

120. **league:** covenant, compact

121. **choler:** bile

123. **By sight:** i.e., at the **sight; baleful:** noxious, malignant

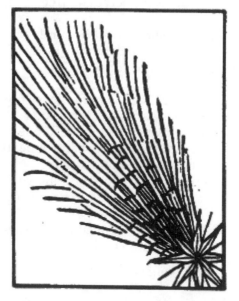

A comet. (1.1.2; 3.2.31)
From Hartmann Schedel, *Liber chronicorum* [1493].

Moved with remorse of these outrageous broils,
Have earnestly implored a general peace
Betwixt our nation and the aspiring French;   100
And here at hand the Dauphin and his train
Approacheth to confer about some matter.

YORK
Is all our travail turned to this effect?
After the slaughter of so many peers,
So many captains, gentlemen, and soldiers   105
That in this quarrel have been overthrown
And sold their bodies for their country's benefit,
Shall we at last conclude effeminate peace?
Have we not lost most part of all the towns—
By treason, falsehood, and by treachery—   110
Our great progenitors had conquerèd?
O, Warwick, Warwick, I foresee with grief
The utter loss of all the realm of France!

WARWICK
Be patient, York; if we conclude a peace
It shall be with such strict and severe covenants   115
As little shall the Frenchmen gain thereby.

Enter Charles, Alanson, Bastard,
Reignier, ⌐with Attendants.⌐

CHARLES
Since, lords of England, it is thus agreed
That peaceful truce shall be proclaimed in France,
We come to be informèd by yourselves
What the conditions of that league must be.   120

YORK
Speak, Winchester, for boiling choler chokes
The hollow passage of my poisoned voice
By sight of these our baleful enemies.

WINCHESTER
Charles and the rest, it is enacted thus:

125. **in regard:** since
126. **Of mere:** i.e., from pure
127. **distressful:** painful
133. **dignity:** position
137. **privilege:** i.e., the rights
139–40. **am possessed . . . territories:** i.e., have taken possession of **more than half the** French **territories   Gallian:** French
141. **therein reverenced for:** i.e., there saluted with deep respect as
142. **for lucre:** i.e., in return for acquisition; **the rest unvanquished:** i.e., the other portion of **the Gallian territories**
143. **that prerogative:** i.e., being **reverenced for . . . lawful king** (line 141)
146–47. **coveting . . . all:** Proverbial: "**All** covet, **all** lose." **coveting for:** i.e., **coveting,** desiring   **cast:** thrown   **of all:** i.e., being king **of all** France
150. **the matter grows to compromise:** i.e., that a **compromise** is being achieved
151. **upon comparison:** i.e., through comparing what you will receive to what you might someday have
152. **the title:** i.e., viceroy
153–54. **Of benefit . . . desert:** i.e., as a gift from Henry VI, rather than something you deserve **challenge:** claim

That, in regard King Henry gives consent,   125
Of mere compassion and of lenity,
To ease your country of distressful war
And suffer you to breathe in fruitful peace,
You shall become true liegemen to his crown.
And, Charles, upon condition thou wilt swear   130
To pay him tribute and submit thyself,
Thou shalt be placed as viceroy under him,
And still enjoy thy regal dignity.

ALANSON
Must he be then as shadow of himself—
Adorn his temples with a coronet,   135
And yet, in substance and authority,
Retain but privilege of a private man?
This proffer is absurd and reasonless.

CHARLES
'Tis known already that I am possessed
With more than half the Gallian territories,   140
And therein reverenced for their lawful king.
Shall I, for lucre of the rest unvanquished,
Detract so much from that prerogative
As to be called but viceroy of the whole?
No, lord ambassador, I'll rather keep   145
That which I have than, coveting for more,
Be cast from possibility of all.

YORK
Insulting Charles, hast thou by secret means
Used intercession to obtain a league
And, now the matter grows to compromise,   150
Stand'st thou aloof upon comparison?
Either accept the title thou usurp'st,
Of benefit proceeding from our king
And not of any challenge of desert,
Or we will plague thee with incessant wars.   155

REIGNIER, ⌈*aside to Charles*⌉
My lord, you do not well in obstinacy

157. **course of:** i.e., **course of** negotiating; **contract:** agreement

159. **like:** i.e., a similar

166. **stand:** hold good

167. **reserved:** i.e., with the reservation that

168. **towns of garrison: towns** where troops are quartered; fortified **towns**

175. **entertain:** enter on; accept

5.5 Suffolk persuades Henry to marry Margaret over the objections of Gloucester. Suffolk plans to control Margaret and, through her, the kingdom.

O SD. **conference:** conversation

2. **astonished:** stunned

To cavil in the course of this contract.
If once it be neglected, ten to one
We shall not find like opportunity.

ALANSON, ⌜*aside to Charles*⌝
To say the truth, it is your policy   160
To save your subjects from such massacre
And ruthless slaughters as are daily seen
By our proceeding in hostility;
And therefore take this compact of a truce
Although you break it when your pleasure serves.   165

WARWICK
How say'st thou, Charles? Shall our condition stand?

CHARLES
It shall—only reserved you claim no interest
In any of our towns of garrison.

YORK
Then swear allegiance to his Majesty,
As thou art knight, never to disobey   170
Nor be rebellious to the crown of England,
Thou nor thy nobles, to the crown of England.
          ⌜*Charles, Alanson, Bastard, and Reignier*
                    swear allegiance to Henry.⌝
So, now dismiss your army when you please;
Hang up your ensigns, let your drums be still,
For here we entertain a solemn peace.   175
                              They exit.

⌜Scene 5⌝

Enter Suffolk in conference with the King,
Gloucester, and Exeter, ⌜*with Attendants.*⌝

KING HENRY
Your wondrous rare description, noble earl,
Of beauteous Margaret hath astonished me.

5. **rigor:** violence
6. **Provokes:** impels
8. **shipwrack:** shipwreck
9. **fruition:** the pleasure arising from possession
10. **tale:** account, enumeration
11. **worthy praise:** i.e., the **praise** of which she is **worthy**
14. **a volume of enticing lines:** a book filled with **enticing** writings
15. **conceit:** mental capacity, understanding
17. **full replete:** abundantly supplied
25. **flatter:** gloss over, palliate
29. **deface:** obliterate
31. **triumph:** tournament
32. **try:** test; **forsaketh:** avoids, shuns; **lists:** arena
33. **odds:** superiority

The Tower of London. (1.1.170; 1.3.1)
From Claes Jansz Visscher, *Londinum florentissima Britanniae urbs* . . . [c. 1625].

Her virtues gracèd with external gifts
Do breed love's settled passions in my heart,
And like as rigor of tempestuous gusts   5
Provokes the mightiest hulk against the tide,
So am I driven by breath of her renown
Either to suffer shipwrack, or arrive
Where I may have fruition of her love.

SUFFOLK
Tush, my good lord, this superficial tale   10
Is but a preface of her worthy praise.
The chief perfections of that lovely dame,
Had I sufficient skill to utter them,
Would make a volume of enticing lines
Able to ravish any dull conceit;   15
And, which is more, she is not so divine,
So full replete with choice of all delights,
But with as humble lowliness of mind
She is content to be at your command—
Command, I mean, of virtuous chaste intents—   20
To love and honor Henry as her lord.

KING HENRY
And otherwise will Henry ne'er presume.—
Therefore, my Lord Protector, give consent
That Margaret may be England's royal queen.

GLOUCESTER
So should I give consent to flatter sin.   25
You know, my lord, your Highness is betrothed
Unto another lady of esteem.
How shall we then dispense with that contract
And not deface your honor with reproach?

SUFFOLK
As doth a ruler with unlawful oaths;   30
Or one that, at a triumph having vowed
To try his strength, forsaketh yet the lists
By reason of his adversary's odds.

34. **poor earl's daughter:** i.e., the **daughter of the Earl of Armagnac** (See 5.1.41–47.) **unequal odds:** i.e., not equal to Margaret

35. **may be broke:** i.e., the engagement of Henry and the **earl's daughter may be** broken off

36. **more than that:** i.e., **more than** a **poor earl's daughter**

42. **As his alliance will:** i.e., that union with him (through Henry's marriage to his daughter) **will**

45. **near kinsman:** i.e., a close relative

46. **warrant:** certainly promise; **liberal:** generous

47. **Where:** whereas

50. **for wealth:** i.e., on the basis of **wealth**

54. **market men: men** who go to **market** to buy and sell

56. **by attorneyship:** through (negotiating) attorneys

57. **will:** insist on; **affects:** loves

59. **affects her:** i.e., loves Margaret

60. **Most . . . us:** i.e., **of all these reasons most** binds **us**

61. **opinions:** i.e., **opinions** that; **preferred:** advanced to this marriage

62. **wedlock forcèd:** enforced marriage

63. **age:** lifetime; long time

A poor earl's daughter is unequal odds,
And therefore may be broke without offense.   35

GLOUCESTER
Why, what, I pray, is Margaret more than that?
Her father is no better than an earl,
Although in glorious titles he excel.

SUFFOLK
Yes, my lord, her father is a king,
The King of Naples and Jerusalem,   40
And of such great authority in France
As his alliance will confirm our peace,
And keep the Frenchmen in allegiance.

GLOUCESTER
And so the Earl of Armagnac may do,
Because he is near kinsman unto Charles.   45

EXETER
Besides, his wealth doth warrant a liberal dower,
Where Reignier sooner will receive than give.

SUFFOLK
A dower, my lords? Disgrace not so your king
That he should be so abject, base, and poor,
To choose for wealth and not for perfect love.   50
Henry is able to enrich his queen,
And not to seek a queen to make him rich;
So worthless peasants bargain for their wives,
As market men for oxen, sheep, or horse.
Marriage is a matter of more worth   55
Than to be dealt in by attorneyship.
Not whom we will, but whom his Grace affects,
Must be companion of his nuptial bed.
And therefore, lords, since he affects her most,
Most of all these reasons bindeth us   60
In our opinions she should be preferred.
For what is wedlock forcèd but a hell,
An age of discord and continual strife?

65. **pattern:** instance, example; **celestial:** heavenly
66. **match with:** i.e., marry to
68. **feature:** graceful and beautiful form
69. **Approves:** proves
70. **courage:** nature, mind
72. **answer:** satisfy, fulfill; **in issue of:** i.e., in providing an heir to
76. **fair:** beautiful
80. **for that:** because
81–82. **attaint / With:** i.e., affected by
83. **but this:** i.e., **but** of **this**
84. **dissension:** violent discord or strife
85. **alarums:** incitements; assaults
86. **As I:** i.e., that I; **working:** operation, action
87. **Take . . . shipping:** i.e., **therefore,** embark; **post:** hasten, hurry
88. **procure:** plead
92. **charge:** i.e., **charge** (weight, load) of money
93. **Among:** i.e., from among; **tenth:** tax amounting to one-tenth of everyone's annual profit or income (or, perhaps, property)
95. **perplexèd:** bewildered, anxious
96. **banish all offense:** i.e., take no **offense**
97. **censure:** judge

Whereas the contrary bringeth bliss
And is a pattern of celestial peace.   65
Whom should we match with Henry, being a king,
But Margaret, that is daughter to a king?
Her peerless feature, joinèd with her birth,
Approves her fit for none but for a king.
Her valiant courage and undaunted spirit,   70
More than in women commonly is seen,
Will answer our hope in issue of a king.
For Henry, son unto a conqueror,
Is likely to beget more conquerors,
If with a lady of so high resolve   75
As is fair Margaret he be linked in love.
Then yield, my lords, and here conclude with me
That Margaret shall be queen, and none but she.
KING HENRY
Whether it be through force of your report,
My noble Lord of Suffolk, or for that   80
My tender youth was never yet attaint
With any passion of inflaming love,
I cannot tell; but this I am assured:
I feel such sharp dissension in my breast,
Such fierce alarums both of hope and fear,   85
As I am sick with working of my thoughts.
Take therefore shipping; post, my lord, to France;
Agree to any covenants, and procure
That Lady Margaret do vouchsafe to come
To cross the seas to England and be crowned   90
King Henry's faithful and anointed queen.
For your expenses and sufficient charge,
Among the people gather up a tenth.
Be gone, I say, for till you do return,
I rest perplexèd with a thousand cares.—   95
And you, good uncle, banish all offense.
If you do censure me by what you were,

99. **execution:** carrying out

100. **from company:** alone

101. **grief:** mental suffering (occasioned by his still unrequited love of Margaret)

102. **grief:** trouble, keen regret

104. **Paris . . . Greece:** In mythology the **Trojan** (line 106) prince **Paris** went to **Greece** and carried off Helen, wife of Menelaus and queen of Sparta, the most beautiful woman in the world; his act precipitated the Trojan War, which ended in Troy's destruction. (See picture of **Paris,** below.)

105. **like:** same; **event:** outcome, result

106. **prosper:** thrive, flourish

Paris. (5.5.104)
From [Guillaume Rouillé,] . . . *Promptuarii iconum* . . . (1553).

Not what you are, I know it will excuse
This sudden execution of my will.
And so conduct me where, from company,   100
I may revolve and ruminate my grief.
                         He exits ⌐with Attendants.⌐

GLOUCESTER
Ay, grief, I fear me, both at first and last.
                         Gloucester exits ⌐with Exeter.⌐

SUFFOLK
Thus Suffolk hath prevailed, and thus he goes
As did the youthful Paris once to Greece,
With hope to find the like event in love,   105
But prosper better than the Trojan did.
Margaret shall now be queen, and rule the King,
But I will rule both her, the King, and realm.
                                      He exits.

Longer Notes

1.1.61. Roan, Orleance: Several names of French towns and French persons are given anglicized spellings in the Folio text of this play. While it is customary for editors to replace these spellings with the appropriate French spellings (so that **Roan** becomes Rouen and **Orleance** appears as Orléans), such a practice disrupts the meter of many lines of dialogue in this play, in which the iambic pentameter rhythm is strongly emphasized. Retaining the anglicized spellings grants the reader or actor the flexibility to place the stress as the line demands, with **Roan** pronounced sometimes as a single syllable (RONE) and sometimes, as in the present case, as two syllables (ROW-an) and with **Orleance** pronounced with the stress on the first (instead of the final) syllable.

Other French names that appear in our edition with their anglicized Folio spellings are **Callice** instead of *Calais*, **Saint Dennis** instead of *Saint Denis*, and **Alanson** (stressed sometimes on the first syllable as AL-anson and sometimes on the second syllable as a-LAN-son) instead of *Alençon*.

We have used the French spelling for Dauphin because the anglicized Folio version, "Dolphin," though the standard English spelling at the time, seems distractingly comic. It is important, though, to accent *Dauphin* on the first syllable (DAW-fin), as the Folio "DOL-phin" indicates.

1.1.65. lead: According to one of Shakespeare's sources, Raphael Holinshed's *Chronicles*, "[Henry V's] body, embalmed and closed in **lead,** was laid in a chariot royal, richly appareled with cloth of gold. Upon his coffin was laid a representation of his person, adorned with robes, diadem, scepter, and ball, like a king."

1.1.133. **Sir John Fastolf:** In the Folio, this character is given the name "Sir Iohn Falstaffe," the same name as that of the famous knight in Shakespeare's two *Henry IV* plays and *The Merry Wives of Windsor.* This more famous cowardly knight is Prince Hal's companion, who dies, in *Henry V,* before Henry first sails to France. The character in *Henry VI, Part 1* betrays Talbot through his cowardice and is stripped by Talbot and Henry VI of his honors.

While it is impossible to demonstrate how two different Shakespeare characters came to share the same name and similar behaviors, at least two possible scenarios can be imagined. In both scenarios, the relevant facts are these: (1) the character depicted in *Henry VI, Part 1* was named, in the chronicles, "Sir Iohn Fastolfe"; (2) the character depicted in the plays about Henry IV was named "Sir Iohn Oldcastle" before his name was changed to "Falstalffe" in the quarto printings of *Henry IV, Part 1* and *Henry IV, Part 2.* (See "Historical Background: Sir John Falstaff and Sir John Oldcastle," in the Folger Shakespeare Library *Henry IV, Part 1,* pages 235–41.) The "Sir John Falstaff" of the *Henry IV* plays, in other words, is a representation of the historical figure Sir John Oldcastle; the "Sir John Falstaff" of the Folio's *The first Part of Henry the Sixt* is a representation of the historical figure Sir John Fastolf. Both were knights with interesting historical connections to Henry V and Henry VI.

In one possible scenario, Shakespeare, in writing *Henry VI, Part 1,* changed the knight's name from "Fastolf" to "Falstaff"; then, when he later wrote his plays about Henry IV and was forced to change the name of Sir John Oldcastle, he simply reused the Falstaff name. In a second, more interesting, scenario, Shakespeare, in writing *Henry VI, Part 1*, retained the name "Fastolf" for that play's cowardly knight. When, in writing the *Henry IV* plays in the late 1590s, he replaced the Oldcastle name, he used a version of the "Fastolf" name—"Falstalffe": a name filled with wordplay, reminiscent of "Fastolf" but different enough to prevent confusion. In this scenario, when *Henry VI, Part 1* was first printed (in 1623 in the First Folio), the Fastolf character was renamed "Falstaff"—probably through a scribe's or compositor's substitution of a name that, by 1623, had become very familiar through the quartos and performances of the *Henry IV* plays and *The Merry Wives of Windsor*.

As complicated as it is, the scenario involving scribal or compositorial change is just as likely (indeed, in our opinion, more likely) than the one in which Shakespeare simply used the name "Sir John Falstaff" as the fictional name for two different historical characters. For this reason, and in order to save unnecessary confusion between two different characters, we have given Sir John Fastolf the name he bears in the chronicles, as have many editors before us. (The first was Lewis Theobald in the early eighteenth century, the most recent Michael Hattaway in his New Cambridge Shakespeare edition of the play [1990]; Edward Burns, in the Arden 3 edition [2000]; and Michael Taylor, in the Oxford edition [2003].) See also George Walton Williams, "Fastolf or Falstaff," *English Literary Renaissance* 5 (1975): 308–12.

1.2.1–2. Mars . . . not known: These lines play on "**Mars his**" (i.e., Mars's) double identity as a planet and as a mythological god. The planet's "**true moving . . .**

in the heavens" (i.e., its precise orbit) was, in a sense, **not known** to early astronomers. **Mars,** as the Roman god of war controlling the successes and failures of warfare **in the earth,** was similarly inscrutable. Lines 1–2 quote Cornelius Agrippa: "Neither hath the true moving of Mars been known until this date" (*De Incertitudine.* . . . , trans. James Sandford, 1569, with spelling modernized).

1.2.64 SD. **la Pucelle:** This French word, which means "the virgin," was the term that the historical Jeanne d'Arc, or Joan of Arc, used to name herself. As the play reminds us, the name sounds like the English word *puzel,* which means "whore." (See 1.4.107.)

1.2.141–42. **Now . . . once:** These lines allude to the following episode in Caesar's life: "*Caesar* in the meantime being in the city of APOLLONIA, having but a small army to fight with *Pompey,* it grieved him for that the rest of his army was so long a coming, not knowing what way to take. In the end he followed a dangerous determination, to embark unknown in a little pinnace of twelve oars only, to pass over the sea again unto BRUNDISIUM: the which he could not do without great danger, considering that all that sea was full of Pompey's ships and armies. So he took ship in the night appareled like a slave, and went aboard upon this little pinnace, & said never a word, as if he had been some poor man of mean condition. The pinnace lay in the mouth of the river of Anius, the which commonly was wont to be very calm & quiet, by reason of a little wind that came from the shore, which every morning drove back the waves far into the main sea. But that night, by ill fortune, there came a great wind from the sea that overcame the land wind, insomuch as the force & strength of the river fighting against the violence of the rage & waves of the sea, the encounter was marvelous dangerous, the water of the river being driven back, and rebounding upward, with great noise and danger in turning of the water. Thereupon the master of the pinnace, seeing he could not possibly get out of the mouth of this river, bade the mariners to cast about again, and to return against the stream. *Caesar* hearing that, straight discovered him self unto the master of the pinnace, who at the first was amazed when he saw him: but *Caesar* then taking him by the hand said unto him, "Good fellow, be of good cheer, and forwards hardily; fear not, for thou hast *Caesar* and his fortune with thee." Then the mariners, forgetting the danger of the storm they were in, laid on lode with oars, and labored for life what they could against the wind, to get out of the mouth of this river. But at length, perceiving they labored in vain, and that the pinnace took in abundance of water, and was ready to sink: *Caesar* then to his great grief was driven to return back again" (Plutarch, *The lives of the noble Grecians and Romans,* translated by Sir Thomas North, 1579, with the spelling modernized).

1.2.143. **Was . . . dove:** This line apparently accepts the account of Muhammad being inspired by a dove. There was also a slanderous story current in Shakespeare's time that accused Muhammad of training a dove to approach him by placing grains of wheat in his ear; when the dove put his beak in the Prophet's ear to get the corn, the Prophet claimed that the dove was the Holy Spirit inspiring him.

1.3.36. **cardinal's hat:** The dialogue in this scene makes it abundantly clear that Winchester here wears the garb of a cardinal. This introduces what for many editors is a serious problem with the text, because the dialogue in 5.1 indicates instead that in Act 5 he is wearing such garb for the first time. Some editors solve this problem by changing the dialogue in 1.3 so that it refers to bishop's purple rather than cardinal's scarlet clothing. Others allow the dialogue to stand, but follow the Folio in assigning Winchester the new speech prefix of "Cardinal" in 5.4. Both of these solutions assume that 5.1 shows Winchester having just been elevated by the pope from a bishop to a cardinal. This assumption fails to consider two historical facts. First, because Beaufort remained a bishop after he was elevated to cardinal, he need not be called Cardinal in 5.4. Second, and more significant, the historical chronicles used in the creation of *Henry VI, Part 1* make it clear that Beaufort was actually appointed a cardinal during the reign of Henry V, whose burial opens the play. Thus, in terms of the history of the period, he is a cardinal throughout the play, just as he is a bishop. Because Henry V forbade Beaufort to be installed as a cardinal in England, Beaufort was prohibited from dressing as a cardinal during Henry V's lifetime and on into the reign of Henry VI, who eventually lifted the prohibition. The play may then be read as showing Beaufort, in 1.3, defying the royal prohibition by wearing his cardinal's hat and scarlet robes outside of court at the Tower of London, though he is not shown wearing them when appearing in court. Only later in the reign of Henry VI, both in history and in the play (in 5.1), does Beaufort appear in the royal court in cardinal's regalia. In this reading of the Winchester/Cardinal problem, Winchester's entrance in Act 5 with three ambassadors, dressed in a cardinal's robes, is not an elevation in his priestly status but instead marks his installation as a cardinal in England. As Essex comments:

> What, is my Lord of Winchester installed
> And called unto a cardinal's degree?

Then I perceive that will be verified
Henry the Fifth did sometime prophesy:
"If once he come to be a cardinal,
He'll make his cap coequal with the crown."

(28–33)

Because this explanation of Beaufort's position is possible, we do not see the change of speech prefix from "*Win.*" to "*Car.*" that takes place in the First Folio (5.4 in modern texts) as representing a necessary change in this character's status. Thus, we do not alter the dialogue in 1.3, nor do we follow the Folio in giving Winchester a new speech prefix in our edition in 5.4.

It is, of course, quite possible that the seemingly sharp discrepancy between the language in 1.3 and 5.1 is instead the result of multiple authorship of the play, with a failure of communication between the authors of 1.3 and 5.1. In this scenario as well, we would choose to follow the Folio dialogue and to regularize the speech prefixes according to our normal procedure.

1.4.50. **fear of my name:** In Geoffrey Whitney's *Emblemes* (1586), the poem accompanying the emblem for the motto "Vel post mortem formidoloi" (those terrifying even after death) concludes with the stanza:

So, Hector's sight great fear in Greeks did work,
When he was showed on horseback, being dead;
Huniades, the terror of the Turk,
Though laid in grave, yet at his name they fled;
And crying babes, they ceasèd [i.e., stopped
   crying] with the same,
The like in France, sometime [i.e., in the past] did
Talbot's name.

2.1.24–26. Pray . . . begun: These lines have been interpreted by editors as sexual quibbling, with line 24 referring to Joan "having sexual relations with men" or to her "becoming pregnant," and with sexual puns (in lines 25–26) on **standard** (as "that which stands up," "penis") and **carry armor** ("bear the weight of a man"). It seems just as likely, though, that the lines mean instead "Pray God she does not become a male, if, as a French soldier, she continues to fight the way she has done so far." According to the *OED*, **prove** can mean "to come to be, become," and the first meaning of **masculine** is "belonging to the male sex; male."

2.3.9–10. Fain . . . reports: These lines, together with line 70, have suggested to Naseeb Shaheen (*Biblical References in Shakespeare's Plays*) that this scene specifically recalls the biblical meeting of Solomon and the queen of Sheba. "And when the queen of Sheba heard of the fame of Solomon, she came to prove Solomon with hard questions. . . . And she said to the king, It was a true word which I heard . . . of thy wisdom. Howbeit I believed not their report, until . . . mine eyes had seen it: and, behold, . . . thou exceedeth the fame that I heard" (2 Chronicles 9.1, 5–6).

2.4.87. the place's privilege: There is disagreement among editors about whether there was a prohibition against violence at the Inns of Court. Perhaps this disagreement arises from changes in the rules governing student conduct there that took place between the late Middle Ages, when this play is set, and the time at which it was written—around 1590, over a hundred years into the next historical period, the English Renaissance. In *The Inns of Court under Elizabeth I and the Early Stuarts, 1590–1640*, Wilfrid R. Prest writes that "while assaults and brawls at the late medieval–early Tudor inns were punished as they occurred, the benchers seem to have been prepared to accept a high level of interpersonal violence within the societies." However, "penalties for acts of casual violence within the societies . . . escalated sharply in the later sixteenth century. . . . [P]ermanent expulsion had also become a standard punishment" (pp. 95–97). It is impossible to tell, then, if Plantagenet is referring to the actual **privilege** that would have protected students at the Inns of Court from violence at the time the play was written, or if he is being made to speak in his own historical time and thus fabricate such a **privilege** as a way of excusing himself from retaliating against Somerset for insulting him.

2.5.82–91. **Long . . . beheaded:** In *Henry V* 2.2, the **Earl of Cambridge** is exposed as a traitor and sentenced to death by Henry V for treason, but not because he levied an army on Mortimer's behalf. Instead, Cambridge is accused of plotting Henry's death in exchange for French money. He claims that he had additional reasons for his treachery (lines 162–64), but does not specifically mention Mortimer.

3.1.44. **bastard of my grandfather:** John of Gaunt was not married to Catherine Swynford when Henry Beaufort, bishop of Winchester, was born. (John and Catherine were later married.) Gloucester was the youngest son of Henry IV, who descended from John of Gaunt's first marriage to Blanche of Lancaster. See page 2.

3.3.30 SD. **sound an English march:** Some editors suggest that the difference between the so-called **English march** and **French march** may have been in the instrumentation. There is evidence, though, that the "**French march** was slower than the **English.**" So writes Michael Hattaway, in his Cambridge edition of the play (1990), noting that "Dekker wrote of the gentleman who 'comes but slowly on (as if he trod a French March).'" In any case, here the "French march" signals the presence of Burgundy's army, not the French army.

3.4.38. **law of arms:** Editors do not agree about how to read this phrase. At the simplest level, this **law** forbids violence in the context in which this scene is supposed to be occurring. The debate arises over which particular context here is the operable one. Some editors relate this **law of arms** to laws forbidding violence near the king or his residence. Others suggest that the context is that of war, in which soldiers on the same side are not allowed to fight each other, on pain of death.

5.3.6. **lordly monarch of the north:** The link between "monarch of the north" and Lucifer is found in Isaiah 14.12–13, where "Lucifer, son of the morning," says of himself: "I will ascend into heaven, and exalt my throne above beside the stars of God: I will sit also upon the mount of the congregation in the sides **of the north.**" Scholars today argue persuasively that the link supposedly made here with the fall of Lucifer is due to mistranslation and a false reading of Isaiah in the light of the Christian story. However, for an English writer in the later decades of the sixteenth century, it would be natural to link Joan's devotion to the devil with a passage in Isaiah in which the then-current English translation has Lucifer/Satan place himself in **the north.**

Appendices

Authorship of *Henry VI, Part 1*

Henry VI, Part 1 was first published in 1623, together with thirty-five other plays, in the first collection of Shakespeare's plays to be issued in a single volume—the book we now call the Shakespeare First Folio. Until Lewis Theobald in 1734, no one suggested that any of the play was the work of someone else besides Shakespeare. After Theobald expressed skepticism about Shakespeare's sole authorship, a great many editors and scholars have echoed his doubts, most influentially the renowned Shakespeare editor Edmond Malone in 1787. Others have contested Theobald's doubts, including the respected Samuel Johnson. Beginning with Jane Lee in 1876, a number of investigators using various methods have attempted to discriminate between those parts of the play to be credited to Shakespeare and those parts to be attributed to other named playwrights of the period, including Robert Greene, Thomas Nashe, and George Peele, or to anonymous writers. These scholars have arrived at no agreement about exactly who wrote which parts, although there is now a growing consensus about Nashe's likely authorship of the first act.

We do not think it impossible or even improbable that other hands may be represented in the play. It is conservatively estimated that at least half the plays from the public theater of Shakespeare's time were collaborative efforts. We respect the labor expended and skill exhibited by attribution scholars, and, at the same

245

time, we take seriously the limitations that they acknowledge necessarily attend their efforts. On this basis we simply set aside the question of whether Greene, Nashe, Peele, or others wrote some of *Henry VI, Part 1* and contest neither those who have argued for collaboration nor those who have claimed the play for Shakespeare.

We treat the play in the same way as the others published in the Shakespeare First Folio, referring to it for convenience as a Shakespeare play. In doing so, we fully recognize that the theater is always the location of collaborative creation, not just among named dramatists but also among members of acting companies and their employees and associates. We are aware of documentary evidence of other hands reaching into dramatic manuscripts in the course of their annotation or transcription, and we suspect that Shakespeare's words could not possibly have commanded in their own time the same reverence they have been accorded in later times. Such circumstances attach to all the Shakespeare printed plays that come down to us. In calling *Henry VI, Part 1* Shakespeare's, we are simply acknowledging its inclusion in the 1623 First Folio.

Shakespeare's Two Tetralogies

When Shakespeare's plays were collected and published in 1623, the volume included eight plays that together dramatize the "Wars of the Roses." This name has been given to a period in English history that arguably stems from the death of Edward the Black Prince in 1376 and ends when Henry Tudor is proclaimed King Henry VII in 1485. Edward, the oldest son of King Edward III, was a valiant warrior and skilled diplomat who held out the promise of continuing his father's rule over England and much of France. When, however, the Black Prince predeceased his father, his infant son Richard became heir to the throne, and, on Edward III's death, was proclaimed King Richard II. His royal uncles began to compete for power, and in 1399 Richard was deposed by his cousin Henry, son of the Duke of Lancaster. In the following years, the descendants of Edward III divided themselves into two factions—those who sympathized with the deposed and murdered Richard II and his Yorkist supporters, and those who followed the Lancastrians. The factions battled each other for the nation's throne with increasing ferocity, with first one faction then the other in the ascendancy. In 1485, Richard III, the last of the Yorkist kings, was killed at the Battle of Bosworth Field. His opponent, Henry Tudor, a descendant of the Lancastrians, married Elizabeth York and thereby brought together the two battling family lines and brought an end to the Wars of the Roses.

The four plays that dramatize the period between 1422 (the death of Henry V) and 1485 (the death of Richard III and the proclamation of Henry VII as king) were written in the late 1580s or early 1590s. Three of them cover the tumultuous reign of Henry VI, who, like Richard II, was named king when yet a child. During the years covered by the three *Henry VI* plays, England was caught up not only in the struggles between the Yorks and the Lancasters but also in an ongoing war to hold on to, or to regain, lands in France. The fourth of these plays, *Richard III*, shows Richard's violent climb to the throne and his equally violent ejection and death. All four plays were published as Shakespeare's in the First Folio, though there is ongoing debate about how much of *Henry VI, Part 1* was actually written by Shakespeare, and though there are many scholars who argue for other authorial hands in *Parts 2* and *3* as well.

The four plays that dramatize the earlier period in this saga, which begins in 1398 near the end of Richard II's reign and ends in 1421 with Henry V in triumph, were written in the late 1590s, and three of them— *Richard II, Henry IV, Part 1,* and *Henry IV, Part 2*—were printed numerous times in individual quarto editions beginning in 1597, 1598, and 1600. (*Henry V* did not receive a full printing until it appeared in the First Folio.) These four plays are generally accepted as not only written by Shakespeare but as being the very best of his history plays. They have a complex and confusing relationship to the plays written earlier, to which they provide a prequel, as is acknowledged in the Chorus that closes *Henry V:*

> Small time, but in that small most greatly lived
> This star of England. Fortune made his sword,
> By which the world's best garden he achieved
> And of it left his son imperial lord.
> Henry the Sixth, in infant bands crowned King
> Of France and England, did this king succeed,
> Whose state so many had the managing
> That they lost France and made his England bleed,
> *Which oft our stage hath shown.*
> *Henry V,* Epilogue, 5–13 (emphasis added)

Part of the complexity of the relationship between the two tetralogies arises from differences in the ways the two sets of plays present certain moments in history. Mortimer, for example, in *Henry VI, Part 1* 2.5, tells Richard Plantagenet that "the Percies of the north" went to war with Henry IV in order to place Mortimer on the throne, that they lost their lives on his behalf, and that the Lancasters continued to imprison

Mortimer because he threatened their hold on the kingship. This version of the story is markedly different from the version presented in *Henry IV, Part 1,* where Mortimer is, indeed, a theme of contention between Henry IV and Hotspur, but where placing him on the throne is merely one of Hotspur's wilder threats (*Henry IV, Part 1* 1.3.138–40), and where the last we hear of Mortimer is that he failed to show up to support Hotspur and the other rebels at the Battle of Shrewsbury (4.4.23). His name is never mentioned in *Henry IV, Part 2* or in *Henry V,* nor is there any mention in this tetralogy of his being imprisoned or considered a threat. (For another discrepancy between the two tetralogies, see the longer note to 2.5.82–91, page 243.)

An added complication is that because the plays covering the later part of the period were written first, editors from the mid–twentieth century onward began calling them "The First Tetralogy" (i.e., the first-written tetralogy). These editors place the First Tetralogy in collected editions before the four plays that depict the earlier years, rather than putting all eight plays in the order in which their historical figures lived, as did the First Folio of 1623. Thus "The Second Tetralogy" refers to the set of plays that depict action that precedes the story told in what we now know as "The First Tetralogy." As a consequence, few readers today, trained to read the plays in the order in which they were written, would ever encounter the eight plays by beginning with *Richard II* and reading through to the end of the saga with Richard III's death and the proclamation of the reign of Henry VII. Thus the full story of this turbulent period of English history as depicted in these eight plays—the fall of Richard II, the rise of Henry IV, and the subsequent violence between Edward III's royal descendants—is rarely experienced with its full narrative force.

Joan la Pucelle, or Joan of Arc

A principal difficulty with the text of *Henry VI, Part 1* concerns the sharp difference in the characterization of Pucelle between the first four acts and the fifth. In the first four, her characterization is complex; she is one thing for the French, quite another for the English. In the fifth act, her complexity disappears, and Pucelle is flattened into an embodiment of the insults that the English have hurled at her for the first four acts.

In those first four acts, the division in her characterization is a deep one. For the French she is a "sweet virgin" (3.3.16), a genuinely holy and chaste woman, who is also a great military leader and strategist: "Divinest creature, Astraea's daughter, . . . glorious prophetess," in the words of Charles the Dauphin, who says "No longer on Saint Dennis will we cry, / But Joan la Pucelle shall be France's saint" (1.6.4–8, 28–29). Nothing could be further from the English perception of her. The first Englishman to encounter her is Talbot. He immediately accuses her of being the "Devil or devil's dam, . . . a witch . . . [and] strumpet" (1.5.5–12). Thus, from the beginning the French and English have opposite views of Pucelle's spiritual and moral nature.

Of course, this difference of opinion between the English and French about Pucelle also arises regarding other characters. Talbot himself is an example. For Salisbury, Talbot is "my life, my joy" (1.4.23), and, for Henry VI, a "brave captain and victorious lord" (3.4.16). Just as Pucelle claims that her power comes to her from the Virgin Mary, whose "aid . . . promised and assured success" (1.2.83), so Talbot is confident that "God is our fortress" (2.1.28). Yet for the French, Talbot is "a fiend of hell" (2.1.49) and a "bloodthirsty lord" (2.3.35). In the words of the General of Bordeaux, he is the "ominous and fearful owl of death, / Our nation's terror and their bloody scourge" (4.2.15–16). It is clear that the opposing views of Talbot arise from the difference in national interest between the French and the English, and it would seem reasonable to assume that the two nations' opposite conceptions of Pucelle have the same origin. Yet Talbot is never flattened into a caricature.

In the fourth act, Talbot dies as a mere mortal, struck down by the French army he has been fighting, but he remains a hero to the English and a hated enemy to the French. In the fifth act, when Pucelle is being taken off to be burned at the stake by the English as a haughty and promiscuous witch, she will not even acknowledge her own father when he visits her before her death. Now the play itself, rather than simply the English in the play, makes her into everything the English have accused her of being. Act 5 has her conjuring up fiends to aid her in defeating the conquering English forces— openly and, to her greater embarrassment, fruitlessly practicing witchcraft among demons who now refuse to abide by her will. She even desperately offers to "lop a member off and give it" to her recalcitrant familiars (5.3.15). When the English capture her and call her "ugly witch" (5.3.34), their words are no longer an insult motivated by nationalism but a statement of what the play has made, within its fiction, fact. In 5.4, the other English insult, "strumpet," is also validated by the play's action when Pucelle attempts unsuccessfully to escape her torture and death at the stake by claiming to be pregnant, naming first Alanson and then Reignier as the father of her unborn child. When the English call her "Strumpet" again (5.4.85), they can be heard not so much to insult her as to identify her.

Readers of *Henry VI, Part 1* have long been disappointed in its fifth-act transformation of Pucelle from an interesting character into the embodiment of an English slur on a French hero. This transformation has motivated some to want to identify any dramatist other than Shakespeare as writer of those parts of the last act that vilify Pucelle, rather than tarnish so great a dramatist's reputation by imputing to him such poor drama. The flattening that occurs in the final act, in contrast to the complex rendering of Pucelle's character earlier in the play, has also been seen as grounds for believing that the play is the work of several different hands, one of whom had a far more hostile vision of Pucelle than did his fellow playwrights.

Textual Notes

The reading of the present text appears to the left of the square bracket. Unless otherwise noted, the reading to the left of the bracket is from **F,** the First Folio text (upon which this edition is based). The earliest sources of readings not in F are indicated as follows: **F2** is the Second Folio of 1632; **F3** is the Third Folio of 1663–64; **F4** is the Fourth Folio of 1685; **Ed.** is an earlier editor of Shakespeare, beginning with Rowe in 1709. No sources are given for emendations of punctuation or for corrections of obvious typographical errors, like turned letters that produce no known word. **SD** means stage direction; **SP** means speech prefix; ~ stands in place of a word already quoted before the square bracket; ʌ indicates the omission of a punctuation mark.

1.1   1. the] F (ẙ)   47. dead.] ~, F   61. Roan] Ed.; *omit* F   82. arms;] ~ʌ F   91. SP SECOND MESSENGER] Ed.; *Mess.* F   94 *and throughout.* Dauphin] F (Dolphin)   105. SP THIRD MESSENGER] Ed.; *Mes.* F   122. continuèd,] ~: F   123. human] F (humane)   133 *and hereafter.* Fastolf] F (*Falstaffe*)   155. I.] ~, F   160. need; 'fore Orleance] Ed.; need, for Orleance is F   170. haste] F (hast)   179. steal] Ed.; send F

1.2   30. bred] Ed.; breed F   47 *and hereafter in this act.* SP CHARLES] Ed.; *Dolph.* F   101, 146. Saint] F (S.)   105 SD *and throughout.* la] Ed.; *de* F

1.3   6. SP FIRST SERVINGMAN] F (*Glost. I. Man*)   8. SP

253

FIRST SERVINGMAN] F (*I. Man.*) 29. Humphrey] F
(*Vmpheir*) 30. Peeled] F (Piel'd) 50. I'll] F2; I F
  1.4 1 *and hereafter.* SP MASTER GUNNER] Ed.; *M.
Gunner* F 25. gott'st] F (got's) 27. Duke] Ed.; Earle F
33. vile-esteemed] Ed.; pil'd esteem'd F 43. scare-
crow] F (Scar-Crow) 69. SD *shoot, and Salisbury and
Gargrave fall*] Ed.; *shot, and Salisbury falls* F 89. Bear
hence his body; I will help to bury it.] *2 lines earlier in* F
95. Nero] Ed.; *omit* F 107. Pucelle or puzel] Ed.; *Puzel
or Pussel* F 110. we] Ed.; me F 111. then try] Ed.;
then wee'le try F
  1.5 16. hunger-starvèd] Ed.; hungry-starued F
  1.6 11. not bells] Ed.; not out the Bells F 22. of]
Ed.; or F
  2.1 8. SD *scaling ladders*] Ed.; *scaling Ladders: Their
Drummes beating a Dead March.* F 24. long,] ~: F 31.
all together] Ed.; altogether F 40. SD *Scaling the walls,
they cry "Saint George! À Talbot!"*] Ed.; *Cry, S. George, A
Talbot.* F, *1 line later* 57 *and hereafter in this scene.* SP
PUCELLE] Ed.; *Ioane* F 81. SD them. | *Alarum*] Ed.;
them. *Exeunt.* | *Alarum* F 81. SD *an English Soldier*]
Ed.; *a Souldier* F 81. SD *The French*] Ed.; *they* F
  2.2 6. SD *Drums . . . march.*] F, *at 2.1.8.* 20. Arc]
Ed.; Acre F 59. SD *Whispers.*] *1 line later in* F
  2.4 1 *and hereafter in this scene.* SP PLANTAGENET]
Ed.; *Yorke.* F 57. law] Ed.; you F 60. meditating∧]
~, F 133. sir] F2; *omit* F
  2.5 35 *and hereafter in this scene.* SP PLANTAGENET]
Ed.; *Rich.* F 84. Cambridge∧ then,] ~, ~∧ F
109. that] F (y̆) 129. mine ill] Ed.; my will F
  3.1 0. SD *Winchester . . . Gloucester offers*] Ed.;
*Winchester, Warwick, Somerset, Suffolk, Richard Planta-
genet. Gloster offers* F 25. Besides] F (Beside)
52. reverend] F (reuerent) 55. SP GLOUCESTER] Ed.;
Warw. F 56. SP WARWICK My lord] Ed.; My Lord F

57. so] Ed.; see F 65, 176. SP PLANTAGENET] Ed.; *Rich.* F 69 *and hereafter.* SP KING HENRY] Ed.; *King.* F 78. What] Ed.; *King.* What F 133. Winchester] *Winehester* F 138. king. ~: F 141. thee;] ~∧ F 172. alone] F2; all alone F 183. SP YORK] Ed.; *Rich.* F 195. SD *All but Exeter exit.*] F (*Exeunt.* | *Manet Exeter.*) 208. should] F2; *omit* F

3.2 13. *Qui*] F (*Che*) 14. *Paysans*] F (*Peasauns*) 14. *pauvre*] F (*pouure*) 21. specify∧] ~? F 59. SD *Those below*] Ed.; *They* F 67, 68. Seigneur] F (Seignior) 83. Coeur-de-lion's] F (Cordelions) 125. gleeks] F (glikes) 139. human] F (humane)

3.3 48. eyes,] ~. F

3.4 0. SD *Winchester . . . To*] Ed.; *Winchester, Yorke, Suffolke, Somerset, Warwicke, Exeter: To* F 27. SD *All . . . exit.*] F (*Exeunt.* | *Manet Vernon and Basset.*) 45. SD *He exits.*] Ed.; *Exeunt.* F

4.1 0. SD *Winchester . . . Governor of Paris, and Others.*] Ed.; *Winchester, Yorke, Suffolke, Somerset, Warwicke, Talbot. and Gouernor Exeter.* F 19. Patay] Ed.; *Poictiers* F 25, 144. besides] F (beside) 26. there] thete F 48. my] Ed.; *omit* F 72. that] F ($\overset{t}{\text{y}}$) 94. cheeks∧] ~: F 113. slight] slighr F 174. SD *Flourish. . . . exit.*] F (*Exeunt. Manet Yorke, Warwick, Exeter, Vernon.*) *For "Flourish," see note to* 4.1.182. 176. orator.] ~.) F 181. iwis] Ed.; I wish F 182. SD *York . . . remains.*] Ed.; *Exeunt.* | *Flourish. Manet Exeter.* F 192. sees] Ed.; that F

4.2 3. calls] F2; call F 12. even] eeuen F 15. SP GENERAL] Ed.; *Cap.* F 55. Saint] F (S.)

4.3 5. Talbot.] ~∧ F 5. along,] ~. F 17. SD *Sir William Lucy*] Ed.; *another Messenger* F 18, 31, 35, 48. SP LUCY] Ed.; *"2 Mes." or "Mes."* F 50. loss∧] ~: F

4.5 12 *and hereafter.* SP JOHN TALBOT] Ed.; *Iohn.* F 42. that] F ($\overset{t}{\text{y}}$)

4.6   57. SD *They exit.*] Ed.; *Exit.* F

4.7   24. breath!] ∼, F   65. Goodrich] F (Goodrig)
70, 71. Saint] F (S.)   91. him.] ∼, F   97. thou] F (y̡) 99.
SD *They exit.*] Ed.; *Exit.* F

5.1   0. SD Ed.; *Scena secunda.* F   15. Besides] F
(Beside)   27. SD *the Ambassador of Armagnac . . .
another Ambassador*] Ed.;   *three Ambassadors*   F
49. where, inshipped] F4; wherein ship'd F   50. SD *All
. . . exit.*] Ed.; *Exeunt.* F   62. SD *He exits.*] Ed.;
Exeunt F

5.2   0. SD Ed.; *Scœna Tertia.* F

5.3   8. speed] Ed.; speedy F   13. silence] silenee F
47. reverent] F (reuerend)   57. her] F3; his F   85. ran-
dom] F (randon)   184. modestly] F2; modestie F
193, 200. mayst] F (mayest)   195. wondrous] F (won-
derous)   197. And] Ed.; Mad F

5.4   28. suck'dst] F2; suck'st F   38. one] Ed.; me F
50. Arc] *Aire* F   59. torture] tortute F   61. discover]
discouet F   62. warranteth] wartanteth F   75. Machi-
avel] F (*Macheuile*)   94. SD *Enter . . . Cardinal.*] 2 *lines
earlier in* F   95 *and hereafter.* SP WINCHESTER] Ed.; *Car.*
F   103. travail] F (trauell)   128. breathe] F (breath)
151. comparison?] ∼. F

5.5   0. SD Ed.; *Actus Quintus.* F   25. sin.] ∼, F
46. Besides] F (Beside)   62. wedlock] wedloeke F

Henry VI, Part 1:
A Modern Perspective

Phyllis Rackin

In recent years, Shakespeare's earliest history plays have been enjoying a minor theatrical revival, but they still have a long way to go before attaining the popularity of their successors. The three parts of *Henry VI* are rarely performed; and on those rare occasions when they do reach the stage, they are typically cut and conflated into either a two-play series or a single two-part play. This neglect is not confined to the theater: the plays are rarely reprinted and seldom discussed by scholars. The current consensus is that they are vastly inferior to Shakespeare's later, better-known English history plays, such as *Richard III*, the two parts of *Henry IV*, and *Henry V*.

This modern neglect is worth questioning, since the *Henry VI* plays—and *Part 1* in particular—seem to have been extremely popular when they were first performed at the end of the sixteenth century. In 1592, Thomas Nashe published a satirical pamphlet titled *Pierce Penilesse his Supplication to the Divell*, which included a defense of stage plays and the earliest reference we have to any of Shakespeare's plays. The play Nashe mentioned was *Henry VI, Part 1*. "How would it have joyed brave *Talbot* (the terror of the French)," he wrote, "to think that after he had lain two hundred years in his tomb, he should triumph again on the

257

stage and have his bones new embalmed with the tears of ten thousand spectators at least (at several times), who, in the tragedian that represents his person, imagine they behold him fresh bleeding."[1] Nashe's claim that at least ten thousand spectators saw the play may actually be too conservative. The records of the initial receipts left by the theater manager, Philip Henslowe, suggest a figure closer to twenty thousand. In fact, only one of the many other plays Henslowe produced earned more.

The play's initial popularity was short-lived. Only one production was recorded during the Restoration and eighteenth century—a period when it was dismissed as a "Drum-and-trumpet Thing," the work of another playwright that was merely "furbished up" by Shakespeare "with here and there a little sentiment and diction."[2] When *Henry VI, Part 1* was revived in 1738, the playbill declared that it had not been "acted these fifty years."[3] In the nineteenth century, no less an authority than Samuel Taylor Coleridge believed that one had only to read the opening speech aloud to "feel the impossibility of [its] having been written by Shakespeare."[4]

This long-standing consensus about the inferiority of the *Henry VI* plays persists, even when they are successfully performed on stage. A case in point is Barry Kyle's 1995 production at the Theater for a New Audience in New York. The critics generally agreed that the performance was a stunning success. The *New York Post* described it as a "thrilling theatrical experience," the *Daily News* as one that no fan of Shakespeare's should miss.[5] Nonetheless, for at least one reviewer, the low status of the plays was unaffected by this clear demonstration of their theatrical power. "Thanks to good performances in the leading roles," the *New York Times* declared, "the productions are effective and surprisingly engaging. . . . [This] is no small feat. There are problems with the plays."⁶ However, none of the "problems" the reviewer proceeds to list holds up under examination. The first two—that the plays contain "few recognizable lines" and that Shakespeare was probably not their sole author—are entirely circular. They rely on the plays' lack of canonical status to explain why they do not deserve that status. The third—that the history depicted in the *Henry VI* plays is inaccurate—is a charge that could be brought against every one of Shakespeare's English history plays, even the most admired.

This is not to say that the reviewer's information is inaccurate—only that it does not justify his low opinion of the play. There is considerable evidence that other playwrights, including Thomas Nashe himself, had a hand in the writing of *Henry VI, Part 1*. The likelihood of multiple authorship is supported by numerous inconsistencies in the only text we have, the one that was published after Shakespeare's death in the First Folio, and also by the fact that at the time the play was written, collaborative authorship was the norm rather than the exception in plays written for the new public, commercial theaters. Moreover, the names of a play's writers often went unrecorded, even on the title pages of printed texts. The reviewer's reliance on sole authorship as a criterion of dramatic merit seems doubly anachronistic, both too modern to reflect the priorities of Shakespeare's first audiences and too old-fashioned to reflect the tastes of current audiences, who are accustomed to seeing both films and television drama that are the products of multiple authors.

Objections to the episodic plot seem equally anachronistic. The chronicle histories that constituted the chief sources for the play's content were organized, as the name "chronicle" implies, by order of time rather than narrative causality, a practice that often resulted in the juxtaposition of events that had no relationship other than chronological coincidence. In addition, sixteenth-century playgoers would have been familiar with numerous dramatic precedents for what looked to post-Shakespearean readers like defective plotting in the *Henry VI* plays, not only in other London commercial plays but also in the traditional dramatizations of biblical history that were performed throughout the country. The neoclassical rule that dramatic action must be unified was known in Shakespeare's time, but it was rarely observed in practice. Sir Philip Sidney, writing at about the same time that the *Henry VI* plays were first produced, cited the failure to observe the dramatic unities as a characteristic defect of the English drama;[7] but very few contemporary playwrights followed his strictures. Playwrights of our own time, ranging from the writers of popular soap operas to the admired authors of elite, avant-garde plays, are similarly indifferent to neoclassical requirements for dramatic unity, which now seem increasingly outdated and inadequate to accommodate the subtleties of postmodern drama.

Whether or not Nashe had a hand in writing *Henry VI, Part 1*, the virtues he found in it provide a useful key to interpretation. Nashe identified the history play as a preserver of "our forefathers' valiant acts" that would otherwise lie buried in "rusty brass and worm-eaten books." In those plays, he wrote, the dead heroes are raised from "the grave of oblivion."[8] Seen in this light, the entire action of *Henry VI, Part 1* can be understood as a series of efforts on the part of the English to preserve the legacy of Henry V against the menaces, both domestic and foreign, that threaten to erase it. At the beginning of *Part 1*, the idealized King Henry V has just died, and the subsequent action shows the death of the chivalric, civic, patriotic, and ethical virtues associated with him—often in the person of members of the older generation, such as Lord Talbot and the dead king's brothers, who exemplify the virtues of that older world. The episodic plot can be explained as a symptom of divided authorship, but it can also be interpreted as the necessary structure for dramatizing a world where authority is likewise divided and problematic. The play has no strong, central character; the young king is powerless to control his unruly nobles, and there is no evidence of a divine providence shaping the outcome of events. In the chaotic world of Henry VI, good intentions are as likely to end in disaster as success. Even the conclusion of the play is open-ended, concluding nothing but simply initiating actions that will be pursued in subsequent plays.

The loss of Henry V's legacy of national unity and heroic conquest is prefigured in the opening scene, when the dead king's funeral is interrupted by quarrels among the nobles and by the arrival of messengers from France. At the point of this interruption, the dead king's brother, the Duke of Bedford, has been attempting to secure Henry's place in heroic history. Invoking Henry's ghost, Bedford declares "A far more glorious star thy soul will make / Than Julius Caesar or bright—" (1.1.56–57). At this point, Bedford's invocation is cut off by the entrance of a messenger, who announces that eight French cities have been lost. With the loss of Henry's French conquests, the messenger laments, half the English coat of arms—the fleur-de-lis that represented England's claim to the French throne—has been "cut away" (1.1.83).

For the characters in the play, as for the playgoers Nashe described, the stakes in the battle for France are explicitly defined as England's place in history. Even the French refer to the history of English heroic conquest. In the second scene, after an English victory at Orleance, Alanson proclaims that the account of English heroism during the time of Edward III, written by the medieval French historian Froissart, has now been "verified" (1.2.29–32). Later in that same scene, when Pucelle arrives at court promising to chase the remaining English from France, she too invokes English history. "Glory," she says, "is like a circle in the water. . . . With Henry's death, the English circle ends" (1.2.136, 139). The French thus fight to erase English heroic history; the English fight to preserve it.

The struggle for Orleance continues. Pucelle momentarily recaptures the city, and then the English hero Talbot retakes it. Having done so, he immediately declares that old Salisbury, who had been killed in the previous battle, will be buried in the city's "chiefest temple." This scene is fictitious, because Salisbury was actually buried in England, but Talbot's determination to bury him in France reiterates what is at stake in the military struggle. In order "that hereafter ages may behold," Talbot says, he will erect a tomb for Salisbury,

> Upon the which, that everyone may read,
> Shall be engraved the sack of Orleance,
> The treacherous manner of his mournful death,
> And what a terror he had been to France.
>
> (2.2.10–17)

The French city will become the site for the inscription of English heroic history.

Earlier, when Pucelle had captured Orleance for the French, the Dauphin declared his intention to celebrate her victory with a monument, but his plans are significantly different from Talbot's. The Dauphin promised to erect for Pucelle "A statelier pyramis . . . / Than Rhodophe's of Memphis ever was" (1.6.21–22); but this monument, unlike the tomb that Talbot plans for Salisbury, will apparently contain no inscription. It is also noteworthy that the prototype of the monument the Dauphin envisions is a pyramid constructed for a Greek courtesan who married an Egyptian king. Here and elsewhere, when the French invoke history, the figures they choose are drawn from a variety of exotic foreign lands. The Dauphin further promises that when Pucelle dies, her ashes will be carried "in an urn more precious / Than the rich-jeweled coffer of Darius" (1.6.24–25), a Persian king. The French Countess of Auvergne declares that if she can capture Talbot, she will be "as famous" as "Scythian Tamyris," who killed Cyrus, another Persian king (2.3.5–6). It is as if the French have no national history of their own.

The French are characterized as opposite to the English in a number of other ways as well, and here too Nashe's claims are suggestive. Talbot, the English hero, exemplifies the aristocratic ideals of chivalric warfare and noble lineage that Nashe associates with a glorious English past. When Talbot is captured, the French initially offer to exchange him for "a baser man-of-arms by far," but Talbot refuses, declaring that he would rather die than be so cheaply valued (1.4.30–33). He will not allow himself to be ransomed until the French agree to exchange him for a brave captive of noble rank. In his defense of stage plays, Nashe castigates their opponents as lacking not only patriotism but also nobility and manhood—two qualities that are exemplified by Talbot but notably lacking in Pucelle. In fact, the play constructs a schematic opposition between the two: Talbot is old, and Pucelle is young; Talbot is a gentleman, Pucelle a peasant. He fights according to the code of chivalry; she resorts to dishonorable stratagems.

Pucelle and the French forces she leads embody the disorderly objects of present fears, the very people and values that Nashe identifies as threatening traditional order. Salisbury's death, which Talbot denounces as an act of treachery, comes at the hands of a French boy sniper. Even at the upper reaches of the social hierarchy, the French have no regard for the chivalric values that animate Talbot. The Dauphin is delighted by the "happy stratagem" (3.2.18) that Pucelle uses to capture Roan: she has disguised herself as the peasant she truly is to enter the city on the pretext that she and the soldiers who accompany her are simply "Poor market folks that come to sell their corn" (3.2.15). The French Countess of Auvergne graciously invites Talbot to visit her castle, but when he arrives, she insults him and treacherously attempts to take him prisoner.

The fact that both Pucelle and the Countess are women is crucial to their identity as opponents to the ideals associated with English heroic history. For Nashe, the sight of "our forefathers" on stage constituted a "reproof to these degenerate, effeminate days of ours."[9] In *Henry VI, Part 1*, the death of Henry V threatens to leave England with "none but women left to wail the dead" (1.1.52). The infant Henry VI turns out to be an ineffectual, effeminate king, and the remaining representatives of heroic English manhood are threatened by enemies who are literally female.

Like Pucelle, the Countess explicitly threatens the historic record of English military glory. It is not simply Talbot that she attempts to destroy: it is also his heroic reputation. When Talbot enters, she mocks,

> Is this the scourge of France?
> Is this the Talbot, so much feared abroad . . . ?
> I see report is fabulous and false.
> I thought I should have seen some Hercules,
> A second Hector, for his grim aspect
> And large proportion of his strong-knit limbs.
> Alas, this is a child, a silly [i.e., feeble] dwarf!

It cannot be this weak and writhled shrimp
Should strike such terror to his enemies.

(2.3.15–24)

Such insults suggest that Talbot's role was originally
assigned to a small actor. In contrast to Nashe's claim
that the sight of heroes like Talbot onstage would inspire the playgoers, the Countess argues that Talbot's
appearance shows that the reports of his remarkable
exploits are "fabulous and false." But she does not have
the last word. "You are deceived," says Talbot: "I am
but shadow of myself" (2.3.52–53). His true "substance, sinews, arms, and strength," he explains, con-
sist of the crowd of English soldiers he immediately
summons to the stage to thwart the Countess's plan to
capture him (2.3.65) and verify the heroic reputation
she has attempted to discredit. The dialogue would
have had a double resonance in Shakespeare's playhouse: the word "shadow" is likely to have reminded
Shakespeare's first audiences that the Talbot they saw
onstage was quite literally a "shadow" of his true self,
since actors were often called "shadows." The French
woman reminds the audience of the inadequacy of the
physical body they see, but the English man speaks for
a heroic history that eludes the testimony of the senses.

Pucelle, like the Countess, also invokes the evidence
of the senses to challenge Talbot's heroic reputation.
Late in the play, Sir William Lucy, not knowing that
Talbot has been killed, looks for him on the battlefield.
He asks the Dauphin,

where's the great Alcides of the field,
Valiant Lord Talbot, Earl of Shrewsbury,
Created for his rare success in arms
Great Earl of Washford, Waterford, and Valence,
Lord Talbot of Goodrich and Urchinfield,
Lord Strange of Blackmere, Lord Verdon of Alton,

Lord Cromwell of Wingfield, Lord Furnival of
  Sheffield,
The thrice victorious Lord of Falconbridge,
Knight of the noble Order of Saint George,
Worthy Saint Michael, and the Golden Fleece,
Great Marshal to Henry the Sixth
Of all his wars within the realm of France?

(4.7.61–73)

Lucy here identifies Talbot by listing the heroic titles
that designate his noble lineage and great military
achievements. It is not the Dauphin who replies but
Pucelle; and, like the Countess, she focuses on Talbot's
body to discredit the idealized history recorded in the
glorious names that Lucy has just recited:

Here's a silly stately style indeed.
The Turk, that two-and-fifty kingdoms hath,
Writes not so tedious a style as this.
Him that thou magnifi'st with all these titles
Stinking and flyblown lies here at our feet.

(4.7.74–78)

Pucelle's vigorous language, based in earthy, material
fact, threatens to topple the imposing formal edifice
that Lucy has erected with his list of titles. Like the
Countess's scornful description of Talbot's diminutive
body, it subjects the proud language of English heroical history to the challenge of a skeptical female voice.
  Shortly thereafter, Pucelle's voice is silenced. After
York captures her in battle, they have a brief dialogue
in which the object of contention is whether Pucelle
will be allowed to speak. First, she curses; York re-
sponds by ordering "hold thy tongue"; Pucelle replies "I
prithee give me leave to curse awhile," but York refuses, leading her offstage instead (5.3.39–44). Pucelle
will appear in only one subsequent scene, and there

she is thoroughly degraded, first denying that she is the daughter of the humble shepherd who has, he says, sought for her far and near, and then attempting to evade execution by a series of frantic, futile, self-contradictory lies. Instead of discrediting English historical mythmaking, Pucelle's speech now serves only to discredit herself, reducing her to the object of her English captors'—and the playgoers'—ridicule.

Nonetheless, the play does not end happily for the English. No sooner does York lead Pucelle from the stage than Suffolk enters with another French woman in hand. Suffolk's captive is Margaret of Anjou, soon to become the treacherous queen of Henry VI and to prove, in the subsequent plays that depict the remainder of Henry's reign, a much more serious threat to the preservation of English heroic history than Pucelle or the Countess. As the Duke of Gloucester foretells, the marriage between Henry and Margaret will be "fatal" to the English nobility, "cancelling" their "fame," "blotting" their "names from books of memory," "razing" the records of their "renown," "Defacing monuments of conquered France," and "Undoing all, as [if] all had never been" (*Henry VI, Part 2* 1.1.104–08). *Henry VI, Part 1* initiates that lengthy process of undoing. For readers and playgoers who prefer happy, triumphant endings, it has long proved a disappointment. But now, at the beginning of the twenty-first century, when triumphant conclusions no longer seem so convincing, the play may well be due for a major revival.

---

1. Thomas Nashe, *Pierce Penilesse his Supplication to the Divell* (London, 1592), sig. H2r.

2. Maurice Morgann, *An Essay on the Dramatic Character of Sir John Falstaff* (London, 1777), pp. 49–50.

3. Quoted in David Bevington, "The *Henry VI* Plays in Performance," in *Henry VI, Parts One, Two, and Three,* by Shakespeare (New York: Bantam Books, 1988), p. xxv.

4. *Notes and Lectures upon Shakespeare and Some of the Old Poets and Dramatists with Other Literary Remains of S. T. Coleridge,* ed. Mrs. H. N. Coleridge (London: William Pickering, 1849), 1:187.

5. Clive Barnes, "Troupe's 'Henry VI' Fit for a King," *New York Post,* March 8, 1995; Thomas M. Disch, "Regarding 'Henry'—Highly," *Daily News,* March 7, 1995.

6. Wilborn Hampton, "3 into 2: History Plays Rearranged," *New York Times,* March 7, 1995.

7. Sir Philip Sidney, *An Apology for Poetry* (London, 1595), sigs. I4v–K1r.

8. Nashe, *Pierce Penilesse,* sig. H2r.

9. Ibid.

Further Reading

Henry VI, Part 1

Abbreviations: *Ado* = *Much Ado about Nothing;*
AYLI = *As You Like It; Cym.* = *Cymbeline;*
1H6 = *Henry VI, Part 1; 2H6* = *Henry VI, Part 2;*
3H6 = *Henry VI, Part 3; John* = *King John;*
JC = *Julius Caesar; Mac.* = *Macbeth;*
MM = *Measure for Measure;*
R2 = *Richard II; R3* = *Richard III;*
RSC = The Royal Shakespeare Company;
TN = *Twelfth Night*

Berry, Edward I. "*1 Henry VI*: Chivalry and Ceremony."
In *Patterns of Decay: Shakespeare's Early Histories,*
pp. 1–28. Charlottesville: University Press of Virginia,
1975.
   Berry argues that a central theme throughout the
first tetralogy is a pattern of dissolution and decay. In
1H6, it takes the form of social disintegration as man-
ifested in the breakdown of ceremony and ritual. The
chapter focuses on the meeting between Talbot and
the Countess of Auvergne (2.3), a scene that articu-
lates through Talbot an ideal of chivalric community
rooted in ritualism that is elsewhere parodied by Joan
la Pucelle's "colloquial vigor and irreverence." For
Berry, it is not simply "the motif of the interrupted
ceremony" (Hereward T. Price's phrase)—first seen in

the aborted funeral rites of Henry V (1.1)—that unifies the play at its deepest level but "the idea of ceremony itself," which serves as "both theme and mode of dramatic action." As the structural rhythm alternates between indecisive battles abroad and social disorder at home, "each communal gathering becomes increasingly divisive" until broken ceremonies break Talbot, the man who embodies ceremony. In *1H6*, the concept of ceremony "serves as a static ideal against which the process of social decay is measured." In the remaining three plays, that decay is explored in terms of justice and law (*2H6*), the family (*3H6*), and finally the self (*R3*).

Bevington, David. "*1 Henry VI.*" In *A Companion to Shakespeare's Works*, edited by Richard Dutton and Jean E. Howard, 2:308–24. Malden, Mass.: Blackwell, 2003.

In his review of the play's scholarship, Bevington notes how the pendulum on the vexed issues of authorship and chronology, which first began to swing from theories of disintegration in the nineteenth century to claims of unity and coherence in the twentieth, seems to be moving back to theories of multiple authorship (e.g., Nashe, Greene, and Peele) and a comparatively late date (i.e., one following the composition of *Part 2* and *3*). The survey begins with the topics of authorship and compositional date because of their relevance to "the central issue of the play's unity and integrity." Is *1H6* "a jumble of fragmented pieces, written in a distracting medley of styles," or is it a cohesive whole? Bevington concludes that increasingly the critical tendency favors coherence, whether in terms of characters (chiefly Talbot and Joan), imagery (specifically patterns involving enclosure, birds in flight, and all sorts of predatory vs. weaker animals), or style (epic, ceremonial, emblematic). Critics have found a unified design in the play's treatment of gender and family, in its reflection of contemporary attitudes toward witchcraft and the demoniacal, and in its rhetoric. Some have used staging to argue for a kind of theatrical coherence. Where E. M. W. Tillyard and his followers emphasize the "Tudor myth" and providential history, anti-Tillyardians point to the undercutting of order, justice, and moral equity in the plays, to pervasive bad luck, and to death as "wanton" rather than "divinely retributive." David Scott Kastan brings a welcome balance to this particular debate with his observation that "providentialism" is present but "as a model of historical causation to be probed and challenged." As a result of the anti-Tillyard corrective, critics opting for integrity of design seek it in themes of disorder, confusion, decay, and social disintegration. The ultimate verdict on the interrelated questions of authorship and aesthetic quality remains to be decided; but "[c]ertainly the debate adds materially to our interest in the play."

Blanpied, John W. *"Henry VI, Part One:* 'Defacing monuments of conquered France.'" In *Time and the Artist in Shakespeare's English Histories,* pp. 26–41. Newark: University of Delaware Press; Toronto: Associated University Presses, 1983. (The chapter is a revision of the essay "Art and Baleful Sorcery: The Counterconsciousness of *Henry VI, Part 1," Studies in English Literature* 15 [1975]: 213–27.)

In his metatheatrical study of *1H6,* Blanpied contends that the confusion and roughness intrinsic to the play reveal a record of the discoveries Shakespeare made about the instability of both the chronicle material he was dramatizing and drama itself, a form that is "fluid, active, temporal." The author claims that the intentional design of *Part 1*, which deals with the decline and fall of England's heroic past, can be found in a "counterconsciousness" and pervasive irony in the face of what spectators and readers experience as a "collapse of order and ceremony." Throughout the play, the authoritative power of the "monumental past" is undermined by the playwright's assertion of "those theatrical techniques [e.g., broad morality-type characters, a persistent declamatory style, and minimal narrative linkage] that seem designed to dignify it." As a result of such theatrical subversion, "everything straightforward and sturdy turns doubtful and inconclusive." Three scenes, 2.3, 2.4, and 2.5—none bound by chronicle matter and conventional styles—show where Shakespeare's interest really lay and thus hold the seeds of his future development as a playwright. In them, we can glimpse the playwright's desire "to show a reality elsewhere in the future—a future that is not merely to be suffered passively, but is to be actively created: made drama." Subjected to the pressures of Shakespeare's dramatizing imagination, the "ground" of the play's monumental, heroic past dissolves and "melts into a kind of dream of the waking present . . . . Stability is always in the past, it seems; the present is always the awareness of falling through space."

Burckhardt, Sigurd. "'I Am But Shadow of Myself': Ceremony and Design in *Henry 6, Part 1.*" *Modern Language Quarterly* 28 (1967): 139–58. Reprinted in *Shakespearean Meanings*, pp. 42–77. Princeton: Princeton University Press, 1968.

Burckhardt assumes that the Folio text of *1H6* represents Shakespeare's deliberate effort to shape his source material into a coherent whole. He addresses the issue of dramatic integrity by examining 2.3, a scene that appears "irretrievably episodic" but that, through its depiction of the "real" Talbot, shows us the "real" play. In keeping with *1H6*'s pattern of interrupted ceremonies, the Talbot-Countess encounter is "a *ceremony* [that of the taunt] . . . startlingly interrupted." The Countess's rhetoric, like the general mode of the play, is given to "'high terms' ceremonially put forward and ceremonially responded to," to hyperbolic self-assertion, and to a style that is "impatient of indirection." The surprise is that Talbot rejects "the verbal gauntlet" in favor of "ironic urbanity," implicit counterplotting, and generous forgiveness, thereby refusing to play his expected "ceremonial" role in the exchange. For a brief moment, Talbot abandons his usual combative self-assertion as "hero" for gracious self-effacement (2.3.62–68) as "servant" in the larger cause of England, his substance lying in the "sinews, arms, and strength" of common, nameless Englishmen and "in the overall design [that begins with the turmoil in the reign of Richard II and ends with the restoration of order under Henry VII] in which they are made to act." What the Auvergne episode proves is that the real hero of the play is not Talbot but the heroine England. Rather than finding the human analogue to God in an earthly king—the correspondence posited in the traditional Elizabethan world picture—Shakespeare, in writing this scene, discovers a new analogy: God as a dramatist who "planned, designed, plotted, employed stratagems, [who] . . . worked by indirection and implication[,] . . . [and who] . . . wrote histories which, though on the surface they might look like savage spectacles, moved in truth by careful plotting toward an ordered conclusion." As the vehicle by which drama triumphs over ceremony, self-effacement over self-assertion, and the implicit over the explicit, Talbot becomes "the sovereign plotter" who has mastered the style and plotting of his divine counterpart.

Harris, Laurie Lanzen, and Mark W. Scott, eds. *Shakespearean Criticism: Excerpts from the Criticism of William Shakespeare's Plays and Poetry from the First Published Appraisals to Current Evaluations*, 3:11–164. Detroit: Gale Research, 1986.

This volume presents significant passages from published criticism on the three parts of *H6*. The set of passages is introduced by a brief discussion of the "date," "text," and "sources," followed by a longer discussion of the "critical history" of the plays. Each entry, beginning with Robert Greene's *Groatsworth of Wit* (1592) and ending with Marilyn French's *Shakespeare's Division of Experience* (1981), is prefaced with a brief historical overview that places the excerpted document in the context of responses to the play. Of the almost sixty entries, early commentary derives from Thomas Nashe (1592), John Crowne (1681), Gerard Langbaine (1691), and such eighteenth-century editors as Nicholas Rowe, Lewis Theobald, Edward Capell, Samuel Johnson, and Edmond Malone; nineteenth-century critics are represented by such figures as William Hazlitt, Samuel Taylor Coleridge, Hermann Ulrici, and Georg Gottfried Gervinus; entries from the twentieth century include excerpts from the writings of Carolyn Spurgeon, E. M. W. Tillyard, Hereward Price, Wolfgang Clemen, Muriel C. Bradbrook, Harold Goddard, David Bevington, Irving Ribner, Robert Ornstein, Michael Manheim, John Cox, and Larry Champion. A briefly annotated bibliography of fifty-five additional items concludes the section. A subsequent volume, edited by Michele Lee (2002), updates the criticism through the 1990s under such headings as

"Character Study," *"Henry VI* as Comedy," "Playing with History," and "Unity and Design" (63:113–218).

Hodgdon, Barbara. "Enclosing Contention: *1, 2,* and *3 Henry VI."* In *The End Crowns All: Closure and Contradiction in Shakespeare's History,* pp. 44–99. Princeton: Princeton University Press, 1991.

Combining performance criticism (mostly of RSC productions) with study of the play-texts, Hodgdon explores "closural strategies" in the three parts of *H6.* In the commentary specifically devoted to *1H6* (pp. 54–59), she draws heavily on Leah Marcus's discussion of the provocative nexus (i.e., the composite sexual identity of the manly woman) linking Joan la Pucelle and Queen Elizabeth I (see entry below) to demonstrate how, contrary to critical tradition dating back to Thomas Nashe, *1H6* is "less the 'Talbot play' . . . than a 'Joan versus Talbot play,'" an opposition central to the text's narrative dynamic, to its displacement of early modern anxieties concerning female dominance, and to its "troubling, less than triumphant, and formally problematic close." On the level of history, the war pits one nation against another in an international conflict. But because Joan functions "as a spectacular . . . site of gender display," and thus condenses contemporary skepticism concerning the queen's "claims to anomalous gender identity," at the level of dramatic representation the international war becomes "a battle for the ownership of masculine gender." The play's most "authoritatively conclusive scene"—Winchester's mandating the terms of the peace treaty whereby the French promise allegiance to the English crown (5.4)— seems to underscore male dominance. But three features demonstrate its "contaminat[ion] by gender": (1) the deflection of attention away from the ritual of the negotiations to the imagined offstage burning of Joan, (2) York's phrase "effeminate peace" (5.4.108), and (3) Lucy's earlier prophecy (4.7.95–96) of a phoenix rising from the ashes to threaten France (a mystically regenerative image associated with Elizabeth). The final scene may suggest a "fugitive" gloss in the reference to Henry's future queen (5.5.70–71), who recalls the unruly Joan and, for some audience members, the "misrule" of Elizabeth herself. That gloss is ultimately suspended, however, as the play ends with a decidedly male fantasy and a reassertion of male dominance in Suffolk's prediction of his future rule over the new Queen Margaret, the king, and the realm itself (5.5.107–8). Later in the chapter, Hodgdon discusses the play's stage life, especially its closing scenes, as performed in John Barton and Peter Hall's *The Wars of the Roses* (RSC, 1963), Terry Hands's "(relatively) uncut and unadapted" revival of the complete *H6* trilogy (RSC, 1977), Michael Bogdonov's *The Wars of the Roses* (English Shakespeare Company, 1988), and Adrian Noble's *The Plantagenets* (RSC, 1988).

Howard, Jean. "Stage Masculinities, National History, and the Making of London Theatrical Culture." In *Center or Margin: Revisions of the English Renaissance in Honor of Leeds Barroll*, edited by Lena Cowen Orlin, pp. 199–214. Selingsgrove, Pa.: Susquehanna University Press; London: Associated University Presses, 2006.

Howard relates the performance of early modern gender roles to the role of theater in early modern culture to argue that in writing the first tetralogy, Shakespeare not only was exploring "the dynamics of civil war and the chaos occasioned by a weak king" but was also "experimenting with stagecraft, with the business of making good plays." Howard's particular focus concerns strategies the dramatist devised for delineating different "styles of stageable masculinity" as he wrote for a particular acting company composed only of male actors, whose physical attributes would be well known to him; at a time when the theatrical practice of doubling was a necessity; and in a genre—the history play—wherein male characters "wildly outnumber" women characters. One of the chief tasks the dramatist faced in differentiating one man from another was how to "create interesting fits" between the male role and the male actor called on to impersonate the character. In *1H6*, the king's "feckless masculinity" contrasts with the "chivalric masculinity" of Talbot and with the "masculinity of modernity" projected by the self-serving courtier Suffolk.

Howard, Jean, and Phyllis Rackin. *"Henry VI, Part 1."* In *Engendering a Nation: A Feminist Account of Shakespeare's English Histories*, pp. 43–64. London: Routledge, 1997.

The chapter appears as part of a section dealing with "weak kings, warrior women, and the assault on dynastic authority." The women in the histories play many roles but never that of protagonist, probably because in the aristocratic world of this genre "patriarchal domination is assumed and female characters marginalized." Even when women enter the battlefield—"the privileged scene of heroic history"—as Joan and Margaret do in the *H6* plays and Eleanor does in *John*, their usurpation of masculine prerogatives "always [runs] the risk of stigmatization." This is especially true of Joan, the most powerful of the three female warriors, who is also depicted as "the most demonic." Howard and Rackin relate the "alien" nature of women in the English histories to residual and emergent versions of national identity. The older model—feudal and

dynastic—is privileged in *1H6*, where "hereditary enti-
tlement authorizes English claims to France, while the
newer discourse of the nation [as defined geographi-
cally rather than dynastically] is associated with
French resistance and a form of subversion that is gendered feminine." When Joan, for example, persuades
Burgundy to join her troops, she appeals to his loyalty
to the French land (3.3.44–57); the English nobles,
however, are appalled by his disloyalty to his nephew,
the English king (4.1.50–54, 62–66). The authors also
connect the marginalized status of women in English
historiography to English antitheatrical invective,
which condemned the "disreputable feminized world
of the playhouse," where boys wore female costumes
and women were a "contaminating presence" in the
audience. In *1H6*, the leader of the French forces is not
only female but also "insistently theatrical" as both an
energetic, memorable stage presence and the embodiment of vices that polemicists associated with the theater. Idealized in heroic terms, the past in *1H6*
becomes "the repository of English honor, and its loss
is defined as a process of effeminization. . . . The entire
play can be seen as a series of attempts on the part of
the English to preserve [Henry V's] fame, along with
the fame of English martial heroes, and with them the
manhood of the English nation."

Jackson, Gabriele Bernard. "Topical Ideology: Witches,
Amazons, and Shakespeare's Joan of Arc." *ELR 18*
(1988): 40–65. Reprinted in *Shakespeare and Gender: A
History*, edited by Deborah E. Barker and Ivo Kamps,
pp. 142–67. London: Verso, 1995.

   In this influential topical analysis of *1H6*, Jackson
neither condemns Shakespeare's misogyny nor defends
him against that charge but rather argues that "the
play's presentation of Joan la Pucelle, like its dominant

ideology, is not clear-cut." The initial portrait as suggested by allusions connecting her to biblical, classical, and mythological figures (e.g., Deborah [1.2.107], Astraea's daughter [1.6.4], and Amazons [1.2.106]) is positive. But because her victory over the English must inevitably be seen in a negative light, the representation worsens in Act 5, where she becomes associated with witchcraft and sexual promiscuity. In the late sixteenth century, fascination with the virago type coexisted with the need to neutralize her power by feminizing her, something seen in Joan's terrified attempts to thwart death and in her claims of pregnancy. The contradictory presentation of Joan in *1H6*—"one man's Sibyl is another man's Hecate"—draws on several topically relevant and interrelated roles: the Amazon, the warrior woman, the cross-dressing woman, and the witch. Such contextual variety permits her "to perform in one play inconsistent ideological functions that go much beyond discrediting the French cause or setting off by contrast the glories of English chivalry in its dying moments." Like Leah Marcus (see below), Jackson calls attention to similarities between Joan and Queen Elizabeth I, which can be read in a variety of ways that make it unclear whether topical criticism is intended. As another example of topical linkage fraught with ambiguity, Jackson cites Talbot and the Earl of Essex, who in 1591–92 had embarked on a controversial French campaign to besiege Rouen. "The coexistence of ideologically opposed elements is typical of the play's dramatic nature, and foreshadows the mature Shakespeare."

Leggatt, Alexander. "The Death of John Talbot." In *Shakespeare's English Histories: A Quest for Form and Genre,* edited by John W. Velz, pp. 11–30. Binghamton, N.Y.: Medieval and Renaissance Texts and Studies, 1996.

The scene depicting the death of Lord Talbot (4.7) reveals a critical moment in Shakespeare's artistic development that "reverberates" not only through *Part 2* and *3* of the *H6* trilogy but also through the dramatist's later tragedies. What is often overlooked, and what is most significant about the scene, is that "it involves the death of not one hero but two," Talbot and his son John. Like young Cato in *JC* and young Siward in *Mac.*, John Talbot is the son of a famous father and seemingly "born only to die"; but unlike those sons, John mirrors his father in being "held up for contemplation." The result of fusing the individual tragedies of two heroes—Shakespeare seems determined to show death as a rite of passage suffered both alone and together—is a sequence that reveals a conception of tragedy as deriving from "the most intimate relations, the most normal passages of life: the need for love, the demands of loyalty and piety, the turmoil of sexual awakening, the need to prove oneself at any cost." As Shakespeare's "first exploration of that kind of tragedy," the Talbot death scene prefigures such later images as the dead Romeo and Juliet lying together and the hanged Cordelia cradled by Lear.

Levine, Nina S. "The Politics of Chivalry in *1 Henry VI*." In *Women's Matters: Politics, Gender, and Nation in Shakespeare's Early History Plays*, pp. 26–46. Newark: University of Delaware Press; London: Associated University Presses, 1998.

While Shakespeare's early histories (*1*, *2*, and *3H6*; *R3*; and *John*) rewrite the Tudor chronicle record so as to acknowledge the importance of women in ensuring patrilineal succession, Levine contends that they also "generate a critique of patrilineal inheritance and legitimacy" that speaks to the Elizabethan present in which the plays are "situated." The author is especially interested in how the *H6* trilogy uses political contexts— "both on- and offstage"—to frame and qualify negative stereotypes of women. The chapter on *1H6* examines the confrontations between Joan la Pucelle and England's heroic warriors "in relation to both Hall's chronicle and to the chivalric fictions of the Elizabethan court . . . to argue that the play points out the limitations of a national identity grounded in gendered oppositions." Levine uses the Accession Day tilting ceremonies, in particular, to better understand Shakespeare's representation of the nation-state in the play. Like these yearly rituals, which allowed the queen and nobility to come together to negotiate long-standing conflicts of power and privilege, *1H6* "rewrites medieval myths of chivalry for the Elizabethan present." But instead of refurbishing the past in an attempt to accommodate chivalric fictions, the play presents a story of loss and division that underscores the very tensions the court sought to control. Levine notes how at the time Shakespeare was writing the *H6* plays, decorous chivalry at the annual tilts was giving way to more militaristic, aggressive displays of masculine courtier power. "Qualifying the authority of both aristocratic males and the ruling female, [*1H6*] endorses no alternative to the double bind of contemporary gender politics. . . . In the absence of a positive, and clearly defined, model of authority, we must locate the play's politics in its double critique of ruling women and self-interested aristocratic warriors."

Marcus, Leah. "Elizabeth." In *Puzzling Shakespeare: Local Reading and Its Discontents*, pp. 51–105. Berkeley: University of California Press, 1988.

In this frequently cited "local" (i.e., topical) reading of Shakespeare through the "lens of sixteenth- and early seventeenth-century events, gossip, [and] personalities," Marcus provides chapter-length studies of *1H6, Cym.,* and *MM.* The chapter on *1H6,* titled "Eliza-beth," deals with the play under the subheadings "The Queen's Two Bodies," "Astraea's Daughter," "Ritual Burning," and "Speculations and Ramifications: Relo-cating 'monstrous regiment.'" Marcus contends that the play's many parallels between the character Joan la Pucelle and the historical Queen Elizabeth I are pre-sented so insistently as to argue a "deliberate strategy"; the result is a subversive meaning that counters the traditionally privileged patriarchal patriotism associ-ated with Talbot. The most important parallel—the "composite identity" of a woman who "acts like a man" and who, consequently, "arouses male anxieties about female dominance"—is evidenced in Joan's male attire and martial bearing and in Elizabeth's use of armor and manly rhetoric in her famous Armada speech be-fore the troops at Tilbury in 1588. Throughout her reign, the queen appropriated the term "prince" to con-struct a manly identity in her vocabulary and sanc-tioned portraits: like all kings she had two bodies, but in her case the public one was male, the private female. The airing and displacing of "suppressed cultural anxi-eties about the Virgin Queen" onto the character of the enemy Joan transforms a post-Armada play into a potentially subversive triumph of English warriors over the ultimate "unruly woman." In *1H6,* "[i]t is as though despising female dominance is a necessary part of being male, English, and 'Protestant.'" But, as Marcus emphasizes, since the parallels are "half-formed . . . [and] equivocal," Shakespeare's intention is ultimately "unreadable because it can be read in too many different ways," a point she illustrates by exam-ining the idol/witch burning ordered by the queen her-self while visiting the home of a Catholic aristocrat in Norwich—an event that resembles the ritual burning of Joan in *1H6*. In light of such events, the "potential for subversion is at least partially defused."

Pendleton, Thomas A., ed. *Henry VI: Critical Essays.* Shakespeare Criticism Series. New York: Routledge, 2001.

The volume's fourteen original essays include two that focus solely on *1H6*: James J. Paxson's "Shakespeare's Medieval Devils and Joan la Pucelle in *1 HVI*: Semiotics, Iconography, and Feminist Criticism" (pp. 127–55), and J. J. M. Tobin's "A Touch of Greene, Much Nashe, and All Shakespeare" (pp. 39–56). Several essays deal in part with the play: Harry Keyishian's "The Progress of Revenge in the First Henriad" (pp. 67–77), Naomi C. Liebler and Lisa Scancella Shea's "Shakespeare's Queen Margaret: Unruly or Unruled?" (pp. 79–96), Nina da Vinci Nichols's "The Paper Trail to the Throne" (pp. 97–112), Frances K. Barasch's "Folk Magic in *HVI, Parts 1* and *2:* Two Scenes of Embedding" (pp. 113–25), Yoshio Arai's essay on the *H6* trilogy in Japan (pp. 57–66), and Irene Dash's "*Henry VI* and the Art of Illustration" (pp. 253–71). The volume also contains several essays on performance: Thomas A. Pendleton's "Talking with York: A Conversation with Steven Skybell" (Duke of York in Karin Coonrod's production) (pp. 219–34), H. R. Coursen's "Theme and Design in Recent Productions of *Henry VI*" (with the emphasis on Michael Kahn's and Karin Coonrod's revivals in 1996) (pp. 205–18), and Patricia Lennox's "*Henry VI:* A Television History in Four Parts" (Peter Dews's *An Age of Kings* in 1960, Peter Hall and John Barton's *Wars of the Roses* in 1965, Jane Howell's BBC revival in 1983, and Michael Bogdanov and Michael Pennington's *Wars of the Roses* in 1988) (pp. 235–52). Pendleton's introduction provides an overview of the scholarship, especially as it relates to issues of text, authorship, date, sequence, relationship of the plays as parts of a tetralogy, and critical assessment. Much attention is paid to the providentialist views of Tillyard (*Shakespeare's History Plays*, 1944), who has served "both as stimulant and irritant" and thus "has had an enormous effect" on the criticism of the *H6* trilogy. The past fifty years have seen scholarly interest move beyond questions of text and authorship; as a result, the three parts of *H6* are now discussed and appreciated more than at any time since they were first performed.

Rackin, Phyllis. "Patriarchal History and Female Subversion." In *Stages of History: Shakespeare's English Chronicles*, pp. 146–200. Ithaca: Cornell University Press, 1990. (The chapter incorporates portions of "Anti-Historians: Women's Roles in Shakespeare's Histories," *Theatre Journal* 37 [1985]: 329–44.)

Rackin describes Renaissance historiography as a male enterprise, written by men to glorify masculine heroism; the goal was to preserve the names of past heroes and record their patriarchal genealogies. Within such a record, "women had no voice." In Shakespeare's histories, women "can threaten or validate the men's historical projects, but they can never take the center of history's stage or become the subjects of its stories." However, Shakespeare does give them a voice to "challenge . . . the logocentric, masculine historical record." Rackin begins her examination of women as "anti-historians" in the patriarchal world of the histories by looking closely at *1H6* (discussed on pp. 148–57, 197–200), where the "pattern of masculine history-writing and feminine subversion can be seen in its simplest terms." By emphasizing the antagonism between Talbot, the English champion, and Joan, his French female adversary, Shakespeare defines the conflict between England and France in terms of mascu-

line and feminine values: "chivalric virtue versus prag-
matic craft, historical fame versus physical reality, patriarchal age versus subversive youth, high social rank
versus low, self versus other." The scenes involving Talbot and his son (4.5, 6, and 7) and Joan's final exit
(5.4), along with Lucy's litany of Talbot's many titles
(4.7.61–73) and Joan's debunking of them (4.7.74–78),
illustrate Rackin's (male) historian versus (female)
anti-historian thesis. Two other women in the play—
the Countess of Auvergne and Margaret of Anjou—
also threaten the values of English patriarchal history.
Like Joan, the Countess is a nominalist, who, in her
desire to confront Talbot, values physical evidence
over historical report. The link between Joan and Margaret has to do with sexual transgression: Joan's
promiscuity and Margaret's future adultery, which is
foreshadowed in Act 5. Although her adulterous relationship with Suffolk has no real impact on the action
of the *H6* plays, it does underscore the fact that legitimacy of the bloodline, so essential to patriarchal authority, depended on the woman's word concerning
paternity: an adulterous woman makes a mockery of
patriarchal succession and thus threatens the masculine historical project. Shakespeare will develop this
type of female subversion more fully in *John*. In *1H6*,
"the subversive female voice . . . prevail[s] for only a
moment," ultimately being contained by the values
and impulses of patriarchal ideology.

Riggs, David. "The Hero in History: A Reading of *Henry
VI.*" In *Shakespeare's Heroical Histories: Henry VI and
Its Literary Tradition*, pp. 93–139. London: Oxford Uni-
versity Press, 1971.

Riggs's analysis of the three parts of *H6* within the
context of exemplary history and heroic drama (as
defined by Marlowe's *Tamburlaine*) leads him to

conclude that the trilogy is crucial to Shakespeare's developing conception of the history play as a dialectic between heroic ideals and ethical and political realities. In his anti-Tillyardian reading, the *H6* plays become "an extended meditation on the decline of heroic idealism between the Hundred Years War and the Yorkist accession." *1 Henry VI* (discussed on pp. 100–113) recasts the latter part of that war as "an exercise in 'parallel lives'"—specifically Talbot's and Joan's, the latter an "extended parody" of the chivalric ideal epitomized by Talbot. The chief contrast of legitimacy versus bastardy plays out in a rhetorical structure conducive to a comparison of the two characters in ethical terms. Both the elder and younger Talbot construe the doctrine of the family name as a timeless dynastic possession to be transmitted from father to son "so literally that valor becomes. . . a test of legitimacy" (see 4.6.50–51). If one of the privileges accompanying "gentle birth" (in both the fifteenth and sixteenth centuries) is the right to bear arms, then "the stain of illegitimacy is presumptive evidence of someone's unworthiness" to do so. This ethical failing is underscored in Joan, whose "shameful" military tactics reveal "the baseness of her origins" and whose final scene before being led off to execution (5.4) "brings to light the fact that she lacks any family name to augment and transmit," thus providing an "ironic counterstatement" to the deaths of the chivalric father and son. In the subplot dealing with domestic factions, "the epic warrior gives way to the fashionable courtier" illustrated by Somerset and York, examples of natural nobility "diverted to trivial ends." "The crowning irony" of *1H6* is that Somerset's and York's trivial sense of honor (as evidenced by the hollow ring of their appeals to family heritage) is more disastrous to Talbot and his ideals than all of the base policy devised by the enemy abroad.

Saccio, Peter. "Henry VI: The Loss of Empire." Chapter 5 in *Shakespeare's English Kings: History, Chronicle and Drama*, pp. 91–113. 2nd ed. London: Oxford University Press, 2000.
The chapter on *1H6* is divided into three parts. The first provides a brief introduction to the trilogy as a whole; the second addresses the end of the Hundred Years War between England and France; and the third discusses Shakespeare's "radical simplification of the narrative" found in Hall and Holinshed. *1H6*, which covers the years 1422–44, deals with the loss of England's French territory; its chief antagonists are the English hero Lord Talbot and the French heroine Joan la Pucelle. "Instead of merely selecting and shaping [the historical narrative, as he does in *R2*], Shakespeare chops the whole story into little pieces, eliminates a large number of them, and rebuilds the remainder into a structure bearing very little resemblance to the original historical sequence. . . . [T]he [resulting] dramatic narrative is analytic rather than historical." The changes made in chronology and episodes, and the unhistorical causal linkage of disparate events, show *"how* France was lost . . . [through] English internal divisiveness and the extraordinary influence of scheming Frenchwomen." Examples of Shakespeare's dramatic license include the following: the telescoping of disasters reported in 1.1; the mingling of events in Act 5 with the capture and execution of Joan (which occurred a decade earlier); an emphasis on Talbot's heroism at the expense of Salisbury's and Bedford's; the decision to make John Talbot younger than he actually was and the only child of his father; the depiction of English civil

dissension as the cause of Talbot's defeat and death; and the turning of Suffolk's motivation for arranging the betrothal between Henry and Margaret into "a full-blown Shakespearean elaboration of a mere hint in Hall." Despite the unwieldy material and the "negative or untraceable character" of Henry VI, the plays themselves, though lacking the poetic and psychological complexity of the later histories, are "sinewy and vigorous" and continue to prove compelling when staged.

Walsh, Brian. "'Unkind division': The Double Absence of Performing History in *1 Henry VI.*" *Shakespeare Quarterly* 55 (2004): 119–47.

Walsh contends that *1H6* deserves attention as "a vehicle for exploring the provocative play of pastness on the late Elizabethan stage." An early reflection on the history genre, *Part 1* characterizes history and performance "as fraught, mutually destabilizing concepts," similar in their shared "reliance on referring." The referent in each case is "dubious and unstable," since neither historiography nor performance can ever objectively render the past "as it really was." This "joint destabilization" is most apparent in the rhetoric of succession as it engages biological, political, and cultural issues. Throughout *1H6*, where the idea of loss is central, we find a breakdown in both lineal succession (as a way of structuring historical narrative) and performance (as a form of presenting the past) that frustrates notions of continuity between the present and the past. The play "proposes that to perform history in the Elizabethan popular theater is not to render the past more accessible but to stage a confrontation with the past's elusiveness that is both troubling and teeming with possibility." The essay pays special attention to Talbot, who is "particularly equivocal about issues of presence and public display"; to factionalism, which not only signals and causes

England's ruin but is also "a dramatic method of introducing contested histories"; and to the ending, with its "precarious" victory over the French.

Shakespeare's Language

Abbott, E. A. *A Shakespearian Grammar.* New York: Haskell House, 1972.
This compact reference book, first published in 1870, helps with many difficulties in Shakespeare's language. It systematically accounts for a host of differences between Shakespeare's usage and sentence structure and our own.

Blake, Norman. *Shakespeare's Language: An Introduction.* New York: St. Martin's Press, 1983.
This general introduction to Elizabethan English discusses various aspects of the language of Shakespeare and his contemporaries, offering possible meanings for hundreds of ambiguous constructions.

Dobson, E. J. *English Pronunciation, 1500–1700.* 2 vols. Oxford: Clarendon Press, 1968.
This long and technical work includes chapters on spelling (and its reformation), phonetics, stressed vowels, and consonants in early modern English.

Hope, Jonathan. *Shakespeare's Grammar.* London: Arden Shakespeare, 2003.
Commissioned as a replacement for Abbott's *Shakespearian Grammar,* Hope's book is organized in terms of the two basic parts of speech, the noun and the verb. After extensive analysis of the noun phrase and the

verb phrase come briefer discussions of subjects and agents, objects, complements, and adverbials.

Houston, John. *Shakespearean Sentences: A Study in Style and Syntax.* Baton Rouge: Louisiana State University Press, 1988.

Houston studies Shakespeare's stylistic choices, considering matters such as sentence length and the relative positions of subject, verb, and direct object. Examining plays throughout the canon in a roughly chronological, developmental order, he analyzes how sentence structure is used in setting tone, in characterization, and for other dramatic purposes.

Onions, C. T. *A Shakespeare Glossary.* Oxford: Clarendon Press, 1986.

This revised edition updates Onions's standard, selective glossary of words and phrases in Shakespeare's plays that are now obsolete, archaic, or obscure.

Robinson, Randal. *Unlocking Shakespeare's Language: Help for the Teacher and Student.* Urbana, Ill.: National Council of Teachers of English and the ERIC Clearinghouse on Reading and Communication Skills, 1989.

Specifically designed for the high-school and undergraduate college teacher and student, Robinson's book addresses the problems that most often hinder present-day readers of Shakespeare. Through work with his own students, Robinson found that many readers today are particularly puzzled by such stylistic devices as subject-verb inversion, interrupted structures, and compression. He shows how our own colloquial language contains comparable structures, and thus helps students recognize such structures when they find them in Shakespeare's plays. This book supplies worksheets—with examples from major plays—to illuminate and remedy such problems as unusual sequences of words and the separation of related parts of sentences.

Williams, Gordon. *A Dictionary of Sexual Language and Imagery in Shakespearean and Stuart Literature.* 3 vols. London: Athlone Press, 1994.

Williams provides a comprehensive list of the words to which Shakespeare, his contemporaries, and later Stuart writers gave sexual meanings. He supports his identification of these meanings by extensive quotations.

Shakespeare's Life

Baldwin, T. W. *William Shakspere's Petty School.* Urbana: University of Illinois Press, 1943.

Baldwin here investigates the theory and practice of the petty school, the first level of education in Elizabethan England. He focuses on that educational system primarily as it is reflected in Shakespeare's art.

Baldwin, T. W. *William Shakspere's Small Latine and Lesse Greeke.* 2 vols. Urbana: University of Illinois Press, 1944.

Baldwin attacks the view that Shakespeare was an uneducated genius—a view that had been dominant among Shakespeareans since the eighteenth century. Instead, Baldwin shows, the educational system of Shakespeare's time would have given the playwright a strong background in the classics, and there is much in the plays that shows how Shakespeare benefited from such an education.

Beier, A. L., and Roger Finlay, eds. *London 1500–1700: The Making of the Metropolis.* New York: Longman, 1986.

Focusing on the economic and social history of early modern London, these collected essays probe aspects of metropolitan life, including "Population and Disease," "Commerce and Manufacture," and "Society and Change."

Bentley, G. E. *Shakespeare's Life: A Biographical Handbook.* New Haven: Yale University Press, 1961.

This "just-the-facts" account presents the surviving documents of Shakespeare's life against an Elizabethan background.

Chambers, E. K. *William Shakespeare: A Study of Facts and Problems.* 2 vols. Oxford: Clarendon Press, 1930.

Analyzing in great detail the scant historical data, Chambers's complex, scholarly study considers the nature of the texts in which Shakespeare's work is preserved.

Cressy, David. *Education in Tudor and Stuart England.* London: Edward Arnold, 1975.

This volume collects sixteenth-, seventeenth-, and early-eighteenth-century documents detailing aspects of formal education in England, such as the curriculum, the control and organization of education, and the education of women.

Dutton, Richard. *William Shakespeare: A Literary Life.* New York: St. Martin's Press, 1989.

Not a biography in the traditional sense, Dutton's very readable work nevertheless "follows the contours of Shakespeare's life" as he examines Shakespeare's career as playwright and poet, with consideration of his patrons, theatrical associations, and audience.

Honan, Park. *Shakespeare: A Life.* New York: Oxford University Press, 1998.

Honan's accessible biography focuses on the various contexts of Shakespeare's life—physical, social, political, and cultural—to place the dramatist within a lucidly described world. The biography includes detailed examinations of, for example, Stratford schooling, theatrical politics of 1590s London, and the careers of Shakespeare's associates. The author draws on a wealth of established knowledge and on interesting new research into local records and documents; he also engages in speculation about, for example, the possibilities that Shakespeare was a tutor in a Catholic household in the north of England in the 1580s and that he played particular roles in his own plays, areas that reflect new, but unproven and debatable, data—though Honan is usually careful to note where a particular narrative "has not been capable of proof or disproof."

Schoenbaum, S. *William Shakespeare: A Compact Documentary Life.* New York: Oxford University Press, 1977.

This standard biography economically presents the essential documents from Shakespeare's time in an accessible narrative account of the playwright's life.

Shakespeare's Theater

Bentley, G. E. *The Profession of Player in Shakespeare's Time, 1590–1642.* Princeton: Princeton University Press, 1984.

Bentley readably sets forth a wealth of evidence about performance in Shakespeare's time, with special attention to the relations between player and company, and the business of casting, managing, and touring.

Berry, Herbert. *Shakespeare's Playhouses*. New York: AMS Press, 1987.

Berry's six essays collected here discuss (with illustrations) varying aspects of the four playhouses in which Shakespeare had a financial stake: the Theatre in Shoreditch, the Blackfriars, and the first and second Globe.

Cook, Ann Jennalie. *The Privileged Playgoers of Shakespeare's London*. Princeton: Princeton University Press, 1981.

Cook's work argues, on the basis of sociological, economic, and documentary evidence, that Shakespeare's audience—and the audience for English Renaissance drama generally—consisted mainly of the "privileged."

Greg, W. W. *Dramatic Documents from the Elizabethan Playhouses*. 2 vols. Oxford: Clarendon Press, 1931.

Greg itemizes and briefly describes many of the play manuscripts that survive from the period 1590 to around 1660, including, among other things, players' parts. His second volume offers facsimiles of selected manuscripts.

Gurr, Andrew. *Playgoing in Shakespeare's London*. 2nd ed. Cambridge: Cambridge University Press, 1996.

Gurr charts how the theatrical enterprise developed from its modest beginnings in the late 1560s to become a thriving institution in the 1600s. He argues that there were important changes over the period 1567–1644 in the playhouses, the audience, and the plays.

Harbage, Alfred. *Shakespeare's Audience.* New York: Columbia University Press, 1941.

Harbage investigates the fragmentary surviving evidence to interpret the size, composition, and behavior of Shakespeare's audience.

Hattaway, Michael. *Elizabethan Popular Theatre: Plays in Performance.* London: Routledge and Kegan Paul, 1982.

Beginning with a study of the popular drama of the late Elizabethan age—a description of the stages, performance conditions, and acting of the period—this volume concludes with an analysis of five well-known plays of the 1590s, one of them (*Titus Andronicus*) by Shakespeare.

Shapiro, Michael. *Children of the Revels: The Boy Companies of Shakespeare's Time and Their Plays.* New York: Columbia University Press, 1977.

Shapiro chronicles the history of the amateur and quasi-professional child companies that flourished in London at the end of Elizabeth's reign and the beginning of James's.

The Publication of Shakespeare's Plays

Blayney, Peter W. M. *The First Folio of Shakespeare.* Hanover, Md.: Folger, 1991.

Blayney's accessible account of the printing and later life of the First Folio—an amply illustrated catalog to a 1991 Folger Shakespeare Library exhibition—analyzes the mechanical production of the First Folio, describing how the Folio was made, by whom and for whom, how much it cost, and its ups and downs (or, rather, downs and ups) since its printing in 1623.

Hinman, Charlton. *The Norton Facsimile: The First Folio of Shakespeare*. 2nd ed. New York: W. W. Norton, 1996.

This facsimile presents a photographic reproduction of an "ideal" copy of the First Folio of Shakespeare; Hinman attempts to represent each page in its most fully corrected state. The second edition includes an important new introduction by Peter W. M. Blayney.

Hinman, Charlton. *The Printing and Proof-Reading of the First Folio of Shakespeare*. 2 vols. Oxford: Clarendon Press, 1963.

In the most arduous study of a single book ever undertaken, Hinman attempts to reconstruct how the Shakespeare First Folio of 1623 was set into type and run off the press, sheet by sheet. He also provides almost all the known variations in readings from copy to copy.

Key to
Famous Lines and Phrases

Hung be the heavens with black, yield day to night!
[*Bedford*—1.1.1]

These news would cause him once more yield the ghost.
[*Gloucester*—1.1.68–69]

Fight till the last gasp.
[*Pucelle*—1.2.130]

Expect St. Martin's summer, halcyons' days. . . .
[*Pucelle*—1.2.134]

Glory is like a circle in the water,
Which never ceaseth to enlarge itself
Till by broad spreading it disperse to naught.
[*Pucelle*—1.2.136–38]

See the coast cleared, and then we will depart.
[*Mayor*—1.3.89]

Let him that is a trueborn gentleman
And stands upon the honor of his birth,
If he suppose that I have pleaded truth,
From off this brier pluck a white rose with me.
[*Plantagenet*—2.4.27–30]

I'll note you in my book of memory. . . .
[*Plantagenet*—2.4.102]

297

Here dies the dusky torch of Mortimer,
Choked with ambition of the meaner sort.
[*Plantagenet*—2.5.122–23]

For friendly counsel cuts off many foes.
[*King Henry*—3.1.194]

Defer no time; delays have dangerous ends.
[*Reignier*—3.2.33]

Care is no cure, but rather corrosive. . . .
[*Pucelle*—3.3.3]

How are we parked and bounded in a pale,
A little herd of England's timorous deer. . . .
[*Talbot*—4.2.45–46]

She's beautiful, and therefore to be wooed;
She is a woman, therefore to be won.
[*Suffolk*—5.3.78–79]